"Robin Grille's *Heart-to-Heart Parenting* has set
literature on early parenting from conception t
foundation in the new science of prenatal psycho
perspectives, and abundant practical wisdom. Mo
here a reliable guide to joyful parenting and the se
relationships."

—David B. Chamberlain, PhD, author of *The Mind of Your Newborn Baby*

"Reassuring, instructive, and inspirational, *Heart-to-Heart Parenting* puts the
focus where it should be, on empathy and connection. Comprehensive and
engagingly written, this compelling book should be read by every parent and
parent-to-be."

—Jan Hunt, MSc, author of *The Natural Child* and *A Gift for Baby*

"In this wonderfully wise and lucid book, Robin Grille gently guides parents to
discover their own childhood stories, informs about the latest scientific
understandings of the marvels of child development, illustrates with moving life
stories, and compassionately advises how parents can nurture their children, listen
and speak from their hearts, and develop life-enhancing emotional intelligence in
their kids and themselves. The author is an amazingly gifted writer, so *Heart-to-Heart Parenting* is a pleasure to read. I love this humane, inspiring book."

—Mitch Hall, mental health counselor for underprivileged youth, yoga teacher,
peace activist, and author of *Peace Quest* and *The Plague of Violence*

Robin Grille has done a brilliant job of giving parents just what they really
need. *Heart-to-Heart Parenting* offers both a clear, scientifically based,
enlightened understanding of how humans develop from the very beginning
and the tools for cultivating healthy self-awareness in adulthood. This is the
perfect guidebook, filled with compassion and wisdom, for parents who are
committed to raising emotionally, physically, spiritually and psychologically
healthy people and unfolding into their most authentic selves along the way."

—Carrie Contey, PhD, author of *What Babies Want: Calming and
Communicating with Your Baby*

"This is so much more than a parenting book! *Heart-to-Heart Parenting* elevates
childrearing to an exciting adventure of the spirit—the most transformative
personal growth journey you will ever have. This book is a treasure-hunter's map,
guiding the reader toward the bliss of deep connection with self, family, and
community. It is a timely blueprint for creating sustainable and happy societies."

—John W. Travis, MD, MPH, author of *Wellness Workbook,* cofounder,
Alliance for Transforming the Lives of Children

"Inside every parent is the blueprint to intuit exactly what is right for their children- beyond formulas and fads. Robin Grille ignites that blueprint, validates its wisdom and provokes it into action in a book that dares to give parents back their dignity and sovereignty."

—Kelly Wendorf, author of *Stories of Belonging: Finding Where Your True Self Lives,*

"*Heart-to-Heart Parenting* talks warmly and straightforwardly to the parent. It powerfully supports the reader to access the deepest love and connection that come from nurturing relationships. This book has given me a simple, yet invaluable process to live by, and pass on to the many generations of parents and children in my life and beyond."

—Sofi Thomson, C.A.R.E. Parent Support Program, Byron Bay, New South Wales, Australia

"This exceptional book rises above the cut-and-dried "cookbook" parenting manuals, teaching parents a warm and nurturing *approach* to parenting that fosters solid emotional development in children from the beginning of life. A great gift for every parent-to-be!"

—Robert E. Fathman, PhD, clinical psychologist and president, Center for Effective Discipline, Columbus, Ohio

"*Heart-to-Heart Parenting* is an exceptional book. Rather than tips and one-size-fits-all advice, Robin Grille offers a gentle guide to the authentic heart of parenting. His step-by-step approach supports parents through each stage to find the joy, fulfillment and immense personal growth that the ordinary task of parenting promises for parents and children alike."

—Sarah Buckley, MD, author of *Gentle Birth, Gentle Mothering*

Heart-to-Heart
Parenting

Heart-to-Heart
Parenting

Robin Grille

Disclaimer:

The information contained in this book is intended as general information about research in the areas of developmental psychology, social psychology, biology and psychohistory. None of the information contained in this book is intended as the definitive source of information on the sciences relating to child development and the care of children, or as a source or substitute for professional advice. Nor does the inclusion of any resource group or company listed within this book constitute a guarantee of quality by the authors. The author and publisher of this publication disclaim all liability and responsibility for any loss, damage or injury suffered by any person, corporation or other entity caused by or arising from reliance upon any statement made or information contained in this publication. You are urged to always obtain professional advice relating to your particular situation, in relation to parenting, childcare or child education, from a qualified child health practitioner. Your use of any of the information contained or referred to in this publication is your confirmation that you do not rely upon same as, or as a substitute for, professional advice. Although the personal anecdotes presented in this book are drawn from the author's experiences as a psychotherapist—any resemblance to specific individuals is unintended and entirely coincidental.

Also by the author:
Parenting for a Peaceful World

Published by Vox Cordis Press
PO Box 388, Avalon Beach, New South Wales, Australia 2107
PO Box 8422, Asheville, North Carolina 28814

ISBN: 978-0-646-57545-2
Cover design and photography by Bea Pierce, jellybeaps.com
Author photo and doctoring by Yaramin Grille
Indexing by Siena Travis Callander
Library of Congress Control Number: 2012937745
Library of Congress Subject Headings:
Parenting
Fatherhood
Motherhood
Attachment parenting

Contents

Part 4

The Toddler Connection

Part 5

Talking and Listening So That We Connect

Part 6

Parents Need Nurturing Too

Foreword

I am thrilled to wholeheartedly recommend this book to parents, grandparents, parents-to-be and students.

Here are three promises I can give you before you start this wonderful book: 1) you will be able to parent with greater pleasure and a greater sense of ease—accepting your self and your baby or children; 2) you can look forward to a time when your child or children will have left your home *without* your then wasting years looking back with guilt; and 3) you will know for certain that your role and the *profession* of parenting—because it deserves that status—is the most important role of all.

Having read this book, you'll feel confident when someone asks you, especially if you're currently an "at-home" parent, what you're doing in your life: "I'm raising a healthy, happy child who will contribute in positive ways to this world."

I also want to see it read—and underlined, discussed and its principles put into action—by the millions of women and men who teach and offer support to parents and conduct research in child development, including child-care workers. We in North America urgently need the wisdom this book contains.

Whether your concern for the wellbeing of children and their parents is personal or professional, I believe that you'll find this book is right on the mark. Robin's voice strikes just the right chord and has the right tone and cadence to resonate with both your heart and your intellect. Moreover, I believe it will elicit an "Ah, Yes!" from that small voice within you, the one that lives in each of us and speaks the truth each moment but which, in this noisy world of confusing ideas, we often ignore.

Why, with so many good books now available to help parents, am I so excited by this book?

First, I speak from the personal experience of having been a mother who had to raise a child on her own. I have also been a nursery school teacher and then head teacher in one of the first Head Start programs in the US. Today I direct a non-profit foundation focused on birthing, recognizing the mother-baby as a whole system, and preventing and healing early trauma in children and their families. I am now also a grandmother who appreciates living in an extended family with my daughter and grandson of fourteen, plus an informal "auntie" and "uncle."

I found it devilishly hard to be a fulltime solo parent, something I never wanted to be, especially after knowing what a fine teacher and nurturer of other people's children I had been. But parenting in today's world all too often means going it alone for hours or days at a time in a tiny unit of just our self and our baby (or child or children). Our infants and children received not only the best of what we modern parents have to give at any moment; they also receive the impact of our worst behaviors, the things we don't like about ourselves as parents. We bump up against each other day after day, especially in the confines of our home or apartment, no matter how many square feet it is. How many of us feel unsupported, isolated and deep down, afraid in our own home, afraid that our children are exposed to our inner shadow?

So I understand parents who feel remorse and guilt and a sense of inadequacy when it comes to parenting, no matter how competent they might feel in other areas of their lives. Robin Grille understands this too and has specific help to offer.

If I had to choose the most important reason for this book to be read widely, recommended and discussed among friends and in groups—and given as gifts too—it is that Robin's point of view is one that we all need to hear and heed. His is the wise view: that parents innately *know* how to be with, and respond appropriately to their children.

Deep inside us all, no matter how well or poorly we ourselves were parented, we do know and remember what we needed when we were young. And our heart knows what a child needs today. Building upon that sturdy truth is where we can best begin. This makes everything so much easier, because when you're working from your heart, you are working from your strengths, not your deficits.

How right is Robin that it is mostly a matter of first stripping away what is getting in the way of our being able to parent heart-to-heart, paying close attention to ourselves and our babies and children, so we get back to what our hearts already know.

My second reason why I think you'll love this book, is that Robin Grille *gets* the big picture. How we parent is of utmost importance in the world today, and in healing the wounds of society and this amazing planet Earth. With this point Robin is also unique, for very few people connect that what happens with children influences the level of dysfunction and violence in the world.

It's also exciting that modern science completely backs what Robin is saying in *Heart-to-Heart Parenting*.

Again, my gratefulness to this book and my well wishes to parent—and others involved in the nurturing and rearing of children—whatever your age, education, income or circumstances. You can be the very best parent possible at each moment, and be proud while you enjoy the journey.

Suzanne Arms, Bayfield, Colorado, author of *Immaculate Deception: Myth, Magic and Birth* and founder-director of BirthingtheFuture.org

Preface

You are the most important person in your child's life. A scary idea maybe, but there's no getting around it. As is now known, when it comes to your child's emotional health, genes play only a small role in both your child's personality and unique way of relating to others. Your relationship with your child matters far more than genes do. This is great news: it means we parents can be an enormously positive influence in our children's lives, from even before conception. So, how will this book help you as you make your way along the wondrous and challenging journey of being a parent?

This is not a how-to book. It doesn't seek to answer questions such as what to do when your child does such-and-such. The purpose of this book is to present the best that has been learned about children and their emotional needs, and then to help you decide how to apply this information—you are in charge. For this reason, every major idea in this book will be based on published scientific evidence and/or clinical experience. So, while the first aim of this book is to give you the newest child development science, the second is to show you how to connect with your own inner expert.

The better we know ourselves, the more effective parents we become. Getting to know yourself better as a parent involves learning how your own childhood experiences have affected you. This book contains a number of simple but powerful exercises that can help you connect deeply with the treasury of wisdom you possess, a wisdom you have gained from having been a baby and a child yourself. Connecting with this knowledge inside you will give you the confidence to weigh the advice of professionals and decide what feels right and what doesn't. This inner journey can bring forth your personal and unique ways of meeting your children's needs, and enable you to discover that your heart is filled with loving impulses and wisdom beyond your expectations. This book is less about what to *do*, and more about how to *be*.

As you get to know yourself better and come to understand more about how your childhood experiences have strengthened you, as well as wounded you, you not only become a far more effective parent, but you are also transformed and healed through the experience of parenting your children. Your relationship with your child, with all its frustrations, heartbreaks and joys, causes your heart to grow and, in the process, you gain in wisdom, humility, patience and humor.

The emphasis of this book is emotional health—yours and your child's. Your child's wellbeing and your own are intricately woven together; we are all better caregivers when we feel cared for. So, although *Heart-to-Heart Parenting* is primarily about your child's emotional health, it is also about your personal growth as a parent. There is help in these pages for the issues you face along the way, and reassuring guidance for the emotional terrain you travel. It covers your journey together from the time your child becomes conscious in the womb, through the crucial time of birth and the bonding that follows, up through the first seven years or so.

This book does not discuss issues of academic or physical development—such as developmental milestones for walking, reading or computing math problems, so you might want additional advice regarding these areas of development. While parenting tips can be helpful, I am offering you something more empowering than that. No matter how handy, tips can be traps. Tips can be a mechanistic approach to parenting, an approach that does not necessarily help you to connect with your child as a person. Tips give you the illusion that when your child does this, then if you do that, the problem will be solved. This pushbutton approach may backfire in the end because your child does not feel connected to you when you are manipulating the situation, however expertly.

Our children do not want us to be techno-whizzes or personnel managers; they want us to be people and they want to be treated as people. So while tips can certainly help, you need more, you need to find ways to make the deepest connections with your child. When you connect deeply with your child, whatever you do will work, and what's more, you will be doing it *your* way.

Our children challenge us like no one else ever will and, if we let them, they make us better people. Even the mistakes we make as parents, if acknowledged honestly and with humility, can bring our children and us toward a closer and more trusting relationship. This emphasis on connection is an approach to being a parent that can be most enriching and transform parenting from a job into an adventure.

Chapters 1 and 2 help you to cope with the conflicting and confusing information that abounds by showing you how to locate and trust your in-built parenting wisdom. You will gain insights into how to use your own experiences of childhood, both the painful and the happy ones, to connect you to your deepest intuition. You will learn that your body-sense of being a child is your most important resource and your most powerful tool for effective parenting. These chapters also explain why the early years are so critical to your child's developing personality and emotional makeup.

In Chapters 3, 4 and 5 you will see how the foundation of our children's emotional intelligence is built during pregnancy, birth and the moments that follow birth. We will look at the most fascinating recent discoveries about the consciousness and remarkable abilities of the unborn and newborn, who are far more receptive, communicative and intelligent than has been realized.

Chapters 6, 7 and 8 deal with how we can create a joyous connection with our growing babies. An enormous body of international research has come to the aid of parents; these chapters offer valuable insights into how we can communicate with our babies, understand their needs, forge the closest and warmest bonds with them, and how we can make this stage of parenting most pleasurable and fulfilling. This is a time in our children's lives when we can, through our responsiveness, most effectively assure for them a lifetime of security, emotional health and loving relationships.

Chapters 9 and 10 are devoted to understanding our toddlers, how they see us and the world around them, and how we can support their freedom to fully explore, play and express themselves while they learn and develop respect and empathy for others.

In Chapters 11–14, we look at how we can set strong boundaries with our children without resorting to shaming, manipulation or punishment, how we can hear and understand them and how we can help them to listen to us in ways that are based on connection rather than control.

We will also discover how emotionally authentic communication with our toddlers and children is the key to the most trusting and cooperative relationships with them. The focus in this section remains on helping parents to enjoy their growing toddler and on gaining the greatest delight from this zestful stage in a child's life. This rite of passage has profound ramifications for children's emotional intelligence, and is rich with opportunities to safeguard their future capacity for self-confidence, vitality and love. When we have all the support we need, parenting is a far more joyous enterprise and we have so much more to give our children.

In Chapter 15, we examine various means of connecting to community support networks, parenting groups and even how to start your own parent-support group if necessary. The wellbeing of children in any society depends to a large extent on how well it supports the parents.

Often throughout the chapters, you will find referrals to the References section of books and websites where you can research more about what is being discussed.

This book is not simply about raising happy and responsible children, it is about joy, an aspect of human potential that is not talked about often enough. Joy is a part of our human inheritance, for which everybody has the biological capacity. The rites of passage that begin in the womb and continue through infancy and childhood, offer powerful opportunities to imbue our children's nervous systems with the capacity for the greatest joy and love. If we cultivate an emotionally alive connection with our children from the beginning, we do more than help them to flourish in emotional health: we also create a treasure trove of fulfillment and joy for the whole family.

I wrote this book because I want to convey the message that the way a society supports its parents and the way we collectively relate to our children are the keys to creating a better world and that parenting is not so much about getting it right but that it can be an adventure, an intensive and transformative journey of the heart and spirit. If we focus on deepening the quality of connection we have with our children, parenting can be full of joy and pleasure, and has the potential to be the most fulfilling thing we will ever do.

Part 1

Finding Your Inner Wisdom

1

Preparing to Be a Parent

Who wants to listen to the experts?

While sitting in a café one day, I overheard two women talking about an article in a parenting magazine. Indignantly, one said to the other, "I'm not going to let some pretentious academic with a whole bunch of letters after his name tell *me* how to bring up my own child." Parenting: there is probably no human task for which people are more put off by the idea of experts.

Some parents do like to seek information about parenting—that's probably why you are reading this book. But information is not always welcome. Parents generally don't like to be told what to do. We resent others intruding into our personal relationships with comments and advice. "This is my son and I'll decide how to raise him."

Most of us probably feel touchy about our parenting style being held up for scrutiny; we fear being judged and found inadequate. We feel we are expected—or rather, we expect ourselves—to know exactly what to do, when to do it, and to get it right for our children.

How did we get the idea that we are automatically supposed to know everything about caring for our children as soon as they are born? This is not the case for any of the other skills we learn in life. Long after learning to drive and obtaining our license, we keep improving our road skills—hopefully—for the rest of our life (insurance companies recognize this, which is why premiums get cheaper as we get older). A gardener, even one with the greenest of thumbs, knows that the more that is learned, the more joy a garden will give. All good professionals know that learning in their field of work continues forever. People who play sports accept the need for regular practice and coaching. But the secrets of how we care for our children are jealously guarded, and we want the world to think we have got it all handled.

So, why do so many parents feel overcome with embarrassment when they hit a difficult patch in their relationship with their children? Too often when this happens, we either blame the child or we blame ourselves. Either way, blame hurts. It does not help anyone. But the alternative seems harder, to ask for, and accept, help or advice. When we do so, we often feel like a failure and ashamed.

When you think about it, the expectations that we place on ourselves as parents (or those placed on us by society) are unrealistic and unreasonable. In the years that I have worked with parents and families, I have been repeatedly awe-struck by the things that parents imagine they are magically supposed to know, understand and accomplish, with little or no help and support. "Kids don't come with an instruction manual," we joke to each other and, as we shake our heads, we invoke the wise old saying: "It takes a village to raise a child." But we carry on regardless, without the help of the village or extended family, and with precious little helpful information. So, if help is so important for parents, why does it sometimes feel like interference? Why does it make us feel disempowered? Why does the idea of ongoing learning seem to hit such a raw nerve?

Parents under a microscope

Information about how children grow and develop, and how we can best address their changing emotional needs, is updated in the parenting literature quite frequently. But this information is greeted with mixed feelings. Some parents receive new information—even if it challenges established beliefs—with great enthusiasm, even relief; they welcome the empowerment that knowledge gives them. Others feel confronted by new information and may react defensively and dismissively.

Why is the possibility of learning new skills so hard to face?

You have probably heard mothers and fathers described as either "good parents" or "bad parents" countless times. The idea of a "good parent" or a "bad parent" is a myth, and a destructive one at that. This kind of comparison places enormous pressure on parents to perform. Not surprisingly, many parents feel as if they are being watched by their community and graded for their skill—or lack of it. There is probably nothing that can more quickly take away the joy, the ease and the spontaneity from parenting. So how can any of us open ourselves to new learning, and to receiving help and support, if we feel as if we are under a microscope, if we feel like failures for doing so?

Why do we end up feeling ashamed when we admit that we get stuck sometimes? Who told us we are supposed to know what to do all the time? How can we benefit from the help of the village if we have to keep our need for help a secret? Many parents carry a great deal of shame, as if their children's behavior will expose their inadequacies as parents. Parent shame and guilt, often the result of unrealistic expectations, gets in the way of learning and growth, and it thwarts opportunities to receive support from others.

The cost of unsupported parenting

Some years ago, Jill came to see me for counseling after having been diagnosed with postnatal depression. She had two children, one 3 years old, the other a 9-month-old baby. She spent most of her day at home alone with her children. Her own parents, her sister and her brother all lived in other towns, hundreds of miles away, and so, apart from her children, her husband was the only family she had with her. Although Jill had two close girlfriends who were very dear to her, each was busy with her own life, so they saw each other infrequently. Jill's husband was the only regular adult relationship she could count on. Each day, endless hours went by in which she faced the joys but also the demands of being a mother alone. Jill's mood became increasingly gloomy, she was bewildered, could not understand why she was feeling more miserable each day. When Jill finally confided in her family members about her deteriorating emotional state, they were surprised. "You have two beautiful children, a loving husband, you live in a nice home. What can you possibly have to be unhappy about?" Not exactly the most empathetic response. People in Jill's life were telling her to cheer up.

Not surprisingly, this response compounded Jill's depression. She had started off feeling lonely and exhausted, now, on top of that, she felt like an ingrate and a failure as a mother for not bursting with joy.

There are so many mothers and fathers who, just like Jill, feel deeply inadequate because they are at home with one, two or more children all day and feel at their wits' end; they frequently lose their temper. This is not necessarily because they are at home. It is because they are isolated, cut off from their vital support networks. Looking after children is supposed to be a communal, cooperative endeavor. Our species is simply not designed to nurture its young in separate, nuclear family units. No wonder parenting is so stressful for so many people.

Parenting is a formidable task. Parents need nourishing social contact and practical help on a daily basis. Isolation is an well-known, major risk factor for depression in parents, yet hardly any prospective parent is told about this; in our culture a parent's need for support has been very badly underestimated.

So, one of the aims of this book is to help you not only to be free of shame about reaching out for help and support, but also to actually feel good about yourself as you ask others for help. Parenting is the most important job in the world, and you should have all the support you need. Parents deserve a whole range of different kinds of support.

Practical support

Practical support can be found in the form of friends and family helping you to cook, shop, or look after your older children when you have a small baby. They can also take care of your baby while you take a nap. In cooperative parenting groups, friends and family can help each other along these lines on a daily basis.

Emotional support

The parenting journey provokes all kinds of feelings—frustration, anger, tenderness, joy, fear, laughter, grief, sorrow and more. Often, parents need a shoulder to cry on when tired or overwhelmed. We need someone to listen to our feelings and show concern for how we feel. We also need someone to share our joys with.

Informational support

It can make a world of difference to learn more and more about how children grow, key developmental milestones that we can expect at each stage and how to address children's changing emotional and physical needs.

Parenting can sometimes be difficult, painful and frustrating, but it can also bring us immense joy, and a host of wonderful new feelings that we could not have dreamt of. Provided certain basic conditions are met, parenting can—and should—be full of pleasure and fulfillment. The basic conditions for joyous parenting involve:

- ♱ strong connections to supportive partner, friends, family and community,
- ♱ a deep sense of connection with yourself (self-love, self-respect, a clear sense of your own feelings and needs),
- ♱ an empathetic and emotionally authentic connection with your child.

Pleasurable parenting is about connection. Throughout this book, I will be further clarifying why each of these connections is so important, and discussing many ways to nurture and deepen these vital connections.

Parents have always been learning

When it comes to parenting, every last one of us is on a learning journey. So what, then, is a parenting expert? Well, there is actually no such thing. No one in the world is a parenting expert, and here's why.

The way children are reared has always been evolving. We certainly have not been doing it the same way since the beginning—far from it. Parents and teachers have been learning new things about how to relate to children from the dawn of human history. Parenting used to be far harsher and more violent than it is today; history is replete with tales of extreme cruelty toward children. The true history of childhood through the ages is very distressing, but it is also quite encouraging: it shows us how far we have come over the centuries. If you were to read this history of childhood (see: *Parenting for a Peaceful World,*

Grille, 2005) you might be surprised to find that you gain a renewed appreciation of and understanding for your own parents. This feeling creeps up on you as you begin to see what their childhoods would have been like, and what their parents' childhoods were like. The historical perspective also deepens your respect for yourself, for your own struggles and your successes as a parent, as you discover that humanity as a whole has for a long time been learning about parenting and often making a mess of it. This is very reassuring—it is OK for you to be learning, it is OK to be getting it wrong sometimes.

From this illuminating history of childhood, I would like to share with you some of the most surprising bits.

PARENTING THROUGH THE AGES

In early Roman and Greek civilizations, parents—wealthy and poor alike—who did not want their children, killed or abandoned them at a rate of up to 40%. Abandoned children were commonly used as slaves, and the sexual exploitation of children was publicly condoned.

During the Middle Ages and later, children had very little to do with their parents. Most babies were sent away to be reared by paid wet nurses, many of whom lived in towns far from the parents; most wet nursed children did not see their parents until they were 3 or 4 years old. Once returned to their parents, most were sent away again soon afterward to live as apprentices with trade masters; others were fostered out for their labor in lieu of debt repayments, or were indentured to monasteries for lifetime service.

When the Industrial Revolution arrived in Europe, children as young as four were forced to work in factories, textile mills, mines and as chimney sweeps. They worked up to sixteen hours a day in appalling conditions. They were cruelly punished if their work was inefficient, and occupational health standards were non-existent. In the UK, child labor was abolished in 1874 through the Factory Act; in the US it continued until 1938. Today, it is estimated that 218 million children are forced to work, and over 100 million of them do so in hazardous conditions.

For much of the nineteenth century, children were to be seen and not heard. In England, children of middle-class or aristocratic parents were raised by nannies, not by their parents. A study involving hundreds of biographies (Jonathan Gathorne-Hardy's *The Rise and Fall of the British Nanny,* 1972) found that the majority of British nannies were cold and strict disciplinarians, and many were physically and sexually abusive.

Until the release of the 1962 article, "The Battered Child Syndrome," in the *Journal of the American Medical Association*, child abuse was a problem that did not rate as a priority; it was, effectively, ignored. These days, even though it is widely condemned, child abuse continues at an alarming rate, despite the fact that most of us are horrified by child abuse statistics, that there are mandatory reporting regulations for health professionals, and that there are a number of government provisions to protect children.

On the whole, mothers and fathers are learning, largely by trial and error, to have closer bonds with their children. Breastfeeding rates have been increasing steadily around the world in recent decades. Presently 43 percent of babies in US, 30 percent in Canada, 56 percent in Australia, and 21 percent in the UK are still being breastfed at six months. Although this falls a long way short of ideal, it represents a massive improvement since the 1960s and 1970s when virtually no babies of that age were being breastfed.

Dads are learning to be far more involved with their children. It would have been very unusual to see a dad pushing a stroller or publicly cuddling his baby only one generation ago. Today, the majority of dads witness the miracle of their children being born, but only forty or fifty years ago, most dads remained at work or waited nervously outside the labor ward.

With every new step we take collectively toward a more intimate and hands-on approach to parenting, it is only natural that we would sometimes stumble, make mistakes and feel lost. Most of humanity is learning how to be better parents. So, even though there are still widespread social problems experienced by children—growing numbers of broken families, high rates of youth depression, bullying in schools, childhood obesity and more—we belong to a generation that has, on average, improved on how our forbearers raised their children. There is no finality to parenting proficiency, no finish line where we can arrive and feel like we are finally doing it all the right way. As parenting will always continue to evolve, there is no reason to put ourselves down when we get things wrong. As you will see in later chapters, there are plenty of valid reasons why each parent sometimes falls short of understanding and meeting their children's emotional needs. The more we understand ourselves—how our own childhoods have affected us, and the circumstances that influence our parenting style—the more we tend to view ourselves with compassion and the more we learn to trust ourselves as parents.

This book aims to help parents feel excited about learning new approaches and new things about how children develop, to help you to feel in control of the information you take in as a parent and to weigh it up for yourself. This book intends to help you find and appreciate the parenting expert inside yourself.

Parenting by instinct
Our instincts come to us as raw material. Each of us is born with a powerful self defense instinct, designed to protect us if we are attacked. Those of us who do not learn one or two martial skills are likely to flail around quite ineffectively if faced with the need to fight.

The sexual instinct is one of our most powerful driving forces, yet as beginners we grope and fumble— sex is more comedy than harmony.

Instinctual as it might be, lovemaking is a skill that we learn, and hopefully continue to learn, from our partners. In fact, all acts of love are learned, not in terms of technique so much as in our abilities to be open, self-expressive, demonstrative, sensitive and empathetic.

This applies equally to our parenting instincts.

We all possess a strong, natural parenting instinct to nurture, protect, empower and, eventually, liberate our children—our brains are hardwired for it. But this does not mean we can expect ourselves, or each other, to know exactly what to do as soon as our children are born.

We learn how to be parents through human contact: we learn it from others. Even breastfeeding, one of the most basic acts of mothering, needs to be learned and role-modeled, and often it fails without careful instruction from lactation consultants, breastfeeding counselors or experienced mothers. Breastfeeding difficulties that are commonplace in modern societies are very rare in cultures where mothers breastfeed openly and together.

We are all full of wonderful parenting energies, but the way we enact those energies is always learned from our elders and our peers. That's why most people tend to parent their children much the same as they were parented themselves. It is also why we should never have to feel ashamed to openly acknowledge our difficulties as parents and our constant need to learn from each other. Parenting is all about learning.

So, why talk about the "science" of parenting?

If all we do is learn to parent from our own parents, or from our own immediate community, we will learn much that is valuable but our learning will be limited to a relatively narrow range of parenting styles. We are limited by what we see and experience.

Child development specialists are called developmental psychologists. There is nothing magical or mysterious about developmental psychology. Developmental psychologists look for what seems to work best for babies and children—what helps them grow to be loving, joyous and playful, warm and affectionate, respectful and considerate, interested in learning and able to focus their attention. They do this by carefully and methodically studying what happens to many thousands of children all over the world.

Such research gives developmental psychologists a tremendous advantage. By collecting information from thousands of studies from around the world, scientists open us up to a far broader range of helpful ideas. With the aid of modern communications, scientists such as pediatricians, immunologists, psychologists, neurologists, geneticists, biologists, anthropologists, psychohistorians and others, help us to reap the benefits of the collective experiences of billions of parents and children from every culture and through history. This can be like asking a million experienced grandparents for their advice and distilling an average answer.

Scientists are a priceless resource for parents. In recent years, advances in brain-imaging technology have helped scientists to gain extraordinary new insights into childhood brain development. The secrets of how children develop emotional intelligence have been unlocked. There has been a veritable explosion of remarkable discoveries, as if someone flicked a switch and illuminated the pathways to healthy emotional development. The conditions that help children to develop emotional intelligence are becoming much clearer. Scientists have located the regions of the brain that produce those qualities, and psychologists are identifying the kinds of experiences that help those particular parts of the brain to grow. Incredible as it may sound, the capacity for love and courage can literally be hardwired into the child's nervous system.

So at the very least, science can help you to feel more confident about the choices you have already made as a parent. The latest discoveries relating to children's emotional health have simple applications, many of which will probably resonate with what you intuitively know, if you listen to your feelings. For many people, the new scientific evidence has supported them in doing what their hearts were telling them to do, even when people around were discouraging them.

Why is there so much conflicting information out there?

Have you noticed that sometimes parenting books and health professionals seem to give out contradictory advice? This can be a source of confusion and frustration, causing some parents to feel as if they are caught between opposing factions. Some health professionals will, for example, tell you that it is best to breastfeed babies for over two years, others that one year is enough. Some professionals will advise you against rocking your baby to sleep, warning that this will make your baby too dependent on you; they'll try to impress upon you that babies should learn to fall asleep by themselves. Other professionals will tell you the opposite, that it is crucial for babies to feel comforted and to sleep close to those they love.

Confusing? Who to believe? Think of it this way: the fact that there are some contradictory sources of information out there might also be a good thing. This is happening because science is yielding new understandings at a tremendous rate, understandings about what children need in order to thrive. The same happens in every area of human endeavor—engineering, medicine or agriculture—when existing practices need to be replaced as soon as new facts come to light.

The way we raise our children has never advanced as rapidly as it is today. We are in a period of fast-paced transition—old assumptions are being abandoned, new practices are being adopted. There is nothing unusual about this. As our glimpse at the history of childhood has shown, childrearing customs have been evolving since the dawn of time. Parenting has undergone many critical periods of transformation and, fortunately, this has mostly been for the better. What is different today is that, thanks to modern science and communications, evolution is proceeding at an accelerated pace.

Until the 1990s, it was widely believed by doctors and many laypeople that newborn babies don't feel pain; now, medical authorities know this is not so, and that, in fact, babies feel pain more intensely than children and adults do. It was also once believed that newborn babies do not have emotional awareness, and we now know that to be false. In both cases, as it often happens, science has finally confirmed what many parents already felt in their hearts.

Never before in our history has the plight of children been considered enough of an issue to merit so much discussion and controversy as it does today. The heat of modern debates about how we should care for our children shows just how much more we have come to value their emotional wellbeing.

Tapping your inner wisdom (you're in charge)

There is now an unprecedented abundance of wonderful and empowering information for parents, the kind of leading-edge, evidence-based information that can help you derive much pleasure and joy from your parenting journey while fostering your child's emotional health.

As parents, we need to strike a balance between absorbing scientific know-how and learning how to trust ourselves. Every parent has a fount of inner wisdom they can learn to access. There are practical steps you can take to tune in to this inner wisdom—the voice of your heart.

You and your child's emotional intelligence

Many people around the world are coming to realize that emotional intelligence is more important in our pursuit of happiness than our mental or academic intelligence quotient (IQ). Emotional intelligence (EQ) is the main ingredient that helps create and maintain loving relationships in our personal lives and workable partnerships in our professional lives. Our abilities to know our own feelings, to express our feelings appropriately, to read others' feelings and to empathize with others—these are the fundamental skills that enable us to find fulfillment in life and work. Emotional intelligence is the key to feeling good about ourselves and loving our own company.

Peak emotional health includes our capacity to give and receive love, to derive pleasure from life, and to experience joy, bliss and even ecstasy.

However, our emotional health rests on our willingness to keep learning and growing—about ourselves and about relationships.

Humanity has nowhere nearly achieved the potential emotional health that is biologically possible. Unlike IQ, EQ can quite readily continue to develop through life.

Early childhood is a time when the human brain and central nervous system are growing at the fastest rate, and children's experiences of human relations have by far the most powerful and long-lasting impact on their emotional makeup. That's why the way we respond to our children's feelings has a powerful influence on the way they perceive themselves as they grow up— and the way they will relate to others.

WHAT IS EMOTIONAL INTELLIGENCE?

No one has agreed upon a definitive and universal definition of emotional intelligence or emotional health, although there is wide consensus about how important it is for our relationships. Just to get a sense of what EQ might be all about, and how it applies to you, do the quiz you will find at our-emotionalhealth.com/ei.html.

Why the early years are so important

You will find that throughout this book, the brain will be discussed a number of times. There is a good reason for this. Much has been learned about the human brain in recent years, and we have discovered so much about how children's relationships with their parents redirect the growth of their brains. In a child's brain, new neural pathways are growing all the time in order to create a personality, and this personality is an attempt to adapt to the kinds of relationships in which the child is held.

Here are some simplified examples to illustrate the point: When a child feels lonely and unheard, her brain might grow in a way that causes her to behave in clingy ways—her way to draw more attention to herself to compensate for the deficit. Alternatively, since she felt early in life that relationships let her down, her brain might grow in a way that makes her reserved, withdrawn and aloof in order to save herself from disappointments in relationships. Or, as a result of considerable punishment and shaming during his earliest years, a boy's brain grows toward making him defensive and hostile. This makes good sense for his survival. Because he has experienced an unfriendly and aggressive world, he learns to cope by becoming more aggressive.

It is important to understand that these feelings, attitudes and behaviors are literally hardwired into the child's rapidly growing brain, which is why some of our characteristic traits tend to last, and can be difficult to change. Our emotional intelligence begins to be shaped from earliest childhood, through our earliest impressions of human connection. Since brain changes develop far more slowly in adulthood, it is very difficult to change traits that have been formed in early childhood. Early childhood gives us the greatest opportunity to safeguard our children's emotional health for a lifetime—their ability to pursue their goals and form loving relationships. It serves us well to understand what, exactly, are our babies' and toddlers' deepest emotional needs.

DID YOU KNOW:

That we are born with only one-quarter of our adult brain mass, and that by our third birthday it has grown to 90% of its full size? The way the emotional centers in the brain develop is directly shaped by our relationships with our caregivers. By six months our stress response level is set, based on how our emotional security needs are met by others. This neurological stress response is set much like a thermostat, and it influences the way we face stressful situations throughout our lives.

The foundations of your child's emotional makeup are shaped over the first five to seven years, when the brain is growing at its fastest. Your child's time in the womb, through birth, babyhood, the toddler years and young childhood are of the most profound developmental importance. Their experiences throughout these early years will be the most formative of their lives.

The brain grows while the child is in the womb, and through early childhood, at an incredibly accelerated pace. Brain growth is experience-dependent, which means that the brain senses how relationships feel to the child, and it decides how to grow accordingly. In an unfriendly or emotionally cold environment, the child's brain will grow quite differently than it would in a home that is full of empathy and affection. That's how our earliest relationships have helped to write our distinctive personalities—by encoding the key parts of our brains that regulate emotion.

As parents there is much we can do to immunize our children from all kinds of emotional, mental health and social problems. There is much we can do to teach our children to create loving and caring relationships, to have a strong social conscience and a life of deep commitment and fulfillment. Parents have power, and the right information—as well as our commitment to keep developing our own emotional intelligence—can make a considerable difference to how we influence our children.

This is not to say that later childhood and adolescence are not formative; a teenager's peer group and schoolteachers also wield a lot of influence over who our children become. In fact, there is a second—though lesser—accelerated spurt of brain growth during the teenage years that makes adolescence another vulnerable time of change. But the growth rate of the brain in early childhood is never again paralleled. That's why the foundations of emotional health can be most effectively set in early childhood. How we nurture our children in early childhood can, to a large degree, prepare them for the challenges of the teenage years, by giving them the self-love and the ability to form trust-based relationships and strong personal boundaries that will protect them from negative influences later.

The deepest fulfillment and the greatest joy are found in parenting when parent and child grow together, in other words, when as parents we are open to our own learning about emotions and about relationships, just as we tend to our children's emotional development. By being themselves, our children are our teachers in very profound ways—as we are theirs. How parent and child help each other to grow and become more loving individuals is explored throughout this book. We will look at your own unfolding and healing and growth, alongside your child's step-by-step emotional development. We best help our children develop emotional health when we are willing to grow at the same time. When you and your child are consciously growing together, parenting can be a transformative and healing journey that transports you to the depths of your own humanity.

What is connection?

Our emotional wellbeing—in other words, our ability to experience joy, love and fulfillment—comes from how closely we are able to connect to one another.

Relationships are about connection. Human happiness is about connection. Your baby's and young child's ability to thrive and grow in emotional health begins with how well they feel connected to you. Your own ability to love and be loved comes from how well you can connect to others. Our self-esteem and self-worth come from how well we are able to connect to ourselves, to our innermost feelings and yearnings.

Connection is what we look for in relationships, whether we are conscious of it or not. The deepest connections we make with one another are facilitated through mutual openness, our willingness to be open with each other about our feelings. The quality of our connections also depends on empathy, on our showing each other that we register each other's feelings, that we are somehow moved by each other's feelings.

You sense when a deep connection with another has taken place because you feel closer to that person. You feel you have gotten to know them a little more deeply. This automatically brings forth feelings of respect, appreciation—perhaps even love. Every time we truly connect with another individual, we feel suffused with wellbeing, as if some inner thirst for contact has been satisfied. Our human connections enrich our lives and fill them with meaning.

If you pay close attention, you will notice that there is a rhythm to our search for connection. We reach out and make contact with others and we (hopefully) have our fill. Then we turn back to ourselves—we seek self-connection or connection with Nature. There are many different kinds of bliss: that which comes from honest connections with each other, with ourselves, in communion with Nature, with music and, if you have a spiritual life, with the Divine. Life is a continual and rhythmic moving toward and away from all different kinds of connection.

Moments of deep connection are what your baby yearns for with you; it is what nourishes a baby at the emotional level. Your baby depends on a deep and consistent connection with you, and on how closely his communications of feeling are attended and responded to. Your baby also depends on how much of you—your essence, your warmth—he feels when you are with him. Making contact with your baby doesn't simply depend on doing the right thing; it is chiefly about the quality of your presence: your self-awareness and your attention to your child's feelings.

As a baby evolves into a toddler, and then a child, the meaning of interpersonal connection starts to become much broader—children begin to thrive from knowing you as a person, with all kinds of feelings, limits and needs. Being a real person, rather than playing the role of authority, is what creates authentic connection. Additionally, toddlers and children find their bliss through self-connection, which comes from the freedom to be playful, to explore the world around them and to express their feelings and unique natures. This exhilarating—and sometimes scary—adventure of self-discovery is, with gradually increasing steps, accomplished independently while a parent looks on.

As will be discussed later, your ability to make these kinds of connections with your child is helped by how well you are connected to your self, your feelings, your emotional vulnerability and your emotional inner world. Your connection to your child is also helped by how well you feel connected to—and supported by—people who are significant in your life—your partner, family, friends, colleagues and community.

You will find that the better you know yourself and the closer the connection with your child, the more you will be able to trust your own intuition about parenting decisions. This is what helps you to feel in charge of how you weigh up the advice you receive from books, health professionals, friends and family.

This might seem like a strange concept, but when you are connected to yourself, when you are in your heart and aware of your feelings, your very presence is nourishing—there are some instances when this is true even if all you do is to sit still. By just being yourself and being here, you radiate an essence that enables your children to thrive.

Connection heals emotional wounds

One of the most painful things about being a parent is that sometimes something we do—or fail to do—hurts our children. As parents are learning, it is impossible to avoid making mistakes. There are also times when our children are hurt by circumstances that are beyond our control.

You can help your children to heal their emotional wounds. The way you connect with your children—by listening carefully to their feelings and by being authentic with them—can be profoundly healing for them.

2

Your Memory Is Your Teacher

Beginning with you

Whether you have children, are thinking of having children or are planning to have more, there are connections that you make with yourself that prime you for deeper connections with your child at any stage. So, before we delve into the nitty-gritty of connecting with your child's emotional needs, let's talk more about you.

The quality and depth of connection you have with your child springs from how you connect with yourself. Preparation for this life-changing relationship and all the gifts it brings you begins with learning how to find the loving and knowing instincts inside yourself. You possess more parenting wisdom than you realize—it is just a matter of knowing how to locate this wisdom within. Preparation also involves making sure that some key emotional needs of your own are well taken care of. To be able to care for others, we must first care for ourselves. Once those two basic conditions are met, a lot more pleasure and joy will flow into your relationship with your child.

Where do our personal parenting styles come from?

Each of us has a characteristic way of responding to our children. Some of us are more demonstrative, some of us more reserved. Some of us are stricter, some more laid back. We all tend to have quite different expectations of our children and widely varying levels of tolerance for their behaviors. Personal thresholds of irritation are quite different, and some parents have a lot more patience than others. But these broad individual differences are not simply about personality.

There are many things that influence the unique ways we care for our children. One of those influences is information: we all read different books or magazines, and we talk to different child health professionals. There are, too, many cultural practices, social customs and religious beliefs that script our parenting choices—and our temperaments imbue the way we respond to our children. But the most powerful influence of all is the way we were parented ourselves.

If you can understand how your own childhood experiences have affected you and your emotional makeup, you will gain many useful insights into your own parenting choices, insights that can help you to better understand yourself and your child.

Our own childhood experiences have affected us deeply and, as you will see later, we are also influenced by experiences that we think we can't remember. Our many beliefs, attitudes and characteristic emotional responses are colored by conscious and unconscious memories of childhood.

The following examples will show you what I mean:

When her children reached primary school age, Heather found herself filled with the desire to bake cookies for them after school. She remembered something she had long forgotten—how her mother had done the same for her, and how nurturing this ritual had felt.

Jonathan had a strong conviction that his son should learn how to make or repair things for himself. He loved spending time with his son teaching him how to use tools. Jonathan recalled how, as a child, he loved spending long hours in the company of his grandfather, tinkering in his workshop.

When his son was about 18 months old, Julio spontaneously remembered what it was like to be teething as a little toddler, how he would cry inconsolably and grab his ears. This helped him to recognize exactly what was happening to his own little boy when he saw him grabbing his ears in a similar way. Julio's memory enabled him to empathize with his son and comfort him.

Not all of our childhood memories are happy ones, or memories that help us to know what we want to do for our children. Some memories help us to know what we'd rather *not* do. There is much to gain from glimpsing our more unpleasant memories. If we are willing to remember how it felt to be a child, this feedback can help us make new choices rather than automatically repeat what was done to us.

Pierre's wife, Monique, would often complain to him that he seemed dismissive toward his young son's opinions. Often, when his son tried to speak up for what he wanted, Pierre would cut him short, protesting to Monique that he was only a child and after all, children's views should not really count. Feeling increasingly hurt for her son, Monique challenged Pierre about this, to which he replied that was he had been raised, and that was how he had learned his place. At Monique's urging, Pierre tried to reconnect with how he actually felt each time his own father ignored or blocked his attempts to have a say. Over time, the helplessness, the shame and the frustration he had experienced came back to him. The emotional aspect of his memory is what finally convinced Pierre to allow and, indeed, to encourage, his own son to speak his mind.

The way we were raised does not necessarily have to determine our every act as a parent. If we try to remember how we once felt as children—the pleasurable memories as well as the painful—our memories lose their hold over us, which empowers us to choose what to pass on and what to leave behind.

From automatic to conscious parenting

The way our own parents or caregivers related to us as children may have produced a mix of positive and negative effects. Most of us can recall some loving and joyous moments—as well as a number of scary or painful experiences. All of these experiences come together as the sum of influences upon our personal parenting styles.

An active interest in our childhood memories expands our appreciation for our strengths as parents while giving us self-respect and compassion for ourselves when we find parenting difficult. This can make an enormous difference to our enjoyment—and our endurance—throughout the parenting journey.

Additionally, the more clearly we remember how we once felt—our joys, our fears, our frustrations and our hurts—the more deeply we can empathize with our own children and the better we can understand them—their fears, their hurts, their passions and their yearnings. Your connection to your "inner child" is the most important tool at your disposal. It is not so important to remember exactly what happened and when it happened; what really counts is that you remember how it felt to be a child. Your ability to truly connect with your child depends on your emotional memory. Your child senses your empathy as well as its absence.

Empathy comes with more difficulty for individuals who seem to have walled up their inner child; they might remember childhood events but are detached from how those events felt to them when they were little. Our emotional detachment from ourselves is what permits us to behave insensitively toward our children.

How our childhood memories unconsciously affect our parenting

Quite often, our childhood memories impose themselves on our behavior without our realizing it. When we are frustrated, we might, for instance, catch ourselves talking to our child in the same tone of voice and using exactly the same words as our father once did toward us ("Oh my God! I just sounded exactly like my dad."). Or we unthinkingly mimic a response that came straight out of our mother's repertoire. Have you ever watched someone you know speaking to a child and suddenly changing their demeanor, adopting a sharper and more staccato tone of voice, so that they remind you of one of your schoolteachers? How often have you heard yourself, your partner or one of your friends morph into one of your parents or teachers when addressing children? Have you noticed how automatically this can happen?

This phenomenon often takes us by surprise. It's not that we never act in ways that are not borne of our childhoods; no parents are totally scripted and predetermined. But it is amazing to see how often we treat our children in a way that reflects how we were once treated without realizing we're doing it.

There are at least three main ways in which our parenting behaviors are negative reactions to our own histories.

Overcompensating

Jenny often appeared to have no boundaries with her five-year-old daughter Helena, who would mistreat her, even hit her sometimes. She was unable to say "no" to Helena with any conviction, and she would not allow herself to sound annoyed or irritated. Jenny was treating her daughter as if she were made of glass. When Jenny was a child, her rather authoritarian parents had regularly punished her, talked down to her and yelled at her in ways that made her feel small, frightened and terribly ashamed. These painful memories were driving her to overprotect Helena; the thought that she might ever cause Helena to feel the same way was simply unbearable. Her refusal to ever sound the slightest bit annoyed was an overcompensation. Jenny was deeply caring but unassertive, which created many difficulties, for herself as well as for Helena.

Passing it on

Martin, who sometimes beat his son with a belt, boasted that his own father's thrashings had done him no harm and had made him the man he is today. How true. Martin remembered every beating at his father's hands, but had no connection whatsoever to how he felt—mostly he laughed it off. He felt no remorse for the way he now "disciplined" his son.

That is, until one day, while talking to a counselor, he got choked up as he remembered how terrified he had been, how small he had felt, how humiliated. The emotional hurt was far worse than the physical pain he had endured. For a long time Martin continued to experience his angry outbursts, but from that point on he was no longer able to belt his son. Martin had lost the armoring that made him insensitive toward his son. Before he could connect to his son's pain, he had to connect to his own.

EXERCISE

If you already have children, try to remember any instances when you have reacted in ways belonging to each of the above categories. It might feel somewhat distressing (even embarrassing) to acknowledge these kinds of reactions. You might feel some regret, some remorse, or perhaps it will make you laugh. Please know that these things happen to all of us as parents and allow yourself to feel some of the discomfort because self-recognition can help you to deepen your connection with your child and motivates you to adopt new ways when necessary.

It can be a relief and reassuring to know that other parents stumble in similar ways. So, share anecdotes with your partner or a friend, and ask them to tell you theirs.

Finding it hard to give what we haven't received

When someone suggested that she breastfeed her baby girl for longer than six months, Claudia complained that she felt exhausted. The demand for so much nurturing and physical intimacy was wearing her thin. She herself had never been breastfed, and her own mother, though loving, caring and protective, was not physically demonstrative; she rarely cuddled Claudia as a child. Claudia was being asked to give far more than she had received and so felt strained without knowing why. What finally gave her the energy to meet her baby's needs was to ensure that she received many massages, hugs and much nurturance from her partner and her friends.

How your child triggers your memory

Our children re-stimulate our own childhood memories very powerfully. In fact, at every stage of our children's development, our closeness with them tends to bring up for us many of the emotions we experienced when we were the same age. This happens right through our journey as parents, from the time of pregnancy, through birth, babyhood—all the way through the teenage years and beyond.

Exactly how does this work? Well, it's not that our children always cause us to clearly remember things that had long been buried—though this does happen to some parents, at times. What our children rekindle in us quite frequently is our emotional memories. In other words, they can cause old emotions, things that we felt when we were the same age as them, to waft up to consciousness. Unless you are used to paying close attention to your own emotions, this emotional memory might resurface without you noticing—you might find yourself feeling and acting in ways that surprise or even baffle you. There are times when, as parents, we behave or make choices that are driven by these emotional memories. Depending on the nature of the memory, this can sometimes be helpful to our children; other times it can interfere or bring unintended consequences. So it pays off enormously to be attentive to our feeling states and to develop an interest in how our own childhood has affected us emotionally.

This phenomenon is very important to remember, since it may explain many of the emotional reactions that you have as a parent. So many of the problems we face as parents—the times we feel stuck, lost, don't know what to do—can be better understood in light of these emotional memories. So much of the love, patience and wisdom that we bring to our children is drawn from our emotional memories of childhood, even when we don't realize it.

At the birth of their child, for example, parents often feel some of the anxiety—or the elation—they felt when they were born themselves. Some fathers have been known to pass out while witnessing their child being born. It is cruel and unjust to criticize them for this. What is going on is that emotional memories of their own birth trauma, and the terror they experienced, have been pushed to the surface by virtue of their sensitive connection to their partner and baby. Far from being a reason to judge fathers or to exclude them from labor, this highlights the need for counseling and support for fathers leading up to and after the birth of their child. By the same token, much of the postnatal elation experienced by mothers and fathers alike is a reliving of the ecstatic feelings surrounding their own birth (more about this amazing phenomenon in the next chapter).

When your baby cries, you might sometimes experience waves of your own baby feelings: the helplessness, the longing, perhaps some of the anger you felt as a baby when no one came to pick you up and comfort you. At your toddler's first day at preschool, you might find yourself feeling some of what you felt when you were first separated from your mother—was it fear, anguish, grief, excitement? All these feelings, the feelings of your inner child, are brought forth through the contact with your child because you two are so close.

The more aware we become of the childhood emotional memories triggered in us by our children, the more wisdom we gain as parents, and the closer our connection with our children becomes. If we can be compassionate and understanding toward ourselves whenever these memories are painful and, better still, if we can share these feelings with people who care about us, we can also free ourselves of old hurts.

CASSIE—AN ANECDOTE

Cassie had a three-year-old daughter, Angie, whom she drove to preschool each day. In the early days of the first year, Cassie watched Angie try to talk to and play with the other kids, but too often the others would not respond to her. Sometimes they ignored her altogether or walked away. Cassie started to feel overcome with emotional pain. Coming home from preschool drop-off one day, Cassie burst into tears. She was fearful for Angie, and could not bear to think how rejected she thought Angie must be feeling. Cassie was consumed with worry that Angie would be marked or traumatized by this experience, and that she would feel awkward around her peers forever.

What Cassie feared the most was that Angie would feel the same as Cassie felt when she was her age. As it turned out, Cassie felt incredibly alone as a child. She was rejected by the kids at her school and was painfully shy as a result. This shyness lasted well into her adolescence and brought much sadness to her life.

When Cassie fretfully consulted one of the preschool teachers, she was invited to sit in the playground and watch Angie from a distance. From doing so, she found out two things that reassured her immensely. The first was that Angie showed almost no distress when another child did not respond to her overtures. Angie was far more secure and content with her own company than Cassie had been at her age. She loved to play alone. The second thing Cassie discovered was that the lack of social graces displayed by the other children did nothing at all to dent Angie's self-confidence. When she felt like it, she still reached out to other kids to play with. To Cassie's great relief, other kids were increasingly coming to Angie to play with her. It did not take long for Angie to make two wonderful and steady friends.

Triggered by Angie, Cassie had relived her own three-year-old emotions. It was beneficial for Cassie then to mourn her own difficult years as a child—and this helped her to let go of Angie and trust that she would be OK. Interestingly, after grieving for herself—having realized that the pain was her own and not Angie's—Cassie found herself spontaneously reaching out more to her own friends.

Cassie's memories certainly helped her to be caring and empathetic. At times her protectiveness would be warranted, but in this instance, it was necessary for Cassie to watch closely in order to realize that Angie's experience was different to hers, so her protection would have been intrusive.

STEFAN—AN ANECDOTE

Although he was warm and loving during the early years of his marriage, soon after the birth of his daughter Stefan became puzzlingly angry, hostile and emotionally distant from his wife. Although Stefan could not consciously recall it, his own parents had been very inattentive toward him as a baby, he was left to wail interminably in his crib and playpen and only cursorily picked up for routine feeding and changing. Stefan's babyhood was a time of anger and despair, which left him vulnerable to feelings of rejection as an adult, although he wasn't aware of the cause.

As his wife diverted much of her loving attention toward their newborn, Stefan began to react like a jilted lover: he was no longer the special one in her life. Each day he was forced to witness his baby receiving the loving tenderness he had been deprived of as a baby. It was as if all the anger and betrayal he felt as a baby had come flooding to the surface and, unwittingly, he focused these feelings on his wife and child.

Deep down, Stefan was no less nurturing than any other dad; he was merely reacting to an old emotional wound. It was very important that Stefan, with the help of a therapist, come to terms with his memories so that he could stop blaming his wife and baby for how he felt. With emotional support, Stefan was able to grieve for what he had missed out on as a baby and to begin accepting compassion from others. As his own healing process unfolded, Stefan found himself increasingly moved by the urge to be tender toward his daughter and to rejoice in the tenderness she was receiving from her mother (see Callander, *Why Dads Leave: Insights and Resources for When Partners Become* Parents).

Happy memories are also helpful

There are few things more enchanting than a dad shaking off the serious demeanor of responsible adult at the office and dropping to the floor to play with his child—more to the point—to play like a child. When dads do this, they are usually drawing from early memories of when someone else joined them on the floor and played with them, acted silly, played make-believe games, built and destroyed things, wrestled.

Every happy, peaceful, joyous memory of childhood adds to our reservoir of parenting fuel. Maybe it's in the way you sing your child to sleep every night, as your mother did for you, or in the surprising treats you put in your child's lunch box every so often, just as the surprises you once found in your lunch box filled your day with delight. Perhaps it is in the way you patiently teach your son how to kick and catch a football, the way your dad did with you. Or in the way you cheer, just as your parents did for you, for your daughter's netball team or your son's soccer team from the sidelines. Or in the way you dreamily rock in your chair as you nurse your baby. When we have our own children, we are drawn to reliving these rich, life-giving memories from the parent's point of view. We yearn to pass on the deep sense of wellbeing that pervaded us when Mom or Dad were right next to us. What greater fulfillment is there than those moments when we can watch our children reveling in the same feelings of wellbeing that we once knew?

What are the benefits of connecting with the feelings associated with these memories? When you recapture these inner-child feelings, you are moved to be emotionally available and fully present for your child. These memories help to bring pleasure back into parenting. Your inner child is the doorway through which you connect to your own child.

EXERCISE

Remember one of the most loving and happy moments you ever shared with your mother, your father or another adult who cared for you. Pick any moment: a favorite memory of wellbeing or happiness from any time in your childhood. Perhaps someone was holding you, rocking you, feeding you or reading you a story. Remember who was there with you, what they said, what they did. Remember how you felt, the sensations of being a child, in a child's body. Now imagine yourself doing the same thing for your child. What do you feel when you imagine this?

We can use our happy and our painful memories of childhood to inform and improve the way we relate to our children. Our emotional memory tells us quite a lot about how we loved to be treated, as well as how we wished we were treated differently. This is the most important source of your expertise as a parent. Your emotional memory is the key to making connections with your children. This holds true even if your memory of what happened and when is not at all clear. Often it is your emotional memory that drives your parenting choices without your knowing it.

The expert is… you

Remembering your own childhood experiences—as long as you are connecting with the *feeling* of the experience, not just the narrative—is one of the strongest sources of your expertise as a parent. You can draw so much from your difficult as well as your happy moments. They give you profound insights into your child's inner world and enable the child's powerful and unrestrained emotionality to become less of a mystery to you. So your memories provide you with an empathy enhancer and a tool for better understanding your child's needs. Knowing how your childhood has influenced the person you have become, and the relationships you have, can give you increased confidence when sifting through all the advice and information you read and help you decide what, according to your intuition, feels right.

How your children help you to heal and to grow

You will often be surprised by the intensity and the variety of feelings provoked in you by your child. If you pay close and careful attention to your own feelings, you are likely to notice at each age of your child some uncomfortable emotions, vestiges of unresolved hurts from your own childhood. You might also find beautiful feelings are provoked, feelings of wonder, awe and playfulness, feelings you had long forgotten. Let all of these feelings come to you.

If you understand this process, you might realize that often, negative feelings toward your baby or child are probably projections from your past. They are feelings that others felt toward you when you were young, and have nothing to do with your child. What's happening is that you are partially reliving an old experience that your closeness to your child has brought into your consciousness. Consider talking about this with people you trust because it is a golden opportunity for healing old wounds.

The nuts and bolts of childhood memory

Many of you will be thinking by now: How does this help me? I can't remember a single thing before I was nine. When I ask a group of people the age of their earliest memory, most people say two or three years. There are many individuals who think they cannot remember anything at all before they were nine, or even older—but this is not the norm; the majority remember back to around three. Not surprisingly, if I said to you that you actually remember everything that ever happened to you since you were inside your mother's womb—that we all do—you might find that preposterous.

There is a good reason why most people think they don't remember anything before three. The brain systems chiefly responsible for organizing memory into something like an audiovisual clip that tells a story with a certain order of events, however foggy, include the hippocampus and orbito-frontal cortex, and these systems are not mature until we're about two or three. No wonder it seems as if we remember little or nothing before that. This is to do with a particular kind of memory called "narrative memory," that is, the ability to retell an order of events.

Aside from narrative memory, there is another type of recall named "emotional memory," which enables us to remember not so much what happened, but how we felt about it. The part of the brain chiefly responsible for processing emotional memory is the amygdala; this part of the brain is fully functional before we are born. Think of the implications. It means that many of our characteristic, individual ways of relating to others are influenced by events that took place long before the reaches of our narrative memory. Many of our attitudes and much of our emotional makeup are influenced by the way we felt before birth, as babies and as toddlers. Our earliest layers of emotional memory contribute much to our personalities—the way we relate to others, our hopes and our fears—and very much to the way we respond to our children. Some psychologists refer to emotional memory as "body-memory" or "implicit memory." It is as if emotional memory, though it might elude our conscious awareness, is recorded forever in our bodies, our muscles, our internal organs.

Emotional memory can manifest in many ways. Usually, it shows itself as a strong emotion that does not seem to relate to what is going on around us here and now. Sometimes it comes up as a physical sensation that seems difficult to understand: a hot flush, a palpitation, a headache, muscle aches and tensions, a tremor, nausea or a stomach ache. Even though we are seldom aware of it, it influences our behavior, our attitudes and our way of relating to each other.

Sometimes it is possible for the emotional memory—body memory—to surface into conscious awareness with a story attached. There are countless incidences of people, under certain conditions such as hypnosis or other kinds of psychotherapy, spontaneously recalling verifiable events that took place while they were babies, even while they were being born (see Chamberlain, *Babies Remember Birth* and Verny, *The Secret Life of the Unborn Child*).

Many people have remembered quite clearly how they felt when they cried out for their mothers to pick them up and no one came. They re-experience the anguish quite acutely. Many have remembered the intense joy that overcame them, lying in their mothers' arms as she gazed affectionately at them. Sometimes the memories are lucid, sometimes fuzzy but charged with emotion. So, what we don't remember consciously is still remembered in our bodies; it continues to touch us emotionally well into adulthood.

Even if you can't recall your early childhood experiences as a movie clip, even if no images come to you at all, these experiences have colored the way you feel about yourself today, and the way you feel about others and the world around you. To some extent for all of us, our beliefs, attitudes and behaviors are tinged by the way we were cared for as far back as earliest infancy and in the womb.

DID YOU KNOW:

That, if, when we were babies, our parents were sensitive and nurturing toward us, our feelings of safety and security remain with us as emotional memory well into adulthood? This emotional memory of security and love can strongly protect us from stress. Trauma counselors have found that people who have had close, warm relationships with their parents in early childhood tend to cope better with traumatic events and are less likely to develop post-traumatic stress disorders.

Memory can be state-dependent, that is, a memory can quite unexpectedly be brought to the surface by a bodily posture, a feeling or an event similar to the original (a similar state triggers the old, forgotten memory). That is why your children trigger your own emotional memory, from a time of your life corresponding roughly to your child's age.

In later chapters, some exercises that can help you tap into the flavor of how it felt to be very little, even a little baby, will be presented. You don't have to immerse yourself in these memories too deeply if it feels scary, but just a taste can help you immeasurably to connect with your own children.

YOU CAN REMEMBER

Until recently, psychologists and doctors told parents that it doesn't matter much what happens to a baby, as they won't remember. In light of new research, this kind of advice has to be thrown out.

Children and adults retain emotional memory dating back to their birth and before, and key experiences from these earliest moments have profound long-term effects on the nervous system and, therefore, on personality.

Why do some people remember almost nothing?

There are many reasons why this might happen, and not all the reasons are well understood. Head injuries or illnesses can interfere with memory. Also, the brain is cleverly able to erase very painful events so the conscious memory and the pain that comes with it does not nag at us. If, when children go through something very traumatic, there is no comforting or escape for them, their brains produce chemicals that anesthetize them from the emotional pain. These neurochemicals also help the brain of the child to bury the painful memory. But it is important to remember this: neuroscientists have confirmed that even without conscious recollection, what we lived through as babies and children affects us deeply for the long term because in early childhood, the way our relationships felt to us actually influenced the way our brains developed—it influenced our brain chemistry. Children's and adults' behavior can reflect emotional hurts, even if the conscious awareness of these hurts is deeply buried.

MEMORY'S HEALING POWER

It is possible for buried memories to resurface, and sometimes life events trigger this spontaneous recall. Under very carefully controlled circumstances, preferably with the help of a therapist, it can be healing to allow some of these painful memories to come up, provided that emotional support is made available in a safe environment. Fortunately, it is not necessary to be plunged back into the depths of unpleasant memories and to totally relive our pain as if it were happening all over again. For healing to occur, for you to feel relieved of a difficult memory, and for compassion to take its place, it can sometimes be enough to merely touch upon the memory until you feel just some of the emotion welling up. But sometimes, when a painful or scary memory comes back to our minds, we may need more of the memory in order to feel healed. We may also need someone to listen to us patiently, someone to hold us and comfort us. As we saw earlier, connection heals. Some of the greatest relief comes to us when we cease to be all alone with our distressing emotions.

Remember through your own eyes

Time and time again, when people recount an anecdote from their childhood, they describe themselves in derogatory language. When talking about themselves as toddlers, they call themselves "little brats," when talking about themselves as babies, they claim they were difficult babies who were trying to control everyone around them. This is not remembering themselves from the inside. Babies and children do not think of themselves in those terms, they simply accept the labels pinned on them by the adults. All too often, we remember ourselves not through our own eyes, but through the eyes of critical parents because babies and children are unable to defend themselves from their parents' projections. So much of our self-image, particularly the image we have of ourselves as children, is a confused memory. We are not remembering ourselves—we are remembering others' judgments about us and adopting these as our own.

You know when you have connected with how you truly felt as a child when you feel your childhood memory from the inside. You won't be viewing yourself from the outside, making judgments about yourself—you will be feeling absolute compassion for yourself as a child, no matter what others told you about yourself.

EXERCISE

Here is an exercise for you and your partner: As mentioned earlier, memory can be state-dependent. Sometimes, by assuming a physical position similar to how it was during some situation a long time ago, this can bring up the old emotions associated with the situation. If, for example, you squat or kneel and look upwards into another person's eyes, it might make you feel like a child, small, dependent and vulnerable. Try this with your partner or spouse, or a friend whom you trust.

Take a few moments to look upward at the other, while he or she stands still a few feet away, silent and impassive. Be aware of the sensation of your breath rising and falling in your chest. Close your eyes for a minute or so afterward and notice any emotions that pass through you, however fleeting.

When you feel ready, stand up again, swap roles with your partner, who will now take a turn looking upward at you. Make sure you take the time to share with each other anything you felt during the exercise.

The deadlock-breaking question

Whenever you encounter a stumbling block with your child that keeps coming up again and again—for instance, when you keep getting into a power struggle, when you can't understand why she is crying, when something he keeps doing particularly grates on you, when you find it difficult to be affectionate—try first asking yourself: What was going on for me when I was this age? Before you rush out to try another technique from the latest how-to book, take a little time out to understand yourself better. You might be surprised to find that this helps to break the deadlock. A better understanding of your own habitual reactions will give you a deeper sense of what your child is going through, and help you to develop your own new ways to respond.

Remember, your child sometimes triggers emotional memories in you. When they are painful memories about unresolved situations, your inner turmoil can make it difficult to clearly see and understand your child. By becoming more aware of what is going on inside you, pressure is lifted off your child and you can see him with new eyes.

JUANITA—AN ANECDOTE

Juanita had problems dealing with her son's tantrums. No one finds tantrums pleasant, but the embarrassment and helplessness they caused Juanita were making the tantrums traumatic for her. Juanita was becoming afraid of her own child. Increasingly, she was alternating between anxiously giving him whatever he asked for in order to avert a tantrum, or avoiding him altogether. Juanita had read all kinds of well-intentioned advice on how to control or calm her son, but none of this advice prevented her from feeling estranged from him since he began to show his anger in this way.

When Juanita was about her son's age, she also would burst into uncontrolled rage every so often, the way most toddlers do when they are frustrated. Juanita's childish anger was deemed unacceptable at home. Her parents punished her tantrums severely, until she became ashamed of her own anger and afraid to express it. Juanita sensed that voicing her feelings strongly would never be welcomed in her family. She grew to feel self-conscious and inhibited, afraid to express her passions. In her close relationships, she tended to be timid, unassertive and obliging.

With the help of a counselor, Juanita gradually learned to be more comfortable with her big emotions. As she found ways to express—even enjoy—her own anger again, Juanita began to feel less intimidated by her son and far more comfortable with his outbursts. By remembering the fury she sometimes felt as a child, and the pain of clamping down on these feelings in order to please her parents, Juanita became far more able to be present for her son.

Juanita's healing process had immediate flow-on effects on him. The more he felt his anger was accepted, and the more he felt his mother's empathy and patience, the sooner his tantrums resolved. Far more than any calming technique, this helped Juanita to truly connect with her son in ways that eased his transit through the tantrum stage. More importantly, Juanita and her son regained the closeness they had temporarily lost.

Even if it proves impossible to consciously remember anything about your life when you were your child's current age, try asking members of your family. Sometimes, by piecing together what others can tell you about your life as a child, it can be possible to recapture at least some of the feelings of early childhood. Alternatively, if you take the time to imagine what it is like to be a baby or a small child, really putting yourself in the booties of an infant, your imagination can bring you a flavor of how this once felt for you.

Whenever you recall something that made you sad, afraid or angry, ask yourself these questions: If you could have had any wish come true at the time, what would you have wished for? What would you have most loved for others to do for you that would have made you feel happy again? Is there anything you wished you could have said or done differently? Your honest and uncensored answers to these questions might give you profound insights into your child's needs and how you can comfort, protect, empower or liberate her.

In the following chapters, we will be looking at the times of pregnancy, birth, babyhood and the toddler years. At each of these stages of your child's life, your effectiveness and ability to connect with your child will be enhanced by your willingness to explore your own childhood history. It would be tremendously useful to you as a parent to familiarize yourself with how your caregivers related to you at each of these stages, and how this made you feel. Share your stories with your partner, or if you are a single parent, with your closest friends. This can help you enormously as parents while deepening your appreciation for each other.

Parenting energy—like any other fuel

Have you noticed how from time to time your parenting energies seem to run low, or even run out altogether? Have you ever, as a mother or as a father, experienced yourself running out of parenting fuel and grinding to a halt by the side of the parenting road? Do you at that point become angry at your child for asking too much of you (driving you too hard), or do you get disappointed with yourself and feel ashamed for not having more endurance?

Could you instead think of calling on someone—a friend, a relative—to act as your tow truck? Better still, are you sure you put enough fuel in your tank to begin with?

Much of what comes naturally for us as parents flows easily because we have once received it ourselves, from loving parents—or perhaps from others who have cared for and connected with us sometime in our lives. We seem to give best what we have ourselves been given.

Those things you haven't received can be the hardest to give. Many parents whose own parents were not, for example, physically demonstrative, find it very awkward, maybe even embarrassing, to give their children hugs. They either avoid hugging their children, or their hugs feel stiff and unyielding. Remember, too, the anecdotes about Juanita and Pierre who were never allowed to voice their feelings strongly, how threatened they felt by their children's passion? And, many mothers, when they have not known this kind of intimacy at their own mother's breast, have found breastfeeding a struggle.

This doesn't necessarily mean we are all trapped by our past, it does not mean it is impossible to give what has not been given to us. The important thing to understand is that it is cruel to expect of yourself to give something you were yourself deprived of. It is natural to find this difficult, and it is not your fault if you can't.

Understand that if you find yourself struggling to give, you should reach out for the kind of support you need. This is an irrefutable truth: mothers' and fathers' emotional fuel tanks must be filled regularly. Be aware of your need for support, for community, for nourishing connection with others. In order to meet your child's emotional needs, your own emotional needs must first be met.

We all have an array of intimacy needs, such as the need for emotional support, affectional touch, sexual love, shared humor, fun and play. Below is a basic list of needs that parents should attend to regularly—why not daily? You might like to add more of your own:

- ☩ To have one or more people with whom you feel comfortable to be yourself, to express your feelings, hopes and dreams, with whom to share the joys, pains and frustrations of being a parent.
- ☩ To be with one or more people who you care about and like listening to.
- ☩ To have one or more people who help you, at least occasionally, care for your child.
- ☩ To have stimulating adult conversation with people whose values and interests you share.
- ☩ To play with, laugh with and have fun with one or more people.

Your connections with your children can at times be very energizing, but since you are primarily in a caring role, parenting demands large quantities of your relating energies. Remember to regularly check your personal fuel gauge and, for the sake of keeping parenting pleasurable, fill up.

Summary

The love and care we received from our parents fuels our ability to love others and to pass on this love to our children. Equally, the love we give our children today prepares and energizes them to be parents tomorrow. So, if some of your key emotional needs were not met for you as a child, it becomes all the more important to have plenty of emotional support now that you are a parent. In some instances, some counseling or psychotherapy may be beneficial.

There are no bad parents; there cannot be. Whenever someone is neglectful or hurtful, it is because life has hurt them or let them down. More than likely, they suffered as children. Our insensitivities toward our children, the mistakes we make as parents, are reflections of the things that hurt us when we were children—just as the love and patience we pass on springs from the love we received.

Your preparation for parenting involves first connecting to your inner child—a bottomless source of love, empathy and wisdom. Secondly, it involves ensuring that you have plenty of practical and emotional support through your close relationships and community. If you are like most people in Western society, you have probably underestimated how much support you need. You know how much support is enough for you when parenting ceases to be a chore and begins to feel more and more of a pleasure and a joy.

What you will learn in the following chapters is what science has to say about raising emotionally healthy and joyous children. This developmental map will also give you important information about your own upbringing and how it may have affected you, so you can deepen your connection with yourself, and perhaps heal and grow as a person.

Part 2
When Does Connection Begin?

3

Connecting Begins Long Before Baby's Birth

This chapter and the next two will be about the most fascinating facts that science has revealed about pregnancy and childbirth, and the moments and days immediately after. It will also look at what you can do to provide a deep foundation of wellbeing and trust for your child that will last for life. The way we welcome a new life into the world is at the very core of emotional intelligence and the way the child will view the world as she grows up.

Can we?

Pregnancy? Birth? What on earth do they have to do with a child's emotional health? Aren't we starting a little too early here? How can a parent have any influence on a child's emotional health when the child is still in the womb? We can't communicate with an unborn child, surely.

Up until the last twenty years most people have not regarded little babies as fully-fledged people, capable of feeling all the same feelings as adults. That notion is certainly changing, but would you think of a fetus as a person that thinks, feels and remembers? Have you ever stopped to think about this?

Very few parenting books and courses talk about parenting as something that begins early in pregnancy. But it does. Connection with your baby begins, for both parents, while the baby is still in the womb. In fact, a child's distinct emotional makeup begins to develop long before birth.

Why have so many people overlooked the emotional needs of the unborn and the newly born child? Until very recently, pediatricians thought that babies were not in control of their awareness at birth, that their minds were a jumble of disorganized and meaningless sensations. The idea that newborns are able to communicate, to interact with their parents and understand them was not generally accepted, though many parents intuited otherwise. For a long time, the only concern about a newborn has been for the baby's medical safety. The mother's feelings at birth did not seem to matter much, as they would—it was thought—in no way affect the baby's wellbeing. As long as mother and baby survive the medical "emergency" of birth, then the job's done.

Modern research has overturned this misperception. Science has now confirmed the reality of the mind and feelings of the unborn child and made it quite clear that a baby's life experiences in the womb have a powerful, long-term impact on the emotional centers of the brain, and on the baby's personality. Now we know that all along, babies have been conscious, intelligent and feeling, and trying their hearts out to communicate with us. A baby's life in the womb is full of emotion, and a baby's birth and the first moments afterward are profoundly important. These very first experiences of the world tell the baby what can be expected from human relationships—and first impressions really count. For a long time, cultural "authorities" told us that newborns were not people; just people-to-be—blobs with no personality. Most mothers, going against the tide of what they were being told, did so because they felt intuitively that this was wrong.

Do these early connections really matter?

So maybe we can have a meaningful connection with a baby before, during and after birth. But surely this doesn't have a lasting impact, does it? They are still so little. They couldn't possibly understand anything. That's what we thought. Yet countless mothers and fathers have somehow known that they could. This idea was generally dismissed, owing to lack of scientific evidence—until recently. Today, science has backed up that age-old intuition: your relationship with your unborn child is every bit as consequential as your relationship with your baby, toddler or child—and probably more so. This means that there is a lot you can do to nurture your baby's emotional health from the earliest days of pregnancy. Even if you don't know you're doing it, you influence your child's emotional intelligence in the womb. Active parenting, we now know, begins around conception, and you make a huge difference in your child's life right from then.

Do you remember being born?

Most people feel that they couldn't possibly remember being born, and yet many people around the world have remembered some aspects of their birth. For over a century now, psychologists and psychiatrists have, with the use of hypnosis or body-oriented psychotherapies, documented patients' birth memories that arise in psychotherapy. Many more have been surprised by birth memories while in deep meditation, while witnessing the birth of a child or in a host of other circumstances. Children have often spontaneously recalled their birth and been able to retell it to their parents in vivid detail. I have spoken to a number of parents who are amazed by the accuracy of their toddlers' memories of birth, despite the fact that the details had never been discussed in front of them. People who have them, tend to keep such memories under wraps, rather than face denial or ridicule.

ALEX—AN ANECDOTE

When attending an intensive course on meditation, Alex shared with the group a life-changing vision that came to him during one of his deepest meditations. One early morning as Alex was enjoying a profoundly peaceful and relaxed state, an image came to him of a flesh-colored sun dawning over a horizon. As the orb reached halfway above, an unknown force pushed it back beneath the edge. This sun dawned a second time, only to be submerged again. On its third attempt, it was finally released from whatever held it prisoner, and at last claimed the sky. As soon as this vision was complete, Alex was flooded with feelings of relief, love and elation so overwhelming he dissolved into tears.

Oblivious to the meaning of this waking dream, Alex left his home to go about his business. For the rest of the day and wherever he went, he felt waves of the most inexplicable love and compassion for every person, friend or stranger, he passed. Alex had no idea what was happening to him.

Some days later, while recounting his strange but beautiful experience to his mother, her eyes misted over and she began to tell him a story she had never shared. When Alex was being born, he had begun to arrive so quickly that the obstetrician had not yet made it to the delivery room. The anxious nurses, when seeing his head beginning to crown twice pushed him back for fear of undermining the obstetrician's strict control. Finally, the doctor arrived; at Alex's third attempt, he was released into the world. Unbeknown to him, Alex had always carried this memory of his stifled entry into the world. The oppressive restraint upon his birth impulse had marked him emotionally, somewhat dampened his spirit and inhibited his passion. Note how after reliving his birth, though only in a symbolic way, Alex experienced a most uplifting emotional release. The release of emotions associated with his birth freed Alex quite considerably to live and love more fully from that day on.

BIRGIT—AN ANECDOTE

Birgit was enjoying a deep-tissue massage; on this day her practitioner was working deeply into her neck and head, where she had long been complaining of tension. As the masseur was mobilizing and stretching her head, Birgit began to feel teary, and soon she was sobbing. Unexpectedly, a birth memory had come back to her of being yanked by the head with forceps, then immediately separated from her mother and placed in a bassinet. The fear and the grief she had felt as a newborn resurfaced, triggered by the neck and head massage. This memory and the emotional release that came with it helped Birgit to better understand the feelings of anguish and separateness that had often plagued her throughout her life. It also helped Birgit to enjoy a more intimate and satisfying connection with her husband.

Do you remember anything about your own birth? If, like most people, you think that you don't, then notice how you feel when you see images of normal, natural birth. Do these images touch off any feelings for you—such as gladness, joy, wonder, affection, fear, disgust, revulsion or anger? The feelings that such imagery brings up for you are quite possibly triggered from your personal store of emotional memory, and may have a lot to do with what you and/or your mother felt at some time when you were being born.

David Chamberlain, PhD, one of the world's foremost psychotherapists specializing in healing birth trauma, and a leading expert on birth memory, has collected many detailed birth memories recaptured by his patients and corroborated by family members or confirmed after reviewing hospital records.

Are we sure a fetus knows what's going on?

If you have any doubts that a fetus and a newborn have a working mind, then let's look at what scientists have only recently discovered about the abilities of a fetus:

- ♱ By week six in the womb, instruments can detect the earliest measurable electrical activity in the child's brain.
- ♱ By week twelve, the fetus is able to feel pain.
- ♱ By week fifteen, the fetus has learned to swallow the amniotic fluid he is floating in. He can discern taste, and even show preferences. If a bitter substance is injected into the womb, he stops swallowing. If saccharine is injected, he doubles the rate of swallowing.
- ♱ By the fourth month, the fetus can teach herself to aim her thumb into her mouth and suck it.
- ♱ Your baby can hear your voice from around twenty weeks into the pregnancy.
- ♱ Between the sixth and seventh months, the fetal brain is mature enough to support conscious awareness and to feel a range of emotions. Brainwave readings show that the fetus can now respond to what he sees, touches and hears. One of the most amazing discoveries is that all the wiring necessary to store memory is available in the fetal brain from the third trimester.

We have to come to terms with the idea that we all have some kind of memory since before birth, and that this memory must affect us all in some way.

By the time your baby is born, she has already learned to recognize the voice of her parents. French researchers have found that newborns can accurately pick out their mother's voice from a field of other voices. If the father has been close to the mother during pregnancy, the newborn can already identify his voice too. Lullabies that you sing or music you play to your baby in the womb will have a more calming effect after birth. Experiments show that babies even respond to stories that they heard you read when they were in the womb. At the university of North Carolina, researchers asked pregnant mothers to regularly read *The Cat in The Hat* by Dr Seuss aloud. Soon after birth, these babies were given a rubber nipple that was electronically connected to a tape player that played recordings of their mother's voice. By varying the speed of sucking, the baby could change the recorded stories playing—and they showed a consistent preference for the familiar one, the one they had learned in their mother's womb.

Why does our time in the womb and our birth affect us so much?

Whenever I travel, or go to a restaurant or stay in a hotel, it strikes me how much effort the tourism and hospitality industries put into making sure that, as a consumer, I feel warmly welcomed. Cabin crew in planes, reception staff and table waiters all go out of their way to beam at me, pull out chairs for me, offer to serve me and generally impress me with how happy they are to see me. Millions of dollars in training are funneled into making us feel special wherever we go. Granted, much of this feels false and contrived, and yet, don't we all feel let down, ripped-off, angry and unloved when we are met with indifference or lack of warmth? We expect, no, demand, to be made to feel welcome—that we are wanted. We even pay for this privilege.

How does the local hospital greet the newly born? If we adults are so sensitive to the way we are greeted, why don't we extend the same kind of care to our newborns as they enter the world and their new lives and meet their family for the very first time? Isn't this all the more important for a newborn, who is infinitely more sensitive than an adult?

Think about it: now that it cannot be denied that infants are fully aware, feeling and wide awake before, during and after birth, how do you suppose some of our modern birthing procedures would make them feel? After spending months in a cozy, perfectly nourishing cocoon, with all sounds muffled and all lights gently dimmed, how would their eyes feel when they first meet the blazing lights of the delivery room? How would their delicate ears take the noisy, reverberating chatter and clatter? What is it like, from a baby's point of view, to be artificially evicted from home with the use of drugs, to have metal forceps clamped on his skull and tugging at his neck, to be taken from his mother and handled by strangers, to be stabbed, weighed and measured, placed in a plastic box—suddenly alone for the first time? What would it feel like to arrive into a room full of people who are all talking to each other but ignoring you, no matter how you plead with them. If people around you don't know that you can feel, think and communicate, it is as if they are denying you are a person. How does that make you feel as an adult? Imagine then, how does it feel for a newborn? If, as most people, you do not have immediate memories of your birth, take a few moments to imagine this scenario, live it through in your mind. How would it make you feel if that was your introduction to the world? What does this kind of experience teach the baby about the world they have come into? How does that prepare a newborn to trust people?

On the other hand, what was it like to be held warmly, to be talked to softly, to be able to extend arms and legs for the very first time, to feel lungs expand with air, to gaze at mother's loving face for the first time? What was it like for us to envelop our mother's nipple with our lips for the first time, to suckle and have our mouths and bellies generously filled with this delicious liquid?

Think about this: if you are a mother, this is your baby's first sensory experience of you outside the womb, her first impression of the outer world. This first connection is the foundation on which emotional intelligence is built. When a newborn feels acknowledged, wanted and communicated with, it makes the difference between feeling that she exists for others or that she is all alone in the world.

DID YOU KNOW:

That an American sculptor recently did a survey of art from around the world spanning the last 700 years, searching for sculptures of pregnant women that actually showed the baby curled up inside? To his great surprise, he was able to find no more than one such example, a medieval piece entitled *The Visitation*. His own works of prenatal art depicting the unborn child were, for many years—until very recently—turned down, often with considerable contempt, by all the galleries he approached. Why is pregnancy, and in particular the reality of the fetus, so taboo?

In 1952, Lucille Ball, the world famous comedian, was banned from saying the word "pregnant" on television, under the media codes for public morals. Not long ago, an Australian television host who had been popular with viewers for many years, took the unprecedented step of continuing in her role while pregnant with her first child. Her show was flooded with angry letters from viewers who found her protruding belly "disgusting"; debates about the "inappropriateness" of her stance raged throughout the Australian media. When Demi Moore posed naked—and very pregnant—for Vanity Fair in August 1991, she caused an uproar, and many stores in the US refused to stock the issue.

These attitudes have begun to change in recent decades; increasingly, we see women happily exposing their pregnant bellies at the beach or through revealing clothing in the streets, shops and cafés. Why for so long did the sight of a pregnant woman make so many people squeamish? What does this say about how many of us have been taught to feel toward mothers, the unborn child, the miracle of creation? Could we not instead view pregnancy as something magical and beautiful?

Birth, as Nature designed it

It is only over the last two decades that scientists have come to understand how truly astonishing and delicately balanced is Nature's grand design for loving connections. Under normal and natural circumstances, when a mother is giving birth, an extraordinary transformative process is unfolding in her body that will prime her and her baby for some of the most profound emotional changes—making them both wide open to, quite literally, falling in love at first sight. The mother's brain, in the moments leading up to, during and immediately after birth, orchestrates the massive release of a cocktail of hormones specifically tailored to induce some of the most profound feelings of love, bonding and nurturance. A similar spike in these hormones affects the baby, released in the baby's own brain, as well as received directly from the mother through the placenta. There is no other time in our lives when these brain chemicals are released in such huge quantities. If the natural process of birth is supported and not interfered with, these chemicals have the power to lull the mother and child into a blissful state of communion.

Why does this remarkable emotional phenomenon happen? Nature does not go to so much trouble just to give us bonuses; it is far too wise and economical for that. This transcendent and life-changing emotional event must have a vital purpose. It is designed to bond the mother and child, fill them with love for each other and prepare them for healthy attachment. Nature has planned for millennia to make parenting as pleasurable and joyous as possible, and provides all the ingredients necessary—we just have to trust this plan. The mother-child connection is the cornerstone of a harmonious society, and the health of this connection depends on it being largely pleasurable and happy. The mother-child connection is also the starting point for our emotional intelligence—for the way we relate to all others as we grow. No wonder Nature has invested so much of its ingenuity to forge this bond and imbue it with blissful emotion. Let's take a closer look at some of these marvelous hormones and what they can do for the mother and child.

Oxytocin

Oxytocin, naturally released in huge quantities before, during and after birth, has been dubbed the love hormone. Oxytocin produces intense, loving feelings and speeds up labor by increasing contractions. Additionally, oxytocin plays a role in reducing the mother's pain. After birth, oxytocin induces nurturing behavior in the mother. If you want to keep reveling in those blissful, loving and maternal feelings, here is a helpful hint: you can maintain quite high oxytocin levels through direct skin-to-skin contact with your baby, so if after birth your instincts tell you to keep your newborn close to you, go with it. In hospitals they call this "rooming in"; you will find that the old practice of taking the baby away so the mother can "rest" is quickly disappearing. Medical authorities and psychologists are beginning to realize how important these primal moments of bonding are, for the mother's and the baby's emotional health.

Prolactin

This hormone, also released in the mother's body in high quantities, brings about tender mothering behavior. It is also related to milk production and immune system functioning.

Beta-endorphin

Beta-endorphin, a naturally occurring opiate, is known as the hormone of pleasure and transcendence. It induces dependency feelings, and helps mother and baby to feel deeply connected and attached to each other. Beta-endorphin is also analgesic, meaning that it is able to reduce the mother's labor pains. Many women have described the effects of beta-endorphin as an altered or transcendent state of consciousness, an ecstatic, trance-like state of mind. If mothers are given the space to surrender to this trance-like state, and if they are not pressured into remaining rational and engaged in conversation, the levels of this beneficial hormone will remain high, and so assist the birth process enormously. In other words, we should cut the chitchat, especially during the later stages of labor, and let the mother focus on herself.

Noradrenaline

There are temporary surges of noradrenaline in the baby and the mother immediately after birth, and for an hour or so this makes them both alert and wide-awake. The baby's pupils dilate to meet the mother's eyes directly, and so they get to know each other. This noradrenaline peak gradually wears off until the newborn falls asleep, having fulfilled the need to bond with her beloved. For decades scientists have observed this brief but critical postnatal period of "imprinting," Nature's way of showing the baby who her mother is.

Michel Odent, MD, Sarah Buckley, MD, Binnie Dansby and other experts describe this combination of hormones as an "ecstatic cocktail." Many mothers also say, particularly after a natural childbirth, that they are overcome with elation, and with uncontainable love and tenderness. Like a hormonal version of Cupid's arrow, this is Nature's way of helping mother and baby fall helplessly in love—an experience that has the power to transform their relationship for life. The intense feelings generated—probably unlike anything the mother has experienced, or will experience again beyond another labor— provide the mother with a deep reservoir of emotional fuel for the challenging venture that awaits her, while marking the new relationship with the most delicious sentiment, right from day one. When conditions are favorable and the birthing process is natural, the resulting rapture can nourish the parenting connection forever, helping both parents tune in more closely to the child's needs.

All of us who are involved with the birth of a child—parents, extended family, friends and health professionals—should be doing everything possible to provide the conditions that ensure the maximum free flow of these wondrous brain chemicals. Further on, we will be looking at some of the specific ways that family and friends can support new parents.

When this natural hormonal process proceeds uninterrupted, it provides for the baby a deep well of good feelings and a foundation of trust in life and love that can reverberate for a lifetime. It is, literally, a happy birthday, the forerunner of many happy returns. A natural and lovingly supported birth gives the baby an injection of emotional wellness that paves the way for strength, resilience, self-esteem and ability to love and be loved. It's as if the child's mind will always be silently murmuring: I was received with so much love and joy, so I must be very lovable, and people are lovable. When this is our core attitude toward ourselves and toward each other, our relationships will reflect this mood. Because these inaugural moments of life are recorded in the child's brain as emotional memory, their effects can be far-reaching and lifelong.

The newborn's earliest images of his mother and his first experience of the outside world give him a point of reference for later relationships. The emotional memories associated with this primal life stage form the basic model of relationships through which we view and interpret relationships. Here are sown the very first seeds of the child's emotional intelligence. That's why it is so important to surround mothers with loving support during pregnancy, to aim as much as possible toward a natural and sensitively managed birth, and to make sacred the bonding process that is to follow.

Early connections that last a lifetime

Here is where the rewards of a respectfully, sensitively managed birth get really exciting. When the hormones of birth are allowed to work their magic, your baby has a far greater chance of becoming a content and smiling baby, one who falls asleep more easily and is more readily comforted through her connection with you. This cannot be emphasized often enough: pregnancy, birth and the moments afterward are the greatest investment in your future together.

When the primal connection is compromised

There are many different things that typically interfere with Nature's best intentions. Mothers do not have a rhinoceros hide, particularly at the time of birth, and the right hormonal balance is highly susceptible to the mother's emotional state. Labor wards can be alienating. The atmosphere of emergency surrounding some hospital-managed births, the cold and clinical ambience, the bright lights and unfamiliar people in masks and gowns, the mother's loss of control when the obstetrician runs the show—any of these factors can stress and alarm many birthing mothers. An intimidating environment produces stress hormones that inhibit the flow of the joyous and analgesic hormones mentioned earlier. Fear produces adrenalin, which interrupts oxytocin production, which often causes complications and slows down labor or, in some cases, even stops it.

Over the years, in my private practice, I have listened to innumerable stories of mothers whose normal and healthy contractions at labor came to a sudden halt the very moment their obstetrician—or any other individual for that matter—with whom they did not feel *emotionally safe*, entered the room. The pressure on the mother to accept medical intervention often begins in response to her body's natural fear responses—and thus her control is taken away. How often are the dramatic "medical complications" at labor, the type that lead to a cascade of invasive interventions, nothing more than misunderstood complications of human relationships and poor communication?

Australian childbirth expert and author Sarah Buckley, MD, says that "anything that disturbs a laboring woman's sense of safety and privacy will disrupt the birthing process," which means that birth complications can at times be due to the mother's emotional needs not being met—her needs for support, trust, privacy, and most of all, her need to have control over the process.

The impacts of the medicalization of birth

There are doubtless many situations that warrant intervention to protect the health or even the life of the mother or baby, however, these days we interfere with natural and healthy birthing processes far too much and too often, and this comes at a price to the whole family.

Artificial painkiller opiates, such as Demerol, for instance, can interfere with the pleasurable and joyous feelings that can be associated with birth, by suppressing the release of oxytocin and beta-endorphins. Of course, the pain of labor is undeniable—all the more reason why it should be balanced with the rewards provided by the natural hormones.

Because it drastically reduces natural oxytocin production—giving artificial oxytocin to induce the contractions of labor, as well as epidural pain relief, increases the likelihood of delivery by forceps or vacuum extraction; and it also lengthens labor.

Drugs delivered by epidural infusion reduce—sometimes sharply the postnatal levels of all the euphoric hormones, and this can have a negative impact on mothering. Remember, bonding is made easier through joyful feelings.

Drugs at birth are costly to the baby as well, with consequences that are physical as well as emotional. Drugs used to induce labor can, for example, interfere with breastfeeding. They can weaken the baby's suckling reflex, which diminishes the amount and duration of breastfeeding. Mothers who have had an epidural are more likely to report that they don't seem to produce enough milk.

Since mother and child are still connected through the umbilical cord, drugs administered to the mother also enter the baby's body, where they can play havoc with the newborn's nervous system. Some effects immediately after birth have been noted: under the influence of these drugs babies seem less alert, listless and uncommunicative. They fail to connect with their mothers, don't meet their gaze and are less available for bonding. This effect can last for quite a while: the baby can appear less responsive for the first month. High-level epidural exposure makes babies more irritable and difficult to settle through the first few weeks; it is not uncommon for their mothers to describe them during this period as "more difficult."

Other suspected effects have been detected years later, probably the result of early re-programming of the child's brain. The use of opiates at birth has even been associated with opiate addiction in young adults.

In caesarean delivery, the peaks of all those hormones are wiped out, for both mother and baby. Sarah Buckley (2009) states: "Natural, undisturbed birth is associated with peak levels of at least four feel-good hormones that contribute to mother-infant bonding, as well as safety for mother and baby."

In our haste to sanitize labor and bring the peaks and troughs of sensation and emotion under strict control, we have crushed the most primal, the most awe-inspiring connection. The ripple effects of undermining this cornerstone of emotional intelligence can be felt in the mother-child relationship for a long time. The foundations of loving relationships need to be better protected, and birthing rites need to be held more sacred. If we are to cater for children's emotional intelligence as devotedly as we cater for their survival and their bodily health, we need to reconsider the trend for defensive obstetrics and pay better attention to the very real emotional needs of the fetus and the newborn.

It troubles me to realize that this information may seem unfair for parents who have already gone through a very unnatural birth, or those who have no choice owing to insurmountable medical circumstances. Obstetric intervention will always have its place, but now that we are faced with so much new information about the vital *psychological* needs of birthing mothers and their babies, it would be wrong to hold back this knowledge—especially as there is so much to be gained from putting it into practice. If an unborn child or a newborn has to go through a scary process, then we are far better off understanding what she feels so we can respond appropriately to any later emotional reactions. It is early days yet, but we are entering an era that will see many reforms to the way children are conceived, carried and birthed.

If the mother has been robbed of the natural hormonal surges because of a medical emergency, or because of difficult circumstances surrounding labor, all is not lost. There is good news. Nature has provided us with many opportunities to heal, and catch up on the sweet feelings of closeness that are every baby's birthright. Breastfeeding, direct, skin-to-skin contact with the baby and loving eye contact all produce the very same hormones, helping mother and baby to relax into an adoring connection. When there has been an emotional wound, connection heals it. Connection is the key.

Over the next several chapters we will see many ways in which healing can happen at every stage of childhood.

DIANNE—AN ANECDOTE

Dianne, a mother of three, gave birth to her first daughter in 1955. When delivering her first baby, Dianne was placed under what she later thought to be a general anesthetic. When she awoke hours later, she could hardly believe she had given birth, as she had experienced none of the labor. Much to her consternation, she felt totally estranged from her baby when the nurse brought her from the crib. At first, she found it difficult to trust that this was indeed her baby, as she had not been there to see her born. Could the hospital have made an error and accidentally given her the wrong baby?

It took Dianne about three months to feel that she had bonded with her child. Their first weeks together contained none of the joy that Dianne had dreamt of and her baby would have needed. As she was to find out later, it was then a common procedure to administer "twilight sleep", a combination of morphine to dim the pain of labor and scopolamine to prevent any memory of it. Dianne felt robbed of her chance to participate in bringing her daughter into the world, and of the joy of attachment in the first few months together. The desire on the part of the hospital staff to eliminate pain meant that the baby's and mother's emotional needs were sacrificed.

ATTITUDES TOWARD MOTHERS' PAIN IN LABOR—A BRIEF HISTORY

For hundreds of years, church authorities insisted that the pain of labor was God's punishment to all women for Eve's transgression against God and her corruption of Man. All women were henceforth expected to bear the pain for their inherited sin. St Augustine taught that "Whatever comes into being by natural birth is bound by original sin." Martin Luther maintained that the pain and danger of pregnancy, childbirth and motherhood are punishment for women's sin, and suggested they should think of this as a "a happy and joyful punishment," in other words, it serves you right, so grin and bear it.

In colonial America, influential hellfire preacher, Cotton Mather, taught that pregnancy was a time to consider the wrath of God and repent. How would it make a mother feel, as she is bringing her child into the world, to be held in such contempt by her community? How would this emotional environment have affected each baby born?

In 1846, James Simpson, a Scottish physician, promoted the use of chloroform to relieve the pain of childbirth. Unaware of any possible negative side effects, Simpson's concern was to alleviate suffering. This was opposed by the church, citing Genesis 3: 16—"I will greatly multiply thy sorrow and thy conception; in sorrow thou shalt bring forth children." It would seem that cruelty to women and children has been a basic building block of our society for a long, long time.

Things were a little more liberal in Massachusetts, where, only two years later, Dr Walter Channing of Boston was spared the religious interference met by Simpson, and so was able to begin to use ether for pain relief in childbirth.

The emerging commitment to relieve women's suffering certainly represents the evolution of a more caring, more humane—or should I say, less brutal?—society. Interestingly, strict control over what had been up until the mid-nineteenth century a women's domain was seized by the male-dominated medical profession. As orthodox medicine took over, childbirth increasingly adopted the feel of a perilous medical emergency—something wrong that posed grave risks to the mother. Midwives, with all their natural expertise and gentle methods, were increasingly sidelined. Childbirth was taken out of women's hands.

At first, the central characteristic of childbirth was *punishment*. Gradually, this was replaced, so that the central feature of childbirth came to be thought of as *danger*. Collectively, we are still not accustomed to thinking of childbirth as natural and beautiful. One would have to be naïve to imagine that such a fearful collective perception of childbirth would not influence how labor unfolds. Our attitudes have a major impact on outcomes. If so many women have been made to feel ashamed, terrified and powerless as they are whisked into the labor ward, could this have increased the rate of obstetric complications?

In 1915 Chicago obstetrician Dr Joseph DeLee, author of *The Principles and Practice of Obstetrics*, the most frequently used obstetric textbook of his time, argued that childbirth is a pathologic process from which few mothers escape some kind of damage. The idea that childbirth is normal was given its deathblow. In an article published in the first issue of the *American Journal of Obstetrics and Gynecology*, DeLee advised complete medical control over labor, as a result of which an armory of routine interventions were imposed, including sedation, episiotomy, forceps delivery, extraction of the placenta and medications to contract the uterus. All these interventions prescribed by DeLee eventually became routine.

Today we understand that the hormones associated with intense fear can slow contractions and even stop labor. Is the fear mongering surrounding childbirth fulfilling its own prophecy? A relaxed and well-supported mother naturally secretes more of the hormones that accelerate labor and reduce pain. Could it be that rethinking labor as normal and natural is the best medicine?

Certainly, there has been some progress and effort to make obstetric procedures less invasive, and infant and maternal mortality rates have been reduced. But there is still one important element missing—we have barely begun to care for the psychological needs of mother and baby, not before, during or after birth. Medical and psychological needs should not eclipse each other, and we need to strike a better balance between the two. In the following chapter we will be looking at some remarkable and proven drug-free approaches to managing and reducing the pain of labor.

DID YOU KNOW?

That the World Health Organization (WHO) states: "There is no justification for any region to have a higher rate [of cesareans] than 10–15%"?[1] Nevertheless in the US, the UK, Australia and Canada, the caesarean rate has exceeded 30%.

The emotional effect of our primal experiences

Primal health is a new field of study that looks at the long-term effects of pregnancy, birth and the first few postnatal months on individuals' physical and psychological health. Much research has been carried out at hospitals and universities around the world—the US, Canada, Germany, France, Sweden, Holland, Finland, Japan, Israel, and Australia—resulting in the accumulation of a huge database, the Primal Health Databank, that tells us much about this fundamental aspect of emotional health.

As a response to this growing awareness of how deeply the primal stage can affect us in body and mind, the Association for Prenatal and Perinatal Psychology and Health (APPPAH) in the US and Canada in 1983, and the International Society of Prenatal and Perinatal Psychology and Medicine was formed in Vienna in 1986. Both continue to expand the public's awareness of this crucial period through conferences and publications.

The way a child feels while still in the womb has a major impact on the child's emotional makeup, and this influences his attitudes, moods, emotional responses and relationships well into adulthood. Mothers' emotional states are passed via hormones through the placenta directly to the baby. When, for example, the mother is highly stressed, the fetus's heart rate goes up, the blood flow to her brain is altered, and she becomes jumpy and restless. Little wonder that when expectant mothers are severely stressed, when they feel unsupported or alone, these feelings can show up in the child's behavior long after birth. Occasional stresses are no cause for concern, but when a mother's stress is

---

1. Appropriate Technology for Birth, *Lancet*, 1985, 2(8452): 436–7.

unending, overwhelming or traumatic, it can impinge on the baby's neurological development, with likely lifelong emotional consequences.

Traumatic birth or severe maternal stress during pregnancy can also be linked to a broad range of psychological problems, including behavioral problems, such as fussy babies who are harder to settle. In more severe cases, traumatic birth has been linked to later development of violence, depression, ADHD, autism, schizophrenia or substance addiction (for more information visit the Primal Health Databank[1] and conduct a keyword search). We can't say that prenatal or birth traumas are the single cause of such problems, but they can be contributing factors.

When, on the other hand, the unborn and newborn child feels wanted, when the mother talks lovingly to her, a profound contentment envelops her, preparing for her a strong foundation of inner security and emotional health. This is the very first building block of emotional intelligence. Though it may always remain unconscious, the emotional memory of feeling safe, wanted and loved, sensitively handled at birth and thereafter, underwrites a person's ability to access feelings of joy and love throughout life. It is impossible to overestimate how much you can influence your child's future emotional intelligence through the way you treat yourself, others and your unborn child.

PREGNANT WOMEN AND 9/11

In 2005, Mt Sinai School of Medicine professor of psychiatry, Rachel Yehuda, PhD, and University of Edinburgh, professor of molecular medicine, Jonathan Seckl, PhD, published a study of pregnant mothers who suffered post-traumatic stress as a result of witnessing or being directly affected by the September 11, 2001 destruction of the World Trade Center in New York. The stress suffered by their unborn children as a direct result of the mothers' stress was clearly evident in abnormal levels of the stress hormone cortisol one year after birth. This effect was particularly strong if the mothers were into the third trimester of pregnancy at the time of the event. These mothers should have received ample counseling immediately after the trauma to help them and their unborn children.

Why are some babies more "fussy" than others?

To many hapless parents it comes as a crushing disappointment to find that life with their new baby is too often an ordeal. Their babies seem to be so hard to settle or comfort—they struggle to fall asleep and are easily woken, they cry disconsolately for ages—and the parents feel exhausted, angry and plagued by doubts about their own adequacy. Moments of joy seem few and far between,

---

1. Primal Health Databank: birthworks.org/site/primal-health-research/databank-keywords.html

and parenting soon becomes a duty rather than a pleasure. Until recently, these babies were dismissively branded as "difficult," "colicky" or "fussy," as if this were an innate aspect of their temperament—just the luck of the genetic draw. Based on this point of view, either the parent or the baby gets the blame, and neither is helped.

The fact is that the baby's fussy "nature" is a genuine emotional response; if we care to listen we will hear that we are being told something important. Today, there is mounting evidence that trauma during pregnancy or birth can leave the baby with a residue of anxiety and anger that makes her over-reactive.

GWYNETH—AN ANECDOTE

When Gwyneth gave birth to twin boys, unexpected birth complications prolonged labor for the second twin, causing him and Gwyneth considerable stress. It wasn't long before Gwyneth noticed how differently the two infant boys responded to the world around them. The one who had been stuck at birth cried a lot more, was less easily comforted and generally appeared hypersensitive in comparison to his more placid brother.

Gwyneth was unusually fortunate in that her older sister, Amanda, whose children were already grown, lived nearby and had plenty of time on her hands. Since they both suspected that the second twin's irritability might have been the result of the difficult birth, Amanda offered to lend her support. Often, when the baby would seem impossible to comfort, she would be on hand to hold him, rock him and walk him around the house. Both sisters had resolved to do everything in their power, for as long as it took, to help the stressed twin to release the emotions associated with the frightening memory of his birth. Their instincts were telling them that he needed to be lovingly held for as long as it took him to, quite literally, cry it all out.

Although this lasted several months, the sisters' commitment paid off. Eventually, the more troubled twin found the same contentment that his brother had enjoyed all along.

A note of caution: If your baby seems unable to respond to soothing, you may need to consult your family doctor or pediatrician to ensure that there are no hidden medical reasons for your baby's distress. Only if your baby's physical needs (warmth, cleanliness, nutrition, health) are taken care of can you deduce that her distress is emotional

What can be done to heal birth trauma?

Labeling a baby as "fussy" or "difficult" risks characterizing him and creating the conditions for a self-fulfilling prophecy. Based on what we know today about primal health, it's about time we considered the real possibility that there is no such thing as an inherently difficult baby. It's not the baby that's difficult. We, the parents, have difficulty understanding and meeting baby's needs, particularly if we don't feel supported enough ourselves or if the baby has gone through a rough patch in the womb, at birth or soon afterward. There are no "difficult babies," but there are babies who are by nature a little more sensitive, and babies who need to express a lot of hurt and trauma. How do we help them so that these feelings won't remain to affect their behavior for the long term?

The main thing to remember is that whenever there has been hurt or trauma, connection heals. Healing is possible only when the baby's feelings are validated—in this they are the same as us, the adults. As long as we are convinced that our baby is "difficult," or trying to be "manipulative"—as many people believe—we are unlikely to behave with the sensitivity and tenderness that can make all the difference. Babies feel connected to you when they understand that you hear their voice, that you take in how strongly they are feeling and that you are willing to respond—if only to stay near them. The most powerful tools of healing are naturally available to any mother or father, in fact to any loving adult. Listening. Touching. Holding. Gentle rocking. Soft singing. Any or all of these ways to connect with your baby can change their world for them.

Neuropsychologists tell us that loving human touch can trigger the secretion of feel-good brain chemicals, such as oxytocin. Sometimes, this will bring immediate relief; other times babies need to cry for prolonged periods. This is the body's way of releasing the stress associated with stressful or traumatic experiences. If all goes well, eventually the grieving process will be complete and the baby's body will relax and settle into a deep, peaceful slumber. That's why the soothing effects of your rocking and holding may not be visible for a while; holding your baby may be helping her to cry out all the tears, as it were. Stay with her all the way, and if this becomes too difficult for you, invite someone else who cares for the baby to take over. It is vital that your baby not be left alone to cry. While connection heals, aloneness is scary and can be particularly traumatic for a baby if she is crying.

Massage
Consider taking a baby massage class. This wonderful new addition to the parent's toolkit is becoming more and more widely available. Baby massage deserves a special mention here as one of the most wonderful methods for soothing an anxious or unsettled baby. Emotional stress is always stored in the body in the form of chronic muscle tension. That's why emotional memory is often referred to as "body memory." A delicious, regular massage can unwind from the baby's body not only the tensions that build up from the day's frustrations and anxieties, but also tension and shock that have been stored

since birth. It would be hard to overstate the treasure trove of additional benefits to the baby's mood, circulation, digestion and immune system from massage.

Somatic treatment

Many families have benefited from cranial-sacral, chiropractic, or other somatic (body) treatments especially tailored for babies. The treatment hinges on the fact that birth trauma is recorded to a significant degree as a traumatic body memory focused around the head and neck of the child, as this part of the body takes much of the impact through the birth canal. The frightening events of a difficult birth can remain embedded in the form of bodily tension and immobility. The practitioner releases rigidities in the baby's skull, neck and spine by using the most imperceptible and gentle of manipulations. Many people have found this kind of release has greatly alleviated their babies' emotional states.

Why do up to one in five mothers suffer from postnatal depression?

If you think postnatal depression (PND) is innate and therefore unavoidable, a curse you inherited through your genes, you need to think again. There is little evidence of an inherited predisposition to PND. That said, there is research available that says that PND could be the result of birth trauma to the mother or interruptions to what the mother and baby innately expect around the time of birth. Contributing factors can include forceps or caesarean delivery and the separation of mother and newborn (Buckley 2005: 11).

Mood and hormones go hand-in-hand. The interruption of natural hormonal flows disrupts the delicate balance and denies the mother the fullness of emotion she would intuitively expect. Little wonder she gets depressed. The emotional needs of the birthing mother are paramount, so we must consider these needs a lot more. PND is preventable (Grille 2005: 368).

In the next two chapters, we will look at how we can care for the emotional needs of mothers, fathers, unborn children and newborn babies in order to ensure the most joyous and stress-free beginnings for new families.

4

Bringing Joy to the Dawn of Life

Nurture yourself—the child benefits

A mother's personal fulfillment and her rich emotionality are precisely what help her child to be emotionally intelligent. That's why I place a lot of emphasis on mothers' emotional wellbeing. Parenting your child begins with parenting yourself.

Why is this?

The baby in your womb feels what you feel. Emotion is carried biochemically in the blood; the hormones are its messengers. The placenta and the umbilical cord bring streams of your feelings to your baby's body. On some level, the baby is directly at the mercy of your stress, your alarm, your tranquility and your love. Your unborn baby would even sense how you feel toward him, if he is wanted or not.

It might be scary if, as a mother, you think of yourself as being solely responsible for your baby's wellbeing, an awesome burden of responsibility. You are not solely responsible: everyone who surrounds you, everyone who cares about you and your child, is also directly responsible for supporting you, nurturing you and honoring your time of gestation. How the world treats you, how the world holds you, has a major influence on how your baby feels. It is we, the people around you, who need to share the responsibility. If we mistreat you, if we neglect you, we are doing the same to the little person in your belly. If we treat you with respect, tenderness and care, your baby directly feels this. And, as we will see later, the emotional world of the unborn child can have long-lasting consequences.

So, here are a few suggestions for how to treat yourself daily in ways that will have direct, flow-on effects to your baby in the womb that will enhance his emotional health—possibly for life. Ask your partner and or whoever is close to you to read this with you.

Do the things that bring you pleasure, physical pleasure as well as emotional pleasure—such as singing, dancing, painting, swimming, lying in the sun, going on beautiful walks, reading your favorite books, making love, and so on. If your work brings you pleasure (be honest with yourself about this) and is not a source of too much stress, with deadlines and obligations, then work. If you have no choice but to remain in a stressful job, do all you can—and others can help you—to balance this with the following suggestions:

- ♄ Take time out, be lazy, relax.
- ♄ Get massaged, a lot.
- ♄ Meditate. The transcendent state of mind that meditation brings is especially good for pregnancy. It can place you in a state of deep communion with your baby; some mothers have said they feel as if they are having a conversation with the baby's soul.
- ♄ If you have religious or spiritual beliefs, pray—for yourself and for your baby.
- ♄ Spend time near or in Nature; immerse yourself if you can. Listen to the roar of the ocean, the bubbling of streams, the rustle of wind through the trees, the symphony of birdsong. Fill your senses with natural beauty. Few things can be more inspiring and restorative than your connection with Nature.
- ♄ Talk to your baby out loud, and tell her how you feel about her coming. Tell her about yourself. Don't concern yourself with the idea that your baby has not learned language. She wants to—and needs to—hear your voice; she receives and understands much from your tone, mood and inflection.
- ♄ Talk to your baby silently too, in your own mind. You can even ask her questions, ask her how she feels, what she would like you to eat today, for the two of you. Ask her if she would like a walk, to go for a swim with you, to be rocked as you rock yourself. It doesn't much matter if you believe such a dialogue is possible, even if you think this is silly. There is something in this for you. This inner dialogue (real or imaginary?) with your baby prepares you for a lifetime of intimate connection with her. It opens you up to her just a little bit more and helps you to include her, to make a space for her in your heart and in your life. It allows you to know yourself better: your thoughts, your questions, your anxieties. And it enables you to feel. As you talk to your baby, your feelings come forward, which connects you to her quite deeply. The bonding has already begun. And be prepared for surprises. In pregnancy, your mind and heart are more open than you are accustomed to. Don't discount this too readily: if you listen inwardly, you might just "hear" a reply.
- ♄ Sing lullabies, your favorite songs, and play lovely music to your baby. The fact that babies remember music they heard often in the womb has now been demonstrated too many times to be denied. Once the fetus learns to associate a particular, soothing piece of music with tranquility

and contentment, this tune will help to settle her as a baby and help her fall asleep. You will be very glad of this.

ɸ   Spend plenty of time with other women, both friends and family. You might notice you feel especially drawn to your mother at this time; if she is not nearby consider cultivating one or more relationships with older, experienced mothers. This is a time when the female elders in your life can be particularly comforting and empowering. In a healthy community, solicitous and experienced women are on hand to help usher new mothers through this life-altering rite of passage. The last thing a pregnant mother should be allowed to feel is alone (except, of course, when she wants to be left alone).

ɸ   Have plenty of hugs, make love, set aside plenty of time to be close to your partner. Make sure you have some light-hearted and fun time together, but also time to share with each other how you both feel about becoming parents: your hopes and dreams, your excitement, your anxieties. You should definitely not worry every time you have an emotion, that this will necessarily trouble your unborn child. You can be angry, even outraged, sad or frightened; it is OK for you to go through all kinds of feelings. You don't have to think every time you get upset: "Oh my God! This will damage my baby." Please take this in very deeply—your feelings don't hurt your baby as long as you are managing them and expressing them. In fact, expressing your feelings can be good for the baby in your womb, because this is teaching his nervous system how to deal with feelings. It is the emotional states that don't get resolved, that linger on and on or get bottled up that can have a negative effect on the unborn child.

ɸ   Talk openly about your worries and fears—to people you trust. If necessary, particularly if you are living through a very stressful situation, speak to a counselor. Don't keep your emotional pain to yourself; reach out to others.

A special note about mothers' mothers

When you are bringing a new life into the world, it is a time of great emotion and many women find themselves feeling all kinds of strong feelings about their mothers, feelings that can rush from the depths to the surface quite powerfully. A pregnant woman's relationship with her own mother becomes very important at this time; their history together and the quality of their relationship come sharply into focus. Pregnant women may feel a deep longing to be close to their mother, reunited if they have been distant. They may even feel child-like at times.

Long-term, unresolved hurts and disappointments might also resurface and the woman might feel awash with grief or anger, which can be a little overwhelming, and can take the mother by surprise if she doesn't understand or anticipate it.

All this is part of a natural and healthy process, so don't be afraid of it—give yourself the space to feel. For millennia, human mothers and the mothers of our more ape-like ancestors have turned to their mothers and other close female relatives for help and protection when their child is born. It is an age-old instinct to band together with loved ones in order to feel well supported in childrearing and give children the best chance at a life of happiness, health and love.

So, let your feelings for your mother come up, without judgment or censure. If painful feelings arise, it's because old wounds want to be healed now. Have a good listener with you and, if you feel the need to, cry on their shoulder—let it all out. This can profoundly enrich your relationship with yourself and with others, and will soon add depth to your relationship with your child, making it more emotionally authentic.

The way your relationship with your mother feels to you is a fundamental aspect of your identity and it profoundly affects the way you feel about yourself as a woman and as a mother. So if the relationship has been fraught, expressing any painful feelings that linger can restore your self-esteem as a woman and as a mother, and free your heart for loving your child. Let yourself weep, grieve, be angry if you need to—and be sure you receive comfort and support from trusted friends and/or your partner. It may help to see a counselor.

Anything you do to heal unresolved issues about your mother ensures that your relationship with your child will unfold quite differently. It is how you ensure that any negative histories are less likely to be repeated. Since your wellbeing directly feeds your child's emotional intelligence, your healing will have a positive impact on his life, beyond what you can predict.

As previously stated, the extent that your relationship with your mother is a positive one, this is definitely a time to rekindle your connection with her. In whatever way you choose to recharge this loving bond, you are calling forth your ancestry of maternal energies and letting them flow through you to your child.

Not every woman necessarily feels the same about this, but don't be surprised if you find yourself drawn to the company of women, particularly more experienced or older mothers. Let yourself have as much feminine company as you can and bask in this genetically encoded, age-old wisdom. *Homo sapiens* are designed to raise children cooperatively in small groups because the burden of parenting alone places an unrealistic load on any pair of parents, reduces the joy and pleasure of parenting and compromises the emotional health of everyone in the family.

DID YOU KNOW:

That anthropologists have known for some time that children who are raised in communal parenting groups fare much better? In the nineteenth century (a time of huge child abandonment rates all over Europe) the island of Sardinia enjoyed one of the best infant survival rates, despite being one of the poorest economies. Unlike most European mothers, Sardinian women joined together in supportive, cooperative mothering groups. Mothers who don't parent alone tend to be much happier. Postnatal depression (PND) is virtually absent in societies where women band together to raise their children in caring, cooperative groups (among the Kipsigi of Kenya, for instance). In the Western world, mothers spend far too much of their time alone with their babies and children, a recipe for depression and exhaustion. It would take little effort to create a better balance between communal life and the privacy and personal space we enjoy at home. If we pay more respect to our natural needs for community—particularly when raising our children—the rates of PND would be drastically reduced.

EXERCISE

This is an exercise for couples expecting a child. Begin separately; you can join up and share the results with each other afterward.

Each of you begins by making a quiet space to be alone with your thoughts and feelings. Take a pen and some paper, and arrange to have no interruptions for a minimum of 15 minutes, but longer is preferable.

Write down how you feel about your mother, or the caregiver who assumed the main mothering role in your life (the same will be repeated afterward for your father or male caregiver). Ask yourself the following questions about her:

• What did she do for you that you loved, that helped you to feel happy?
• What did she do for you that felt hurtful, sad or frustrating?

Do your best not to censor any of the thoughts and feelings that present themselves, and don't judge any of your thoughts and feelings as negative or positive. You don't have to share all of the details about this with others if you prefer to keep them private, so give yourself permission to be as honest as you can. The key is to give yourself unlimited freedom to be honest, so if it helps, tell yourself you can destroy the piece of paper afterward.

Begin with the just the things that seem to stick out most, the things that have had the biggest effect on how you feel about your relationship with your mother. Write down memories that feel important to you, memories of love, memories of hurt. Try not to impose any particular order on this, just take note of memories, thoughts and feelings about your mother as they come up, one by one. Don't overdo it or exhaust yourself—if you wish you can always come back and write more later.

For each one of your memories, ask the following questions:
- How do you feel about this when you recall it now?
- If the memory is a painful one, what would you have wished your mother to have done differently?
- How do you feel this has affected you as an adult, in your relationships, in your ability to fulfill your dreams?

Make sure you note and honor all your feelings; nothing you feel is without good reason. You'll find that if you allow yourself to feel whatever comes up, you may end up feeling better toward yourself. Knowing yourself involves knowing your innermost feelings. Knowing how you felt as a child is, as I said in an earlier chapter, the main ingredient that helps you as a parent.

Don't leave yourself holding these feelings without giving them some vent. Make sure that if you feel angry at the end, release—draw a picture of your anger, write down your angry feelings. If neither of these gives you a sense of release, do something physical: take a walk, hit a pillow or a punching bag. If you feel sad, let yourself cry. Letting yourself express emotion can bring you profound relief and a sense of emotional freedom, especially if this is followed by a hug with someone you love. If joyous, loving memories have come back to you, then let yourself bask in the feelings they bring with them. Let your heart be bathed in the happy memories for as long as you can.

Some time afterward, when you both feel ready, come together and share at least some of the results of this exercise with your partner. Even if there are some details of your story that you'd rather keep to yourself, share how things made you feel. Make a pact first that you will take turns listening without interruption, without criticism and without judgment. What you both want right now is to feel listened to, cared for and respected.

Take a break if necessary. If you prefer, come back to this exercise on another day. The next time, repeat this exercise and this time make it all about your fathers, or the main male caregivers during your childhood.

There is a great purpose in doing this together: it will bring you closer, help you to understand each other better, and hopefully give you more compassion for each other's vulnerabilities, as well as appreciation for each other's strengths. This can help your parenting partnership more than you can imagine. It will help love and understanding—the basic fuel of parenting—to flow between you. It will help you to know how you can be a support for each other whenever your personal difficulties as parents come up.

Our parents, our selves

This is not the kind of exercise that should be done just once; I recommend repeating it from time to time. You can approach it more informally, in your own style, simply as a conversation if you prefer. It will keep your partnership as parents alive, growing, healing and improving. You will find that you keep learning new things about yourself each time you dialogue on this level and enrich your relationship with yourself and with each other enormously. Your child will be the ultimate beneficiary.

As parents, every one of us has some specific areas of parenting that we find more difficult than others. Usually, this will have something to do with painful things that happened to us as children. Some parents find it difficult to hug and comfort their children if they never received this themselves as children. Other parents find it difficult to be patient if their own parents were pushy and demanding. All of our parenting difficulties can be improved on and healed, but only if we begin by being absolutely honest about them. In the meantime, this is why it is so important to think of parenting as teamwork. If we can accept that both partners have different strengths and vulnerabilities, we can take over for each other when necessary. If we cultivate understanding and compassion for each other, if we understand why our personal difficulties arise, we are less likely to criticize each other, and more likely to help each other.

There is another reason to share your childhood stories and feelings with each other. It is always too easy to judge another person for what we perceive as the weaknesses in them. I know of no faster way to make all our judgments dissolve than seeing the other person as a little child. If you can glimpse how your partner felt as a child, compassion replaces judgment very quickly.

Sharing these feelings with a friend you trust or a counselor—anyone who is a good listener—will comfort you even further. Sharing your deepest feelings with others who care about you is the key to intimacy, a sense of belonging and emotional wellness.

If you have a very close and trusting relationship with your parents, share with them what came up for you in this exercise. Whether you find some difficult feelings that need to be aired or that there are great feelings of love and gratitude—you'll probably find some of both—consider writing this to them, phoning them, telling them in person. Pregnancy and childrearing can bring families together and deepen relationships.

What we should do for expectant mothers

French obstetrician and head of the Primal Health Research Centre, Michel Odent (2001: 65), says "one of the main roles of health professionals should be to protect the emotional state of pregnant women." Notice that the *emotional* wellbeing of the mother sits at the very center of what is needed to give the baby the best start in life. Her emotional state also plays a major role in the way labor unfolds. Any person's emotional intelligence begins with his or her mother's emotional wellness from conception. Responsibility extends to the father, family and friends, to health practitioners and to the wider community: we should all guard and cherish every expectant mother.

What we should do for expectant fathers

The fact that mothers play the leading role in the parenting partnership in the earliest days, does not mean that the father is any less important. There are many issues that are particular to fathers, who deserve a special kind of support. Like mothers, fathers can only be emotionally available to the extent that they themselves feel loved and supported. Children benefit directly from their father's emotional wellbeing.

There are many things that typically challenge expectant fathers. They feel anxious about being good enough providers and good enough fathers. They harbor many questions about how they got on with their own dads; if there were disappointments, they worry about whether they will make better fathers. They feel left out of the cozy, mother-baby duo. They feel the loss of the special intimacy they thus far enjoyed with their partner, and in retreating a little to make room for their newborn, some men feel the sting of loneliness, as if they don't belong any more. They fear that the arrival of the new baby will mean a loss of sexual intimacy with their partner, and at times when it does, they feel frustrated. These and many more issues come to the surface.

Fathers, I encourage you to speak your feelings openly with your partner, your friends and your family. Share your worries with them, your fears and your joys. Learn all you can about labor so it is not too scary and alienating an experience. Consider talking to a counselor. If you are planning a hospital or birthing center birth, enquire about what counseling services they have for new fathers.

It helps fathers if we lend them our ears and offer them respect for how they feel without encumbering them with our expectations that they should feel better, or more positive. Listening is only listening if it carries no judgment or expectation. Any of us who are friends or relatives can contribute enormously to the wellbeing of a new family if we share the father's joy and if we listen to his fears and doubts. Sharing his feelings with us is vital for his emotional health and his availability for his family. It is vital for his ability to be a support for his partner, and vital for his ability to bond with his child.

Creating the right emotional climate for labor

So, what are the conditions surrounding labor that best help to make the good hormonal juices flow? Over thousands of years, mothers and midwives have collected a huge repository of wisdom by getting it right and by getting it wrong an untold number of times. The result is an emerging clarity about how mothers can be helped to trust themselves and their inner knowing, to trust the strength in their bodies and to surrender to the instinctive, animalistic states of mind that transform her experience of pain and pave the way for uncomplicated labor. There is more to birth than the mechanics of contraction: the intensely physical act of labor is enabled by an altered state of mind, one that is unusually inwardly focused and meditative. As some of the deepest and most primal emotions will be coursing through, complete freedom of expression is most important.

The script for this awesome event is written in her body: if only she can be helped to trust this rather than taking away her control. Childbirth experts who specialize in birthing mothers' psychological needs recommend the following:

- ♇ The mother needs to be allowed to take charge when she feels the need to, and only be guided when she asks—in other words, guidance on her own terms. Rather than passively follow orders from ward staff, she needs the space and the encouragement to follow the powerful impulses that arise in her body, such as what position to be in, how to move, and so on. She needs procedures and suggestions explained to her, possibly ahead of time, so she fully understands the nature of and reason for them.

- ♇ The mother needs privacy. It may be particularly disturbing at this time to be looked over by strangers.

- ♇ Additional to the professional help (midwife and/or obstetrician), the mother is likely to need the support of a carefully chosen doula (birthing-support person or coach) or friend, as well as the father of the baby. An older, trusted and more experienced woman can be immensely reassuring and encouraging. All who are present should bear in mind that support is only truly supportive when it is on the mother's terms, in other words, non-invasive. There may be moments when the mother prefers to connect with a particular person, other moments she may desire to be left alone.

- ♇ The mother needs to feel safe and comfortable to be as noisy and as passionately emotional as her body needs to be. Grant her full permission—and encouragement if necessary. Pain and anxiety can be made worse by bottling it up. Letting it all out can really help to move things along and create release. Bear in mind, too, that the fullness of joy can be diminished if we hold back from letting it show. Permission is the key—freedom to be noisy, freedom to scream, to laugh, to cry, freedom to be animalistic and passionate, freedom from having to be rational. Letting go of all social inhibition—with the encouragement of others if necessary—literally reshapes the mother's body and alters her brain chemistry in ways that greatly ease the labor.

- ♇ The less we use drugs and other medical interventions, the more natural the labor and the higher the concentration of the natural hormones, which lead to a richer experience of bonding.

ቀ   A home-like, non-clinical and familiar environment, soft lighting, her
     favorite music if she so desires, and that her senses (vision, hearing,
     touch) are treated tenderly—provide anything that helps the mother to
     feel at home. These needs are particularly well attended to in
     homebirths and some birthing centers.
ቀ   A well-informed mother who has been helped ahead of time to
     understand what she can expect at every stage of labor will feel
     empowered, more in control of the process.

In the reference section for this chapter is a list of helpful books and websites. I
urge prospective parents to avail themselves of the enormously helpful
information that abounds.

HOMEBIRTH

Homebirth midwives are available free of charge for families in the
Netherlands, New Zealand and the UK; in the US they are covered by some
healthcare providers. In most Australian states and territories, the cost is
borne entirely by the family, Western Australia being the only state that is
expanding subsidized homebirth services.

SQUATTING

Legend has it that today, the reason women give birth lying down is the
result of the caprices of seventeenth century French King Louis XIV, who is
also credited for initiating the demise in Europe of midwives in favor of
doctors. It is said that Louis wanted a better view of his baby being born, and
henceforth this mode became fashionable around Europe.

True or not, this practice has continued, presumably because it enables
the obstetrician easier access. Some birthing experts say that lying down to
deliver can make labor more difficult. Today, midwives say that women find it
easier to give birth in the traditional positions: half submerged in water,
squatting or kneeling, all of which agree better with the angle of the birth
canal and allow gravity to do more of the work. Some research indicates that
simple measures, such as supported sitting or squatting instead of lying
back, plus some pelvic movement such as rocking or swaying, can
accelerate birth and prevent the need for caesarean deliveries.

Natural birth

The ideal birthing situations recommended by Dr Sarah Buckley (for low-risk
mothers) are homebirth, birthing centers adjacent to hospitals and one-on-one
midwifery care. Midwives who have homebirth and hospital experience say that
babies born at home are more alert and more receptive and calm. According to
Buckley, they have lower rates of complications and interventions, and perinatal

mortality rates are at least as good as hospital rates. These views are shared by an increasing number of childbirth specialists.

Natural birth is not artificially induced, and the baby is not delivered surgically or with the use of instruments. Instead, the mother's own bodily impulses of parturition are facilitated in order to move the baby naturally through the birth canal. Natural birth is drug free, although alternative methods may be used to ease any pain. The umbilical cord is not cut at least until after it has stopped pulsing. The newborn is never removed from contact with the mother, and he is helped to latch on to the mother's breast within half an hour of birth. Baby and mother remain in close, uninterrupted bodily contact thereafter.

The parents' and their baby's emotions are far more supported and attended to in the natural birthing setting, and since there has been no pharmaceutical or instrumental interference, the most sublime emotions are free to flow.

DID YOU KNOW:

That homebirth was the norm in many Western societies until fifty years ago? In the Netherlands today, one-third of babies are born at home under the care of a midwife. Outcomes for homebirths there are better even than those of low-risk mothers in hospitals.

Alternatives for dealing with the pain of childbirth

What if there were an abundance of drug-free methods for alleviating the intense pain of labor? What if pain could be managed without spoiling the joy that comes with natural birth and healthy bonding? Would you then consider natural childbirth?

All prospective parents should avail themselves of as much information as possible about alternative approaches, such as acupuncture and hypnosis, which have already been established as beneficial. Why not also interview one or more homebirth midwives and ask them how they help mothers in pain? Why have one-third of Dutch mothers opted to return to homebirth, and how do they manage?

Here are just some of the methods commonly used for drug-free pain relief:

ተ Hydrotherapy or water birth—submersion in water can bring considerable relief.

ተ Massage during labor.

ተ Reflexology.

ተ Homeopathic pain relief.

✝   Bioenergetics, including body movements such as pelvic rocking, changing positions, deep-breathing techniques and vocalization (screaming, moaning, singing—whatever sounds come naturally).

Finally, it is worthwhile challenging the common belief that childbirth always dooms mothers to excruciating pain. What if that is, to some degree, a myth made real through cultural expectation? Remember that for centuries our leading religious authorities constantly proclaimed, mantra-like, the righteousness of woman's agony. Today, every time you see a re-enactment of childbirth on television or at the movies, you see a totally helpless woman—on her back, under bright lights, screaming in agony, with hospital staff at their panic stations snapping orders at each other. What do you suppose happens to your deepest, subconscious expectations about childbirth when virtually every image of childbirth you ever see looks like a woman being tortured? Images such as these, when seen repeatedly, work hypnotically. They program women's minds to anticipate childbirth with terror, and accordingly, their bodies brace in preparation and the prophecy of suffering keeps fulfilling itself.

The Navajo say that labor is not painful for everyone. In fact, pain-free natural birth was reported in a study of 475 pregnant Navajo women. Not long ago, the drug usage rate in labor in Holland, a modern and sophisticated nation, was 5% while at the same time it was 95% in the UK.

British childbirth educator, Sally Inch, suggests that for many mothers the experience of pain in labor is made far worse than it need be because of what women have been led to expect; the pain is real and every bit as painful as the mothers say it is, but often the extremes of the pain are caused by the body's reaction to fear and the expectation of pain. In 1968, neurologist Sir Henry Read stated that the mental state of the mother has a profound influence over the pain in her pelvis. Today, it is understood that a mother's alarm, her expectation of great pain, her separation from the places where she feels safe and the people she feels safe with, all contribute to the release of stress hormones. These stress hormones can bring about the wrong kind of contractions around the uterus, contractions that interfere with normal processes—and, more to the point, increase the pain. As Inch explains, this is just one example of how fear of pain can be the cause of the pain. Protecting the mother's emotional wellbeing and attending to her emotional needs might turn out to be the best painkiller of all.

It is an absolute must for every expectant mother to read about, hear about or see examples of natural, midwife-managed labor in a home-like setting. Mothers-to-be should fill their minds with such imagery in order to counteract the fear mongering that has surrounded labor over the last few centuries. They need to daily repeat the mantra: "Childbirth is a healthy, natural process," and hear the same sentiment repeated by others. Reassurance can be the greatest pain management strategy, and can make a huge difference to the progress of labor.

Can birth be orgasmic?

Many readers would find this suggestion outlandish, bizarre—even outrageous. And yet, there are countless reports of women experiencing deeply orgasmic and ecstatic sensations during childbirth. In fact, this phenomenon has been so well documented and discussed at so many conferences on prenatal and perinatal medicine and psychology, that it is a mystery why so few people know about it. Somehow, this common experience has been almost secretly guarded, as if it were sacrilegious to mention it. Mothers who have described orgasmic birth have often been met with skepticism, repugnance and outrage. Perhaps this has to do with the fear and shame that surrounds pleasure in our culture. Perhaps it is an unacceptable image for women who have suffered intolerable pain. But orgasmic birth is not such a crazy idea, considering that the oxytocin released in torrents during natural labor is also the hormone released in lovemaking.

I cannot insinuate that birth should be orgasmic for all women; not enough is known about this yet. But even if this experience is not attainable for all, if the possibility of blissful birthing exists, and if labor does not have to be anticipated with fear, shouldn't this phenomenon be investigated thoroughly and with open minds? Shouldn't there be vigorous research to find how more and more mothers can be introduced to orgasmic birth? What if there is a psychological basis for this experience? What conditions produce the state of mind that makes this natural process available? What if all it takes is more natural birthing methods, a better quality of feminine support and a change of expectations about what labor is supposed to be like? This may be the most powerful argument for birthing mothers' need for privacy, a safe, home-like environment, and a natural, midwife-assisted birth.

Imagine how world changing this would be. How much of the trauma of birth, for mothers, fathers and babies, could be eliminated? What would it do to the way we live and the way we relate to each other if our lives and our children's lives began in ecstasy?

What happens to dad?

Fathers play an invaluable role in the birth of their child. Even though they are not directly joined as are the mother and baby, through being close by in a supportive role, fathers' bodies also produce a rush of oxytocin and prolactin. Their emotional connection to their partner and child has a powerful and transformative effect on fathers that is biochemically recorded.

As always, there is wisdom and purpose in Nature's way. New fathers with higher prolactin levels are more responsive to babies' cries. That's why it is so important for them to be at the birth. They are changed by the experience in ways that help them to bond with their child and be more closely engaged and sensitive as fathers.

One of the greatest signs of our evolution toward more child-friendly societies is the rapid rise of fathers who attend labor. If your own father was there to witness your coming into this world, you are very unusual—or very young. Until right up to the 1980s and 1990s it did not often occur. Today, in the space of one generation, around 90% of fathers are there to see their children born. There can be no doubt what a life-changing experience this is, and how it cements the bond between father and child. Take a look around in any public place and notice how many babies and toddlers you see being held, kissed, carried or pushed in strollers by their fathers. This is a radical departure from the way things were not long ago, when dads were so much more detached from their children and the "mushy," tender side of parenting was a mother's domain. These days, dads are far more hands-on—and they are enjoying it. I am convinced that the presence of dads at labor has much to do with this wonderful revolution.

Fathers don't always cope well with attending labor, however. Some men feel overwhelmed by the intensity of emotion and the pain they see their partners experiencing. To some extent this is about our own emotional memories of being born and any unhealed fear or hurt we once experienced, now being evoked by what we are witnessing. Additionally, men can feel quite helpless or inadequate at a birth; we stand before an awe-inspiring process that we cannot control. It can be quite confronting to see our partners wracked with pain one minute, contorted with the effort of labor the next, particularly for the first time. This is the ultimate rite of femininity, utterly unfamiliar and mysterious territory for the male. And although fathers play a central role, sometimes as a sentinel or protector, sometimes as physical or emotional support, this role is essentially passive—the father follows the lead.

Many expectant fathers are overwhelmed by a bewildering array of emotion, terror, panic, anticipation, love, unspeakable joy, and much more. If there are difficult feelings to face, fathers should receive counseling and support, and at least talk openly with friends about any fears or misgivings. Difficult emotions only get in the way when we bottle them up or suffer in private. Fathers' feelings need not separate them from their family, and in fact it is their capacity to feel that makes them good nurturers. Fathers deserve all the support they can get. Support for fathers would help them enormously in their striving to support their partners. New fathers need to select an experienced and trusted buddy, keep him close, and share his concerns with him as the big day approaches.

Counseling services for expectant fathers would be a welcome addition at birthing centers and hospitals. Since most men have not been given much space to be emotional, they may need a little help to accept the powerful feelings evoked at the birth of their child; and if they find themselves spontaneously weeping with joy or relief, or immersed in uncommon peace and tranquility, to allow these feelings to take their course.

Birth and your child's emotional intelligence

A happy time in the womb, when the baby feels wanted, recognized and loved, and a sensitively managed birth—these are the ingredients of primal health, the first step in building your child's emotional intelligence. A joyous beginning prepares the ground for a harmonious parenting relationship and a fulfilling life together. Happy, even ecstatic, memories of life in the womb and birth form a reservoir of emotional wellbeing from which children can draw strength for life, filling them with a healthy optimism. A joyous beginning gives our children the strongest chance of enjoying:

- ♄ being a less fussy, more responsive baby
- ♄ a deep and abiding trust in the goodness of life
- ♄ unshakeable self-confidence
- ♄ access to a deep sense of inner calm
- ♄ a broad and healthy emotionality
- ♄ a compassionate and empathetic nature
- ♄ emotional resilience
- ♄ a zest for life, get up and go
- ♄ a willingness to face new beginnings, and to face life's challenges.

The first moments of life in the outside world are also critical for the parent-child connection and for the child's emotional intelligence. These moments give us, as parents, a golden opportunity to be showered, along with our new baby, in feelings of love so powerful as to affect us for the rest of our lives. In the next chapter, we will look at how to make the most of these magical first moments together.

5

The First Hello

Why the first moments after birth are so important

Up until recently psychologists and pediatricians thought that newborn babies were pretty much out of touch with the outside world and preoccupied with themselves. The mind of the newborn, if there was one at all, was nothing more than a confused and meaningless jumble of sensations that would never be remembered. What a newborn child experienced was not seen to matter much more than what happens to a houseplant.

Boy, were they wrong.

With the help of scientific observation, we seem to have discovered what so many mothers and fathers have been saying all along: infants tune in to their environment and are very sensitive and watchful from the moment they emerge through the birth canal. For the first hour or so immediately following birth, the mother and the baby are under the effect of a powerful and natural hormonal infusion that makes them both super-alert; their senses are highly focused, their hearts open. What is Nature's reason for priming mother and child for their first encounter in this way?

As soon as your new baby opens her eyes, she will be looking to connect with you, her parents. You might be astonished by your baby's ability to look deeply into your eyes, and within moments, to know you and be able to tell you apart from strangers. Unless emergency procedures at birth have disturbed your newborn's wakeful alertness, you might also be blown away by the intelligent awareness you will perceive in her eyes. Just minutes after being born, babies can pick out, from a group of photos, a photo of their mother. She is the one they prefer to gaze at.

Carefully controlled experiments have shown that a breastfed baby can recognize—and prefer—his own mother's odor at three days. When placed lying down between two used breast-pads, one of the mother's and one of another woman, three-day-old infants keep turning their heads toward the mother's pad, even when the experimenters keep swapping the sides where the pads are placed. When he is helped to latch on to the mother's breast within the first hour after birth, his mouth quickly learns the contours of her nipples and begins quickly to adapt to their unique size and shape.

Every one of your baby's senses are switched on at birth, ready to be permanently imprinted by the look of you, the smell of you, the feel of you and the taste of you. And, as we saw in the last chapter, the sound of you is already recorded in your baby's mind before birth. Every part of the journey so far has been carefully orchestrated by Nature so that you, the mother, become indelibly imprinted into your baby's mind and heart through each of his five senses. This is the original act of falling in love, and to the baby, you are *The One.* The hormones that produce intense alertness recede to normal levels after an hour or so, when, if everything goes well, newborns tend to slide into a deep and restful slumber. Having worked hard and found his beloved, he can sleep peacefully. The most supercharged window of opportunity for primal bonding is gently closed.

There is a purpose behind this plan that has been honed through millions of years of evolution. The first and all-important goal of the baby is attachment, and he is born eager to cement this lifelong attachment from the very beginning. The quality and intimacy of a baby's attachment to his mother and father is at the very center of his wellbeing. The first layer of your child's emotional intelligence is about emotional security: the ability to trust that no matter what happens, a loving person is always on hand ready to hold him and comfort him, that he will never be abandoned. Healthy attachment is what gives a baby his emotional security. Attachment is the main imperative of this first stage of life outside the womb, for it has consequences—both physical and emotional—that last a lifetime. The trusting and affectionate mother-child attachment is the prototype of all human relationships, and it gets its start at this first embrace.

Your child's emotional intelligence, and her way of relating to others as she grows up, is highly dependent on the strength of this primary attachment. Most mothers find these moments unutterably beautiful, a joyous first meeting they will never forget.

The earliest days of forging attachment have a remarkable impact on the child's nervous system and brain chemistry. His biology reflects his attachment history like notes in a diary, and the neurological changes that take place at this critical time are manifested in his personality. His emotional memory of how he was ushered into the world lives on in his body and in his unconscious mind, shaping his attitudes and behavior and coloring his emotionality. For all of us, some of our deepest hopes, loves and fears have their roots in the primal stages of our lives.

As the medical profession comes to accept how utterly important these first moments of bonding are, thousands of maternity hospitals around the world are scrambling to reform their practice to ensure that mothers and their newborns remain together at all times. This practice is called rooming-in. Before you choose a maternity hospital, ask if they have rooming-in. Everything about a newborn—her abject vulnerability and dependence, the genetically programmed distress call the moment she is separated—is geared to remaining in contact with her mother, and to a lesser extent with her father, at all times after birth. The classic image of rows of newborns interred all alone in plastic bassinets and being viewed through a windowpane, screaming, deprived of human touch—is one of unimaginable despair and bereavement for a baby. The pace of change is such that this method will soon be a thing of the past.

BREAKING THE BOND

Many of the world's cultures have ritually disrupted postnatal bonding, denying newborn babies the vital opportunity to bond with their mothers when their consciousness is most open, and denying them colostrum, the first and most highly nutritious milk, now understood to be essential for a healthy immune system. This widespread denial of primal bonding has interfered with a most potent means of imbuing the child's brain with peaceful and loving impulses. Could it be that this is one (of many) means to create a population that is more willing to fight? The Spartans, who were among the most warlike of early civilizations, used to drop newborns on the ground. Survivors were expected to become good warriors. The early disruptions to the mother-child connection have been always thought to produce more war-capable societies.

Kangaroo care

These days more and more hospital staff around the world are encouraging mothers to keep their newborns right next to them with direct skin-to-skin contact, for as much of the time as they can. We call this "kangaroo care," since it reminds us of the luxuries enjoyed by baby kangaroos (joeys) inside their mother's pouch. The benefits of kangaroo care can be dramatic and long lasting. Skin-to-skin contact babies tend to cry less and sleep more than those wrapped and placed in cots, and they smile more. Since newborns are not equipped to handle separation, doesn't it make sense that they would fare much better when closely held?

The benefits do not stop there. Lying in contact with her mother helps the newborn to regulate her own body temperature, metabolic rate, hormone and enzyme levels, heart rate and breathing. Her whole body is downloading its vital rhythms through the mother's skin. Some studies show that infants who are handled more gain weight faster and develop muscle coordination sooner. Even premature babies who are touched regularly each day gain weight much faster and show fewer neurological problems later. Touch is just as important as food. Another study found that at two years, and again at five years, kangaroo care children had higher IQs, better vocabulary and better comprehension. Literacy starts early. It is a wonder that we ever allowed infants to spend hours all alone in cribs. As I will continue to show you, a surprising number of customary practices throughout history have been damaging for children's emotional health. Thankfully, parenting practices are continually being upgraded, mostly for the betterment of our children.

Rarely does the baby gain anything without a pay-off for the mother too. Direct skin-to-skin contact in the early moments and days switches on the mother's intuition and helps her to learn the baby's communication style and rhythms. This investment goes a long way toward helping mothers to respond more appropriately to their babies' cries, and so to soothe them sooner. The benefits last; one study found that, two years after the birth, kangaroo care mothers were more responsive and spoke more soothingly to their babies. Closeness and touch can also help the baby to synchronize his sleep cycles to his mother's—the advantages need no explanation for any parent who has felt the sting of sleep deprivation.

Kangaroo care and rooming-in will give your child a base of emotional security that lasts a lifetime. But when you and your baby are separated after birth, as was done in hospitals around the world for decades, it is not always easy to repair the child's damaged trust.

A revolution in primal healthcare

Breastfeeding is one of the best insurance policies to protect the baby's physical and emotional health for life (see Chapter 7). So, another major reason why newborns should remain with their mothers is to establish a strong and healthy breastfeeding pattern. If mothers are to breastfeed successfully, it is very important to allow the baby to latch on quite soon after birth (within the hour), to keep the mother and baby close together, to provide all the professional support necessary and to keep infant formulas and pacifiers well away.

WHO and the UN Children's Fund (UNICEF) have been deeply concerned about the crucial need to improve bonding and breastfeeding rates everywhere; they see this as an urgent public health issue. To this end, they joined forces to promote the Baby-Friendly Initiative (BFI). This is a global initiative to restore breastfeeding and early attachment by accrediting maternity hospitals that formally agree to ten pro-breastfeeding steps.

The ten-step Baby-Friendly Initiative

Some of the ten steps that accredited birth facilities must provide include:

 ✝ mother and newborn to be kept together 24 hours a day

 ✝ breastfeeding to be initiated within half an hour of the birth

 ✝ substitutes, such as baby formula and pacifiers, to be kept away from newborns and their mothers unless medically indicated.

So far this scheme has been a huge success. In 2002, there were around 15,000 baby-friendly facilities worldwide. In 2011, there were 121 in the US, 77 in Australia and over 200 in the UK. Meanwhile, 100% of hospitals in Malaysia, Sweden and Iran are certified as Baby-Friendly. In Sweden, where all maternity centers have been baby-friendly since 1997, the breastfeeding rate at 6 months has increased from about 50% to 73%. The number of BFI facilities is growing rapidly, and will continue to make an enormously positive difference to public health and wellbeing.

If you are thinking of delivering your baby in a hospital or birth center, ask if it is BFI-certified.

Preparing your newborn to be a sound sleeper

By keeping your newborn close to you throughout the day and sleeping close together—close enough so your baby can hear you breathing—your infant learns the difference between night and day, and starts to adapt to your sleep-wake rhythms early. Newborns who room-in with their mothers in hospital learn this faster than those sent to a crib (see Chapter 7 for the pros and cons of cosleeping).

Talk to your newborns—they talk back

If you want to connect with your new baby, watch closely and stay open to surprises. You will see that she looks at you, if only briefly, and says all kinds of things through her changing facial expressions—sometimes in response to yours. Don't push, expect too much or try to make it happen. Just let yourself be natural, allowing whatever facial expressions come to you spontaneously.

BABY SEES MORE

Until recently, pediatricians thought all that babies could see was light. Newborns can, in fact, identify their mother's face, gaze at her and, at times, imitate her expressions. Infants can visually track objects, and prefer to look at faces or face-like diagrams. Newborns are less likely to respond in this way if they are under the influence of drugs used in labor or exhausted from a long and complicated delivery.

To connect with your infant:

☩ Try talking with him when he is fully awake and not preoccupied with hunger or tiredness (the "quiet alert state").

☩ In the first few weeks, the baby's attention is more likely to be quite fleeting; don't expect a sustained conversation.

☩ Use simple words, wordless sounds, simple expressions, such as sticking out your tongue or making an "O"—be creative and playful. Be sure to be gentle, not hyped up and don't try to rev up your baby.

☩ Repeat things a few times and wait; give him space to take it in—it is possible he might even mimic or reply in some way.

☩ The eyes are the windows of the soul. Even when there is not much going on in terms of expression, just notice who you see in your baby's eyes when he gazes back at you, however briefly. His infinite, quiet curiosity, his perfect innocence and lack of judgment. Infants don't perceive, they simply see. They have very little ability to interpret, so their minds are pure. If you catch him in a moment when he is calm and alert, you will see boundless wisdom and peace in his eyes. There is so much that passes between you in just moments of unadorned eye contact.

☩ Be sensitive to your baby's signal that he has had enough, so he is not over stimulated. He will, for instance, turn his eyes away, or his facial expression will show some discomfort. Let him rest and have his space. Under two months the attention span is quite brief, and you would not want to over stimulate him by demanding more.

☩ If you do this a few times every day, and remain quietly watchful, making this your special, tender and intimate time together, you will find you will learn your infant's language, and you will feel so much closer to each other. These conversations are the precursor to literacy. The more your baby feels that his attempts to communicate are met, the more he feels rewarded for reaching out. This prepares a strong foundation for him to be a good communicator.

Psychologists call this dialogue with your infant "healthy mirroring," and it is the main thing that helps the baby to establish a sense of self. More than anything, babies need to feel that someone out there is seeing them, hearing them and caring enough for them to respond to their attempts to communicate. They learn about who they are—their "me"—through the way they are looked at, spoken to, responded to. These earliest memories will be recorded in the baby's brain for life, quietly telling him: "I am loved, I am lovable, I am wanted, I am worth listening to, I am worthy of others' attention...." In no uncertain terms, this is the foundation of a strong self-esteem, the core attitude that enables an individual to create and maintain loving relationships for the rest of his life.

All aspects of emotional intelligence spring from these earliest impressions of human connection. When we give our babies this kind of attention from the beginning, it is the greatest gift. Our time, our loving attention and responsiveness make a universe of difference. Quite literally, this early connection transforms the baby's brain and, in so doing, transforms the baby's future.

Take the time to be self-aware when you are connecting with your infant. Breathe gently and relax, notice what happens around your heart, notice how you feel. If you allow yourself to feel, you will find that, without words or big gestures, your infant has touched you—he has moved you deeply. Your wordless conversations build a most mysterious and rich connection between you. Trust this process, it will help to create a more harmonious relationship between you and your child for years to come. It adds layers of bedrock to the foundation of the love that moves between you.

As babies look out into the world, sometimes they simply explore the landscape, discover and learn about their environment. But often what they look for is connection, someone who sees them and cares for them—they look for mirroring. If an infant's reaching out is not met, she feels a huge sense of loss and begins to feel uncertain—insecure. Her fast-growing brain records the sense that relationships are unreliable. Later on her emotionality and her behavior will reflect this. She may, for instance, develop more clingy behavior in order to catch up on extra attention or, alternatively, she might become resigned, quiet and withdrawn in order to defend herself from disappointment. In the baby stage of our child's life, nothing could be more important than encouraging their communication by responding to them, promptly, tenderly and consistently.

It often catches parents by surprise to discover that their infant, even their newborn, can actually respond to them. Many parents tend to invest little energy on interacting with their babies until several weeks after the birth, when they can get a big, sustained smile out of them, and some giggles. The infant has all his basic bodily functions attended to but tragically is not related to as a person until he can produce the kind of obvious gestures that his parents can recognize. It is sad that many infants are treated as yet-to-be-inhabited bodies. Simply servicing an infant's bodily needs without actually connecting with him is probably not very rewarding for the parent either. That's why it is so important to add this dimension of connection to your relationship. This is how you really get a feel for the person in your baby. Meanwhile, your baby will feel rewarded for communicating, encouraged to reach out to you, to trust.

To connect so intimately with your baby promises to bring you both untold wonders and delights.

Mother's and father's intuition

Long before they can form their first words, babies have a rich vocabulary with which they communicate. From the beginning, their many facial expressions, body postures and gestures, their cries and their little noises are speaking volumes about their feelings and needs. And yet, as parents we all struggle to understand them from time to time.

Over time, we come to decipher what they are saying to us, we gradually become familiarized with their different expressions, though quite a bit of trial and error is involved. Parents' intuition is not always spontaneous; it is developed, sometimes painstakingly, with time. Intuition is not magic. It is no more than learning your baby's language and it comes to you from your willingness to be quietly watchful and fascinated with your child.

Intuition comes from connection, and connection with our own feelings is the first ingredient. If we listen to our own feelings, this helps us to access our body-memory of childhood, bringing us empathetically closer to our child.

Secondly, the flood of natural hormones generated at birth and afterward—the hormones of connection—is designed to help both parents to attune to their baby. That's why an unfailing raft of support and a natural birth with the father present—conditions that favor the greatest flow of these hormones—can make such a dramatic difference to the quality of the parent-child connection, with lifetime benefits to the child's emotional intelligence.

Thirdly, there is no substitute for closeness. For both parents, their intuitive ability to "understand" their baby's communication is honed by spending their hours close together, learning each other's patterns, personal tastes and changing moods. The modern trend for putting babies in daycare makes it very difficult for mothers to develop the intuition and attunement of which they are inherently capable.

How newborns communicate

It was only until two to three decades ago that medical authorities and psychologists still assumed that infants' cries were random and meaningless, just some kind of rehearsal. Now it is clear that their cries are varied, that they have a rich vocabulary loaded with meaning and that their facial expressions and body language are full of meaning too. By spending time together and being observant, mothers and fathers soon learn the many meanings of their baby's different cries. There seems to be no alternative but to experiment with different responses, to be watchful for the baby's reactions and learn from our mistakes ("Are you hungry?" "Do you need your diaper changed?" "Are you cold?" "Are you bored?" "Do you just want to be held?"). Babies don't hold back. They let us know loud and clear—if they are healthy, that is—when what we are giving them is not what they want. The main thing is not necessarily to get it right the first time, or all the time. If this is what you expect from yourself as a parent, you will place enormous pressure on yourself and all the joy and pleasure of parenting will disappear. The main thing is that you are there with your baby, offering your interest and care, gently trying different things, offering a range of goodies to see which one was the one she was asking you for. Yes, sometimes it can be a guessing game, and every parent feels confused and helpless sometimes.

Even if from time to time you find that no matter what you do, your baby keeps crying—and you are sure that she is not injured or ill—there is plenty of reason to remain calm. If you understand that the most important thing for a baby is to not be alone, your caring presence helps her to deal with her feelings. Remember: connection is the key. Stay with her, hold her, rock her a little and talk with her. Let her know how you feel about not being able to console her. Your voice carries your emotion, and this really makes a difference for her, even if you can't see it.

Over time, you will learn your baby's broad vocabulary. If you pay attention and trust yourself to experiment, you will learn to distinguish her cries of boredom from her cries of frustration, when she is cold or physically uncomfortable, her protest when she feels bothered or invaded ("I don't like the way you change my diaper"), when she feels sad or lonely and wants to be held, her cries of fear or of colicky tummy pain, her sounds of hunger, or her grizzles of tiredness. Sometimes she just needs to cry for a while as you hold her in order to release any accumulated stress from the day. The more time you spend together, without rushing yourself or putting pressure on yourself to be a perfect interpreter of your baby's language, the more naturally and easily you will come to understand each other and synchronize your daily rhythms.

Infants don't only want their cries responded to. They want you to see their quiet peacefulness, their joy, their pleasure, their awe and fascination with this wonderful new world they are discovering. Sometimes, they just want to talk, to exchange little noises with you that say little more than "Hello, I am here." Though their attention span is limited and they tire of interaction sooner than older babies, they often look for your eyes and thrive on your attention, your responsiveness to all their feelings. When they see that their joy touches you and is reflected in your eyes, it multiplies their joy. This mirroring is what helps them to grow into joyous children and adults. Your responsiveness is what ensures for your baby a lifetime of contentment and emotional health.

Do newborns get stressed?

You might be wondering: Stress? What stress? Why might infants feel stressed?

Anyone who has had a glimpse of their own memories of babyhood needs no explanation here. They can recapture the joys and the stresses they felt in their tiny bodies as infants. But for most people these memories remain covered, so it is worth reminding ourselves what can stress a baby:

☿ Getting born can be stressful, scary and exhausting for babies.

☿ Babies' brains are not able to compute object constancy, which means that when they see you walk away, they are unable to imagine you coming back. When you are gone, you are gone, and this can frighten them.

☿ Babies don't have the ability as we do to suppress emotion or sensation. Whatever they feel, they feel to full intensity, which means that hunger, or the longing to be picked up and held, are powerful sensations that travel through the baby's entire body.

☿ Waiting is unbearable. Babies cannot understand time at all.

☿ Diaper changes can be invasive; babies tend to hate being fiddled with and cannot possibly understand why they are being messed around with.

☿ Stress is all about losing control and babies are entirely helpless. Their every sensation, satisfaction and comfort are wholly dependent on the goodwill of others. Imagine yourself in that position for a few minutes. Would you not find this stressful?

There is another side to this. Babies are just as defenseless in the face of joy and pleasure. When they are held, connected to, massaged and generally when their needs are met; they can be overcome with joy, suffused with bliss, or transported into the deepest states of peace. Watch a baby who is fulfilled at the breast and you might see the bliss in her eyes. By the way, if you ever experienced this as a baby, your baby's bliss might trigger your own body-memories and help you to tap in to your own bliss.

Can newborn babies smile?

How many times have you heard: "The baby is not smiling, she has gas," or, "Babies can't smile until they are six weeks old"?

It has always seemed strange to me that infants are talked about as if their feelings were not real. It seems odd that an infant can show exactly the same expression as a smiling adult, using the same facial muscles, but somehow on an adult the smile says, "I am happy," while on an infant the very same smile says "Hey, it's not that I'm happy, I'm just trying to fart!" If every time a friend greets you they said, "Is that flatulence, or are you just glad to see me?" you'd be forgiven for feeling a bit miffed.

It seems all the more strange that people should deny the feelings that underlie an infant smile when the neural networks that support emotion are already developed and perfectly able to produce all kinds of emotion by the sixth month inside the womb.

On our bulletin board at home there is a photo of our daughter when she was just a few hours old. She was sleeping peacefully; her slight Mona Lisa-like smile showed a deeply pleasurable and fulfilled state.

Guess what? With the aid of ultrasound imagery, babies have been seen to smile inside the womb. We all need to get over the denial—this is not a practice smile; it is the real thing. To say that a fetus does not feel pleasure has no basis in neurological fact. If a fetus can feel and react to pain (which they can at 12 weeks of gestation), then they can feel pleasure.

Here is the good news: the human body is, right from the start, capable of delicious states of pleasure; our nervous system is capable of deeply fulfilling states of bliss from the earliest moments of consciousness inside the womb. When babies feel cherished, nourished and comfortable, no wonder they smile. Don't you smile when you feel that way?

Meticulous studies of brain activity and facial movements show that infants smile more enthusiastically at their mothers than at anyone else. They know who you are and are hooked on you right from the start.

So, that's what was going on for our newly-born daughter when the photo was taken—she was blissfully smiling, a smile of deep restfulness and satisfaction. It is pleasurable to be in a body, to breathe air, to be able to expand beyond the confines of the womb and to be in the arms of loving parents.

And the goodies just keep coming—the brain chemicals associated with pleasure actually nourish the baby's brain. Pleasure, love and joy cause new neural pathways to develop in the parts of the brain that regulate emotion. A baby's joy builds the neurobiology of emotional intelligence; it contributes to a lifetime of emotional health.

What else can newborns do?

From the first day a healthy baby can imitate some of your facial expressions just a little bit. If you slowly stick out your tongue, for example, and wait patiently a few moments, you might find that he does the same back.

Newborns learn to recognize faces very quickly. They have been observed turning to look for the mother when the father is holding them. Moments after birth, if allowed to, a newborn can instinctively drag himself up to his mother's chest, find her nipple and self-attach. The reason why these abilities have not been generally recognized is that they can be disorganized or reduced if drugs have been used in labor.

The more we can tune in to this reality of our babies' emotional inner world, the more fulfilling parenting can be, and the more our babies feel connected to us.

To circumcise or not?

It stands to reason that the human body does not invest its energies to build a body part that has no use and in fact is likely to cause disease. It was once thought that the appendix and the tonsils, for instance, were useless and problematic bits of flesh. Now we know that both perform an important role as part of the immune system. The same is true for the foreskin; it has an important purpose. For tens of millions of years, all male mammals have had a foreskin. If it were useless and posed health risks, why has it not naturally evolved away? Why did it evolve in the first place?

So, why do we continue to circumcise baby boys? Until the 1970s, doctors assumed that routine infant circumcision was harmless, painless and that it protected the boy from many diseases. Today, no national medical organization in the world recommends routine circumcision of male infants. Many medical authorities around the English-speaking world have spoken against it (see References).

While there are a number of studies purporting to show that circumcision prevents a variety of diseases, none hold up to rigorous scientific scrutiny. But even if we were to accept the discredited idea that circumcision offers disease prevention, that is not enough to justify the amputation of healthy tissue as a pre-emptive strike. We don't take out the appendix at birth in order to prevent peritonitis, or the tonsils to prevent tonsillitis. Since circumcision also poses risks of medical complications, the possible benefits don't seem to outweigh the damage done to the penis. The foreskin is also meant to protect the head of the penis from infection or irritation, particularly in childhood. In almost every case, circumcision is a needless mutilation of the penis.

While many boys are spared circumcision by conscious parents, their foreskin is later damaged by naïve health professionals who retract the foreskin prematurely, tearing the membrane that is meant to dissolve over time (sometimes as long as into the late teen years). The only person who should retract a foreskin is its owner.

The foreskin contains an especially high concentration of nerve endings responsible for pleasurable sensation. With one of the highest concentrations of fine-touch nerve endings in the body, it is the most sensitive part of the penis (lightly stroke the back of your palm, then your palm itself to feel the difference that these nerve endings make). It evolved for a purpose, and its loss diminishes sexual pleasure considerably. Lacking a protective foreskin, the head of the circumcised penis is forced to develop a callus-like outer keratin layer in order to cope with this unnatural exposure, reducing its sensitivity even further. To be sure, many circumcised men are still able to enjoy the heights of sexual pleasure, but they lose some aspects of the normal crescendo of pleasure such as would normally be experienced during foreplay. With an intact penis, the full range of pleasure is more profound and more sustained.

Babies feel pain more acutely than we do, but until recently this was not understood and babies were circumcised without anesthesia. The anesthesias that are employed today (though many circumcisions are still done without) are only partially effective, and do nothing to prevent the post-operative pain caused by diaper changing and urine in an open wound. To an infant, wouldn't this feel like torture? Is it possible to think of circumcision other than as traumatic? Infants' heart rates go up during the procedure, and levels of the stress hormone cortisol also increase. What a way to welcome a child into the world. Since babies are so developmentally and emotionally fragile, we should be pausing to think of the possible long-term emotional effects. It is also worth asking whether circumcision might be part of what troubles babies who seem particularly "fussy" or cry persistently, a kind of infantile post-traumatic stress syndrome.

Non-religious infant circumcision is a uniquely Anglo phenomenon. In the middle of the twentieth century, the US, Canada, UK, Australia, and New Zealand circumcised the majority of their baby boys, but this has now changed greatly. Accordingly, circumcision is disappearing around the world. In the US, until recently, over 50% of boys were circumcised, but the numbers are dropping dramatically—especially in the western states.

Ironically, the most drastic change has been in the United Kingdom (it was a British doctor who first medicalized ritual circumcision in 1865). In 1947 it was declared an unnecessary procedure and defunded from the national health plan leading to sudden drop in the rates. For more than 60 years, British boys have been spared the insult and injury of circumcision, with only about 3% there now being circumcised.

In Canada during the mid to late 90s, the rates dropped to about 30% when no longer covered by the national health insurance plan.

Similarly, circumcision rates appear to have peaked in Australia at around 80% in the 1950s, and dropped to about 12% as a result of statements by pediatric authorities in 1971 and 1981.

New Zealand also had high rates at over 90% in the 1950s, but due to enlightened medical policies, almost no one circumcises there today.

The US is the only Western nation where a majority of males is circumcised (for any reason). Non-therapeutic circumcision is almost non-existent in most other developed countries, many of which enjoy far better health statistics than the US.

CIRCUMCISION AS RITUAL

Ritual mutilation of the penis has been widespread among many traditional cultures in Africa, Australia, New Guinea, Peru, Polynesia, ancient Greece, and among Arabs and Jews. Since the Jewish religion permits progressive questioning and debate, this has made room for a new and growing rabbinical perspective that favors an alternative ritual, sometimes referred to as a naming ceremony or *bris shalom*. It has all the joy of the traditional ritual without the pain and damage of circumcision (see References).

Although the justifications given for non-religious circumcision changed over time, it first became immensely popular in the US, the UK and around Europe in the eighteenth and nineteenth centuries in the belief (and fervent hope) that it would inhibit masturbation. Doctors commonly held the bizarre belief that masturbation would lead to a host of diseases, such as epilepsy, spinal tuberculosis and sterility.

The gift of what your infant can teach you

Feelings are contagious. If you let yourself be still, open and watchful around your new baby, you might find that his simple, utterly non-judgmental attention, his Buddha-like calm and disarming innocence, will transport you into a similar state of mind. Your time with your baby can give you access to states of consciousness that many people spend years meditating, praying, doing yoga or other practices in order to reach. Once you have found these moments of fathomless peace, your nervous system is more likely to remember the pathway to it. In our hustle and bustle we forget how to access this natural state; babies can remind us—if we let them. Spend quiet time together, often, and you'll find you are nourished by this experience as much as your baby is nourished by you. A baby's uncluttered and untroubled mind can teach you that simply being present, here and now, can be a delicious experience.

The psychology of bliss

We all look for contentment and happiness. Since this is, tragically, a rare state of affairs in our world, we give thanks for passing moments of happiness and basic contentment. But the human body has evolved to be capable of far more. Our nervous systems and hormonal networks are innately capable of producing far more intense levels of joy, even if only as peak experiences. We have been designed to follow our bliss, and this seems to have something to do with honest self-expression and loving relationships.

In light of these recent understandings about the brain we need to update our definitions of what it means to be emotionally healthy. The capacity for natural states of bliss, deep calm and profound love is the unacknowledged cornerstone of emotional health and part of everybody's potential. That doesn't mean that we should all be able to be blissed out all day long—life causes us to feel myriad emotions and some of these are painful. But much has been learned about how a number of key childhood experiences can train our brains to have more access to these wonderful feelings throughout our lives. Science has drawn for us a map for how we can become more peaceful and more loving as individuals and as societies.

Loving connections at the dawn of life give us our resilience and our ability to love—and this is what keeps us going through our hard times. If for one reason or another these opportunities for the healthiest start are missed at the perinatal stage of parenting, then it becomes all the more important to take advantage of the many later opportunities for loving connection—as you will see in later chapters.

Mom and Dad, take care of each other

Just as your baby has special emotional needs at the start of her life journey, you the parents are likely to discover some new needs of your own. Don't be too surprised if you both feel unusually open and emotionally sensitive. You might feel as if your emotions are turned up—you'll feel teary, more prone to irritability, more tender and affectionate, and certainly more protective. You might also be unusually happy, and might find yourself smiling and laughing more. This process is both natural and helpful, so respect and honor it.

To some extent, what you might be experiencing are fleeting glimmers of your emotional memories of babyhood, evoked through your connection with your child. This is also a natural part of your transformation as a parent; your added sensitivity helps you to be better attuned to your baby's needs.

Your "babymoon" with your new family is a precious time of bonding and getting to know each other, and it should be preserved as sacred. If you feel the need to be private, honor that. Don't allow your visitors to overstay their welcome; your needs come first right now. Hang out together, chat, talk to each other about your experiences as new parents, hold each other and be tender. Don't come out of your cocoon until you are ready. The first few days or weeks are precious and you should have them together, uncluttered by obligations. These moments will enrich your family life and give you sweet memories, and your baby will benefit immensely.

What friends and family ought to do for new parents

There are so many wonderful things that a community can offer new parents. Taking care of a new family in our midst can be as special a gift for the giver as it is for the receivers. We can cook a meal for them, shop for them, we can offer all kinds of practical support that will allow them precious time to rest, and get to know their new baby. We should not exhort them to place their new baby on exhibit, and instead let the parents introduce us to their child in their own, good time. Certainly, some new parents are keener to socialize than others, but some can feel smothered by the flocks of well-meaning relatives bearing flowers and asking to take turns at holding the little infant. We are all drawn to give our blessing to the new baby of those we love—but we need to tread lightly and be sensitive to their space. Helping parents with a new baby can be a wonderful act of humility and love, and creates a deeply heartfelt feeling of community.

The long-term benefits of healthy bonding

Perinatal bonding is at the heart of our psychological health and wellbeing. It is the springboard to a closer, more harmonious parent-child relationship. This is the child's very first impression of what the world holds for him. The more the infant's primal emotional needs are met, the more readily he will be soothed and comforted as a baby and child. The baby thus begins his life with these attitudes: I am welcome, I am wanted, I belong here, I am a part of the people and the world around me. This pervasive sense of belonging and of being wanted helps the baby grow into a loving, confident and assertive individual.

Wounded by an inadequate early connection, some people spend their lives looking for a place to belong; they find it hard to maintain lasting and loving relationships. It cannot be stressed enough how important these first moments of life in the outside world are. We must do everything possible to protect this foundational parent-child connection.

Part 3

The Baby Connection

6

Creating a Joyous Connection with Your Baby

Where does emotional security come from?

Your newborn is now your baby, and you are beginning to emerge from the giddy first few days together. Your growing family is beginning to find its feet, to settle into a new rhythm, to accommodate a whole new person who has come to live with you. The months spent in babyhood are vastly different to any other stage of childhood; this will be a special time together, unlike any other stage of your child's life. So, what are your baby's emotional needs and how do they differ from the needs of toddlers and older children? How can you best nurture your baby's emotional intelligence and prepare him for a life of loving relationships and personal fulfillment? How can you connect with this amazing and delicate little person in the most mutually enjoyable way?

You probably want more than a set of instructions on how to get it right for your baby, so she has the best chance of growing up happy. This wonderful time is not only for investing in a future outcome but is also a time you and your baby will want to enjoy. Every parent deserves to have a close and joyous relationship with their baby, one that will enrich yours and your child's lives with a treasure trove of fond memories.

For your baby, the first year and a half are almost exclusively about developing an inner core of emotional security. Understanding this as the baby's main developmental concern helps us to orient everything we do as parents toward this goal. Emotional security is about trust, it is the conviction that as lovable and worthy beings we are never alone, that our call for connection with others will always be answered. Emotional security focuses our eyes in a special way as we look out into the world—helping us to see a friendly and nourishing world. It is the very foundation of happiness and success, and the engine of good relationships. Your baby's and your own joy spring from your availability to respond to her communications, helping her to feel secure and well connected to you.

What helps babies feel secure?

If you go to almost any shopping mall and watch parents who have a baby in a stroller, you might see that many do not respond to their baby's cries. They continue chatting with others or going about their business as if the baby's cry has no meaning. Some parents respond by pushing the stroller back and forth to calm the baby, but the baby is not touched, he is not looked at or talked to. Now, if you were in a busy shopping mall and you saw an adult sitting alone and weeping openly while people walked by, impervious, as if the person was not there, how would this feel to you? When someone's distress is ignored, is it worse if that person is an adult?

Imagine a table at a café, a number of adults talking and eating, but there is one 10-year-old child there who is crying disconsolately. Meanwhile, none of the adults at the table pause to look at this child; nor do they ask why she is crying, let alone offer comfort. Instead, they continue to talk animatedly to each other, entirely unaffected by the child's sobbing. When you see this, how do you feel? Does it seem at all strange or surreal that the adults are behaving as if the child is not there? Is it not obvious that the child needs some kind of attention? So, why does the same not apply to a baby?

What we need to ask ourselves is: Do babies' feelings count less than those of adults? Should a baby be considered less of a person than an older child? Historically, this is exactly how it has been. You'll recall that, until recently, authorities thought that babies did not even feel pain. Psychologists and doctors were telling parents not to be concerned about what happens to children under two, as they won't remember anything. Even in recent times, adults have tended to deny that children have real feelings, at least until they can talk, which would be like treating a stroke victim as a fool or as someone with no feelings because he has lost the power of speech. As a result, many of babies' most important needs are ignored.

There is a commonly held myth that as long as a baby is kept clean, warm, fed at regular intervals, and occasionally rocked and touched, this is enough. "He knows he's safe," people say, "he's just fussing. It's nothing." The truth is, a baby's cry is never nothing. Babies need more than their physical needs met. They have emotional needs, they need to be held, touched, talked to and seen. What is the one source of a baby's emotional security? The feeling that whenever he or she reaches out, someone will be there, reliable and sensitive. Babies need to feel connected to those they love. If your baby could speak in words, you would hear this: Help me to feel safe—see me, hear me, and don't leave me alone.

Attachment research—a background

In the 1950s, as a result of the collaboration between Mary Ainsworth, later a professor of developmental psychology at the University of Virginia, and psychoanalyst, John Bowlby, Deputy Director of the Tavistock Clinic in the UK and mental health consultant to the World Health Organization, an inquiry into how infants attach to their mothers began, which resulted in a revolution in the way childhood is understood.

Bowlby and Ainsworth shook the world with their "discovery" that the way parents respond to their baby, right from the beginning, has a very noticeable effect on the child's behavior, with consequences that last a lifetime. Though this may have come as no surprise to anyone who felt this intuitively, the scientific world took decades to accept this idea—and still doesn't entirely, though the dissenting voices are down to a whisper.

What followed on the heels of Bowlby and Ainsworth's groundbreaking work was a veritable avalanche of research that ricocheted all around the world. Hundreds of studies were done internationally to look at how the quality of infant attachment affects the way children feel and behave later. Today, attachment theory has become the dominant framework for studies in early childhood development. This new field of study has changed our understanding about babies forever. The first three years of a child's life have been identified as the most delicate and the most formative of his or her life. This means that what we do *as* parents—and what we do *for* parents—matters the most during the child's first three years.

As this realization continues to take hold among the world's scientific community, it is beginning to revolutionize the way we raise our children, and the way public health policy addresses the needs of families. More importantly, all that has been learned about infant attachment needs to be applied to the day-to-day art of parenting. Pediatrician, William Sears, MD, and his wife, Martha, two of the world's most prolific parenting writers, were the first to interpret this new knowledge for parents in a practical way. It was they who coined the term "attachment parenting." Since Dr Sears' books became popular, the trend across the whole parenting bookshelf is, increasingly, to reflect the results of attachment research.

Babies are people

You may have you noticed that all along I have been referring to babies, infants, newborns and even the fetus as "he" or "she"? I can't stand calling a person "it."

Why do we do that? Take a moment to imagine someone talking about you at a dinner party and referring to you as "it"— "Make sure it has enough food on its plate." What would that do for your digestion?

Take this one step further: imagine somebody calling a toddler "it": "It is learning to read today," or, "It is jumping in a puddle." What does that make you feel? A little outraged, perhaps?

So, why is a baby an "it"?

If you have been hearing babies talked about as "it" all your life, it probably won't strike you as remarkable, or even worth thinking about. It's automatic. For me, since English is my second language (as a child, my first was Spanish, which has no "it"), the first time I heard a baby called "it," it hit me like a bolt of lightning. To this day, I squirm when I hear a baby or a fetus referred to as you would a lump of clay. Words have power. Every time we use "he" or "she" for a baby, we subtly remind ourselves to recognize them as real people. Yet until recently, babies have not been validated as people. It is no accident that anyone would find it unthinkable to call a toddler "it," and yet, babies are constantly referred to in that way. The idea that a baby and a fetus are people still hasn't sunk all the way in.

CHILDREN AS THINGS, CHILDREN AS WORKERS

In the US, children were legally classed as property until the Supreme Court declared them to be persons in 1969. Universal schooling was legislated in most Western countries around the turn of the twentieth century, separating for the first time the world of children from the adult world. Until then, as we saw in Chapter 1, children were commonly sent out to work, some from the age of four.

When it comes to appreciating children's needs we "civilized" humans are often only beginners.

Understanding a baby's mind

If you can understand the way a baby's mind works, you are closer to seeing the world as he sees it. Here is a rough sketch of what goes on in the consciousness of a baby:

- ☩ Babies feel everything—pain, pleasure, joy and sorrow—far more intensely than do adults. Their feelings are a total-body experience; every muscle tenses or vibrates with emotion.
- ☩ Babies cannot lie, put on an act or pretend like toddlers, older children and adults can. What you see is what you get—complete emotional honesty.
- ☩ Babies cannot plan or think ahead. All they can do is react. They cannot make deliberate choices.
- ☩ Babies are incapable of influencing or manipulating anyone, all they do is show their feelings—because they can't help it.

- ☦ Babies can't understand time. When they are made to wait for something they need, like feeding, or being picked up, to them it feels as if it will never come.
- ☦ If you walk away from a baby, she can't make a mental image of you coming back, until she is at least around 18 months old.
- ☦ Babies have very little ability to soothe themselves—there's sucking their thumb, but not much more. When it comes to soothing, they are completely dependent. That means that it is not appropriate to expect baby to settle himself down. They learn to self-soothe later, as older children, based on how well you soothe them now. If you comfort them consistently, they will be better at comforting themselves independently later. The more their dependency is supported in babyhood, the stronger and more independent they will be when they grow up.
- ☦ Babies have no strong defenses against pain or sorrow; they cannot do "fight or flight." When distress is overwhelming, all they have is the "freeze" response, or the "defeat response." That means they collapse, give up and go numb. If this happens a lot, the defeat response becomes habituated; in other words, the neural pathways that facilitate the collapse are trained to activate this more easily and more instantly, which can make them more prone to numbing out their feelings later in life. Psychologists call this: "learned helplessness."
- ☦ If babies learn that reaching out is rewarding, they will become strong communicators, able to connect with people more effectively.

Baby interpreted through distorted adult eyes

Every time I hear of a baby being accused of trying to control or manipulate her parents, or demanding to get "its way," I feel deeply disturbed. And I hear this kind of commentary often.

The idea of a "manipulative baby" is delusional. Babies can't make decisions or plans, let alone devise ways to cleverly play upon the parents' heartstrings. They are utterly helpless.

Of course, caring for a baby can be trying and draining for anyone who does not have enough available support. Babies are too often blamed for this because they cannot talk back. When we are overstretched, tired and cranky, we tend to view our babies through a muddied lens. We project our strained emotions onto them: we see them as devouring monsters, screaming tyrants, selfish little parasites who want everything and give nothing. Because it is human to project in this way, we each have a responsibility to recognize our projections, to not believe them and to view them as symptoms of our need for more support.

When we view our babies with judgment, they appear unpleasant to us—and this makes it harder to give them the affection they need. Babies sense our ambivalence and, understandably, they become insecure, more "fussy." Perception shapes outcomes in any relationship, and so our projections about our babies become self-fulfilling prophecies. In other words, when we judge them for being needy, they are more likely to become even more needy.

Whenever someone describes a baby as a manipulator, you can bet that this person has at one time felt disempowered in the hands of someone else's manipulation. Someone has controlled or manipulated them: their parents perhaps, their siblings, perhaps their spouse. The emotional memory of feeling manipulated—and possibly abused—is being triggered by the baby's demands and the baby gets the blame.

Whenever we feel overwhelmed by the demands of caring for our baby and we notice ourselves disliking our baby or even being angry with him, it is likely that the emotional memory of some unresolved issue is being stimulated. This is a great opportunity for healing ourselves. At this point, we need to ask ourselves pointedly: Who am I really upset with? Who do I know—or remember—that really asked too much from me and was too demanding or domineering? Who made me feel entrapped? Or perhaps: Who made me feel emotionally drained? More than likely you will discover that you have long been needing to express some strong feelings toward someone who has upset you, or that there is a situation in your life from which you wish to be free. Either way, anything you do to express these feelings—writing them down, talking with a friend or counselor—will transform your relationship with yourself and with your baby.

For this process to work well, it's important to not just think about your feelings, but also to let yourself feel them in your body, and finally, to give these feelings some form of expression. Feelings only find release when you relate them to the original situation—in other words the original relationship—in which they arose.

The reward of this kind of process is that it frees you to see your baby through loving eyes again. Projections are dispelled when you can understand the viewpoint of a baby from the inside. This requires your ability to remember or otherwise tune in to what it feels like to be a baby. Later in this chapter, and in Chapter 8, you'll find exercises to help you get a glimpse of how you once felt as a baby. Emotional memory is what gives you your empathy, it is the inner wisdom that helps you decide what is right for your baby.

DWARVES WITH BAD MEMORIES

Revulsion and blame of babies is an age-old tradition; it runs right through our ancestral societies. In an era when 20 to 40% of children born were cast out or killed by their parents (with legal consent), Greek philosopher Aristotle described children as "dwarves with bad memories." St Augustine was possibly the greatest influence on medieval Christian ideas about children. He said of a needy baby, "Is it not a sin to lust after the breast and wail?" Juan Luis Vives, a leading Spanish preacher and educator in the sixteenth century, denounced maternal affection, saying, "Mothers damn their children when they nurse them voluptuously." Around the same time, French theologian John Calvin taught that infants' "whole nature is a sort of seed of sin and therefore it cannot be but hateful to God." Little changed in the next century, when educationist Pierre de Berulle said, "Childhood is the... vilest condition of human nature." Anglican clergyman John Wesley, in his eighteenth century "Sermon on Obedience," quoted from a letter written by his mother: "Let him [the baby] have nothing he cries for; absolutely nothing... Break his will now, and his soul will live." The most widely read parenting manuals in early twentieth century Germany were the works of Dr Daniel Schreber, who advised parents to stop their babies crying through "physically perceptible admonitions." His purpose was for parents to subjugate their baby from the beginning, so as to become "the master of the child for all time."

In the early part of the 20th century, the founders of behaviorism theory, (e.g., JB Watson, BF Skinner, and Truby King) developed a child-control philosophy that denied the value of children's internal emotional world. Now scientifically debunked, behaviorism, with its mechanistic approach to parenting, was for decades the most powerful pedagogical influence throughout the English-speaking world.

These views come from some of Western civilization's leading thinkers. Not only were they immensely influential, but they were also a reflection of the mood of the times. As shocking as it may seem, kindness toward babies and children—as a general trend, at least—has only become a common feature of Western civilization in the last half-century. It is an aptitude that we are all still learning. In the modern world, it seems we have evolved far beyond our forebears in our capacity for empathy. But have we progressed far enough?

The basics of attachment

Decades of research have taught us more about the importance of early childhood than humanity has ever known. Today, there is broad agreement among child development experts about how attachment works and why it is so important. The early years give us the biggest opportunity to influence a child's life; this gradually diminishes as the child gets older. Here is the gist of what the attachment researchers have found:

✝ Babies are genetically programmed to seek attachment to parents or parent figures. Their emotional security depends on the strength of this bond.

✝ The quality of attachment is based on the caregivers':
   o responsiveness,
   o dependability,
   o warmth.

✝ Disturbances in attachment can have a long-lasting, negative effect on feelings, attitudes and behavior. Serious gaps in attachment may have serious psychological and social consequences.

✝ Healthy attachment in early childhood is the mainstay of an individual's future happiness and capacity for loving relationships.

The Australian Association of Infant Mental Health (AAIMHI) has produced Position Paper #2 (see References) that clearly explains babies' attachment needs and what parents can do to meet those needs. The following is taken from Position Paper #2.

Children who are securely attached to their parents are more likely to:

✝ be able to cope well with stress
✝ have satisfying relationships
✝ have healthy self-esteem
✝ have good mental health
✝ reach their full intellectual potential
✝ have fewer behavioral problems
✝ have fewer discipline problems
✝ have fewer problems separating from parents when it is developmentally appropriate.

Should we reward a baby's dependency?

We are living in a period of great change. The scientific insights into early childhood attachment are quite new. Some readers may think this new information merely confirms what they already knew. Others will view it as innovative. You might feel that the attachment research has added little to what is already known in the depths of the human heart; however, this is the first time in history that this perspective on early childhood has received widespread scientific agreement. Before attachment was properly understood, the established attitudes toward babies were fundamentally different and parenting looked quite different to the way it looks today. In some ways, it is as if we were discovering babies for the first time, and, in so doing, have begun to transform the act of parenting.

Among academics this new knowledge has forced an overhaul of established approaches to early childhood development. It takes longer for new approaches to be absorbed in the community, yet gradually the advice given by psychologists, doctors and nurses is beginning to sound different. Most importantly, our approaches to parenting are changing as a result of this paradigm change. This is not unusual, as parenting has always been evolving.

Some of our most basic ideas about babies have been turned upside down. Many people still believe, for example, that if you consistently give babies what they ask for, you are training them to be dependent—so they will never grow up and they won't give you a moment's peace. For decades this was the established and dominant belief among psychologists, and our culture accepted it. As the core guiding principle for raising babies, this idea has been turned on its head. We now know that this principle might be true for older children, but the very opposite is true for babies. The best thing you can do for your baby is to respond to her reaching out as promptly and consistently as possible. We should honor and respect our babies' dependency—that's precisely what helps them become truly independent when they grow up.

It's not surprising that so many parents feel confused. Because we are in the middle of an historic transition, the old thinking is clashing with the new. It is unsettling for many parents to see that, on some issues, professional advice is doing an about-face. Take heart; all this is for a good reason. For the first time, we have lots of know-how for nurturing our babies' emotional intelligence. Our children and, ultimately, our society, will benefit enormously.

Responding to your baby

So, how do we best support our baby's attachment to us? Our baby's emotional security rests entirely on our willingness to hear what he is saying to us and to respond.

More than at any other stage of childhood, the baby months are a time to let your baby take the lead. Following your baby's lead is at the center of what creates healthy attachment. Your baby knows more about what he needs from you and when he needs it, than all the world's experts combined.

So, whether a baby is asking to be picked up and held, or wanting to play a little or interact, or wanting to be fed, changed, rocked, etc., his connection to us depends on how promptly and how warmly we answer these needs.

SECURE ATTACHMENT

Secure attachment is more likely to occur when parents... respond promptly and sensitively to their children's cues... Infants are well aware when their attempts to communicate are ignored by a caregiver, and can become confused, frustrated and distressed if this occurs. If this happens consistently, infants may cease to express their needs in an open and healthy manner.

—AAIMHI Position Paper #2

Babies are not equipped to wait; they simply don't have the capacity to cope with being ignored or denied. The ability to withstand delayed gratification begins to build in the toddler years.

Benjamin Spock, a pediatrician of the post-Second World War era, was probably the most influential parenting guru of all time and his name became a household word. Dr Spock advised parents that it was fine to leave a baby to cry unattended for up to half an hour. Since then, many parenting authors repeated the same thing, to the extent that this advice became folk wisdom, even "common sense." The advice may have been well meant, but it was arbitrary—a wild guess. There was nothing to back it up. It was what people genuinely believed without the benefit of later discoveries about babies' brains. It is now understood that when your baby really needs you, even five minutes feels like an eternity, since they do not understand time.

Babies' cries are always a sign of distress, so it is particularly important not to leave them alone when they are crying. They feel connected to us when all their calls to us are met with our reply. This includes their happy conversations with us. If we join in with them when they show us their joy, their joy is multiplied. They squeal and giggle, kick their legs and wave their arms as if their ecstasy is too much to bear. And the bonus for us is that a baby's joy is contagious—if we get close to them, we catch it.

What is separation anxiety?

You might notice that at roughly six months, your baby starts to protest a little more vigorously at being separated from you. We saw earlier how newly born infants show subtle signs of recognizing their parents. Well, at around six months, all of a sudden your baby seems to really wake up to the idea that you are his parents—and other people are not. It's not that he didn't sense this before—he was probably always less than comfortable away from you—but now he is more consciously aware of the difference, and his reaction to being picked up by a stranger, even a well-known person that he has not bonded with, is suddenly much stronger and more immediate. There could be anxious, sideways glances, followed by crying that ends in howls of protest if he is not soon returned to your arms. When you hold him again, usually he settles down and is enjoying himself in a few moments. Separation anxiety increases after six months, peaking at about one year, though for many children it can last well into the toddler years (and let's face it, separation anxiety lasts into adulthood where it manifests itself as jealousy, possessiveness and co-dependency—we need only look inward to get a hint of how babies feel.)

Why does this happen? Human babies have evolved to become highly anxious when separated. Our brains have learned, over millions of years, that we are much safer in our parents' arms, and less likely to feel well-nurtured by strangers. Separation anxiety happens to babies all over the world. It is a healthy, natural and instinctive reaction for babies to feel unsafe with strangers. Our babies' emotional security depends on us taking them seriously. Their alarm at separation needs to be taken at face value; it means that they are not emotionally ready to be separated, and they should not have separation forced upon them.

Separation is probably the most painful and scary thing a baby can endure, and if they face it repeatedly, it can seriously undermine their sense of security. Babies who are separated from their loved ones often react with rage. They can feel heartbroken and terrified. After some time, some give up and collapse emotionally, entering a state of emotional numbness. Levels of stress hormones (cortisol) have been seen to spike in babies who are taken from their loved ones. Separation from attachment figures can have negative, long-term consequences on the child's emotionality (see "Non-responsiveness can cause many problems," page 148). On the other hand, when a baby's needs for connection are respected, this gives her the strength to be self-assured and independent as a toddler and child.

Before 18 months, babies' brains are too immature to soothe themselves with the idea that if you go, you will come back. Because they are unable to anticipate your return, separation is particularly scary for them. When you need to leave your baby for a while, she will cope far better when she is left with someone familiar, someone else she is attached to. The most painless and empowering ways to help your child to separate from you will be discussed in Chapter 9.

What's all the crying about?

Crying is one of the main ways that babies communicate their needs to us. Although it certainly is not the only way they talk to us, babies do cry a lot; they need to, up until the time they can truly master language. There are huge differences between babies but generally speaking the amount of time spent crying tends to increase for the first few weeks after birth, peaking between three and six weeks; much of the crying happens in the late afternoon or evening. As babies get older, the amount they cry tends to go into decline, but they still tend to cry frequently. These patterns of crying tend to be more or less the same around the world. Since crying is a baby's way of communicating to us, it usually signals that there is something they need, so all their cries deserve to be taken seriously.

Aside from being a tool for communicating needs, crying is also the body's natural means of stress release, restoring the nervous system to balance after a stressful experience. Sometimes, your baby might keep crying no matter what you do to help. Don't despair; she just needs you to hold her. She may be crying out her stress, stress that could be accumulated through the day, picked up from the stress of others in her vicinity, perhaps even stress left over from birth or earlier. Once you've made sure that she has no unmet needs (hunger, pain, in need of a change, etc), just let her cry in the comfort of your embracing arms.

How do we soothe a crying baby?

This question is best answered by asking another: How do we as parents remain calm, peaceful and centered around our baby? A room full of old-fashioned mechanical ticking clocks, will, over time, all fall into synch, ticking in perfect unison with the strongest and loudest grandfather clock. The same goes for the moods in your home, as mood states are highly contagious. Anyone feeling grounded and serene will be broadcasting these vibes to whoever else is around. Unfortunately, this tends to work the same for moods of all colors, including grey moods.

The key to being a soothing presence for your baby is to understand that your baby is sensitive to how you feel. He picks up on your cues through your touch, the tone of your voice, the rhythm of your breathing and the expression on your face and in your eyes. Body language cannot lie. If you are highly stressed, you will find it is harder to transmit calmness to your baby, but if you are feeling centered, peaceful and calm, sometimes your baby will settle down merely by being in your arms.

Few of us can feel calm simply by deciding to—there are steps we need to take to calm ourselves, involving self-care and supportive relationships. This means that to be comforting to our babies, we need to make sure we are looking after Number One. Don't expect to be a great comforter of babies when you are wound tight as a spring.

Settling techniques are not enough. When you are overwhelmed by stress, even the best technique can be a failure. Remember, connection is what works. When you are feeling peaceful and loving, there is a naturally calming effect carried in your voice, your touch, your eyes and your face. Your baby feels connected to you when he feels your empathy and your validation, in other words, that you understand his crying is real and has a genuine meaning. If empathy is what you feel, then the techniques you use are likely to work far better. You can cradle your baby and rock him gently. If at first this does not settle him, try a different position: lying across your arms or up looking over your shoulder. Caress him very softly, pat or rub him rhythmically and gently on his back. Sing a sweet lullaby. Take him for a walk with you, or swing from side to side as you hold him. Of course, if his crying is one of hunger, tiredness, cold, pain or illness, or some other physical need, then soothing will only come through having those needs attended to.

The more sensitively and immediately you respond to your baby, the easier to calm he will be and the better able he will be to soothe himself as he grows into a toddler and older child. He learns to soothe himself through the way you soothe him. Your sensitive responses are immediately helpful for your baby, as well as being a good long-term investment for your relationship.

You might be feeling that these so-called settling techniques are no more than what you could have figured out yourself. Your parenting instincts are switched on. People have always known, for instance, that holding a baby close and giving him gentle, rhythmic movements (rocking) can be profoundly and immediately calming. It's not our parenting instincts that have left us; what we have lost is the trust in those instincts. I am amazed by how many parents are still told not to pick up their crying baby, not to rock them to sleep, and generally not to do what comes naturally—or the baby will end up like an overly dependent leech. This kind of talk is a remnant of harsh bygone days, when children were literally to be seen and not heard. It does not surprise me that, when people—often the experts—constantly tell them not to, parents sometimes find it difficult to follow their hearts and be affectionate and responsive. When someone tells you not to go to your crying baby and pick him up, know that this is old—and dying—advice.

And when soothing isn't the answer

What about the times when your baby is crying and nothing you do seems to comfort her? What she needs then is your company: she needs to be held, comforted, spoken to gently and perhaps walked around in your arms, while she lets out all her stress. Babies are not able to cope with being alone, especially when they are upset. At those times the main thing they need is to be connected to somebody they know. Your holding hands and arms are saying to your baby: I see how you feel, and I will never leave you. I am here for you no matter what. This quality of holding is the ground of your baby's self-worth. He will carry this sense of his own worth deep inside for the rest of his life.

Sometimes we need to ask ourselves: Am I trying to answer my baby's need or am I just trying to stop that noise he is making? These are two very different motivations, and they feel different to the baby. We connect far better with our babies when we mean to be affectionate, rather than just aiming to quiet them. It's important to tell yourself that stopping the crying should not be the goal. The goal is answering his need. Sometimes, what babies need is just to be held while they cry, cry, cry and cry some more. At these times, nothing you do will actually stop the crying; it stops in its own good time, when, as my daughter once explained to me, "The last tear has been cried out." As we saw earlier, this is an important means of stress release, and your baby should not be left alone to do this. If you find yourself tiring from holding a crying baby too long, ideally, there should be another trusted person near you who can take over. That's why it is so important not to do our parenting in isolation. If your baby's crying persists and you are worried, see your pediatrician, doctor or local nurse to make sure there is nothing medically wrong.

Holding your baby

Whenever you are interacting with your baby, your hands are doing quite a bit of the talking. The language that passes between you is largely the language of the body. One of the main ways your baby absorbs the sense that the world is a nurturing place is through the signals that her body receives; in other words the way her body is touched, held and carried. Your touch can be saying: 'I am in a hurry; you are less important right now," or "This world is a harsh place; get used to it." Alternatively, your hands can be saying: "I've got you; you are safe and secure."

Take a moment to look at your hands. Your hands speak volumes, and babies, more than any other persons, are able to pick up so many qualities of emotion through the way you touch them.

Your baby's body, like yours, has memory. Her muscle fibers and sinews retain a sense of how she has been held, which she records as information about relationships and what she can expect from them as she grows. This information is fed to the baby's nervous system in a feedback loop that helps to set her response to stress and her ability to relax. A baby who has been tenderly and respectfully held will benefit from this experience for the rest of her life. She will feel vibrantly connected to her body, yet also able to let go of tension and relax.

So, when you pick up your very young baby, be mindful of not grabbing her, but gradually enclose her in your hands. If you pick up your baby without cradling her head, you will see that, initially, her head drops back. This can feel a little shocking or alarming to her. Always support her neck and head before you lift her up, especially until her neck muscles are naturally strong enough to hold up her head herself.

A better way to pick up your baby is to gently lift her bottom with one hand first, just enough to make room underneath her so you can slide your other hand under her upper back and shoulders, her neck and her head. The neck is a part of the body that can accumulate and store immense amounts of tension. Just as for adults, when we are stressed, the muscles in our necks and jaws tend to contract quite powerfully without our noticing, so it is for babies.

Once her head is securely held, then lift her toward you. When you hold her and chat with her, keep her head cradled in one or both of your hands. Your careful hands can keep your baby immersed in feelings of safety and tranquility—and help her to remain settled and contented for longer periods.

EXERCISE

Many adults carry chronic tension in the neck and head, which leads to headaches, irritability, tiredness and difficulty in focusing.

Try this with your partner. Set aside twenty minutes when you can be together quietly, with no interruptions. Lie comfortably on the ground or on a mat with your partner sitting cross-legged behind you. Ask your partner to take both hands, rest them palm up on the ground together (or on the mat) underneath your head and cradle your head very gently. Their fingertips should be roughly at the top of your neck, just under the large bone at the base of your skull (occiput). Your partner's thumbs should be making contact with the sides of your head, just above your ears. An important note for the person doing the holding: it is essential that you make no sudden movement; just hold your partner's head steadily. Your partner will not be able to fully relax and let go unless they can completely trust that they will not be startled.

Make an agreement that when it is time to stop, the holding partner will speak softly to let you know, and then very gently slide their hands out from under your head. Until then, simply rest in this position with your eyes closed for a few minutes, breathing naturally. Invite your head and neck to let go completely, hand the weight over entirely to your partner's hands—and notice if there is any part of your neck that refuses to let go. If this happens, imagine your breath going to this spot, and with the exhalation, imagine all the tension leaving. You will find that your neck and head gradually trust your partner's holding more, and they let go. Notice what happens to your breathing, notice any sensations that move through you, or any emotions.

When it is time to finish, your partner should gently and slowly slide his or her hands out from behind your head. Resist the temptation to help by lifting your head. Let your head remain heavy, hand it over completely to gravity, and allow it to rest on the ground or mat. Make sure that you take a couple more minutes to rest in this position. When you feel ready to get up, open your eyes slowly and, without lifting your head at all, roll in a slow and lazy way onto your left-hand side. Curl your legs up and rest a few more moments, then turn over onto your knees, so that your forehead remains resting on the ground or mat. Lift yourself up gently by pushing your hands against the mat. By letting your head be the last thing that comes up, you can, in this position, retain the deep relaxation longer, so that it filters right into your day.

Most people find having their heads gently cradled one of the most beautifully relaxing experiences. It is as if your thoughts, your mental strain and worry are lifted from you. It is not unusual, however, to find that one or two places in your neck cling on, as if afraid that your head will be dropped if you don't hold it up yourself. This is a body-memory, and may mean that early in your life you felt insecurely held when you most needed it. You can use your out-breath to gradually cajole your neck into letting go and trusting again—and your partner needs to help you by holding you reliably. This can be enormously beneficial to your emotional state and your stress levels. Make sure you and your partner take turns with this exercise, so you both experience the benefits.

Once you have experienced how pleasurable and restful it can be to have your head held in this way, you will love to pass this sensation on to your baby. Consider that this kind of holding is infinitely more important for her, since her neck muscles have little strength.

Learning your baby's language

Long before your baby can form her first words, she speaks to you regularly. She has a broad array of signals, and if you really take the time to quietly observe and hear her, you might be amazed by the range of her expressions. You will notice, for instance, the way she turns her head toward your breast and reaches with her lips when she is hungry (breastfeeding specialists call this the rooting reflex). Sometimes, you will know she is hungry because she makes sucking noises with her mouth, or tries to suck on her fists.

You might notice a specific kind of restlessness and irritability when she is tired, she might frown, yawn, rub her eyes or become agitated and fussy. When she is stressed, she might make jerky or thrashing movements, spit up or even arch her back and scream.

Since every baby has her own unique language, these examples are only guidelines to get you started, but there is no substitute for your own patient observation. If you decide to trust your baby and to trust that nothing she says is random or meaningless, you will be able to learn a lot about how she speaks to you and what she is trying to tell you. The time you spend together is your teacher.

Learning to decipher your baby's language may always be an imprecise art, and it is usually a trial and error exercise. You need to be prepared to get it wrong sometimes—everybody gets it wrong from time to time. Learning comes through experimentation, offer your baby a range of options when she calls out for your help: "Do you want to be held?" "Do you want a rest or sleep?" "Are you cold?" "Do you need a diaper change?" "Are you hungry?" "Do you want to play and chat with me?" Most of the time you will know when you hit the bull's-eye—she will show you through her relaxation and contentedness. Inevitably, she might be a little distressed as you go through the motions, trying a number of things before you finally find what she was asking you for. Don't despair, and don't rush yourself. Your baby can handle some frustration if you are there with her, talking to her soothingly as you offer her your best guesses. Your intention to care is palpable.

It's not too different to learning a simple and basic sign language (see next section); your mutual understanding will come if you simply watch, listen carefully and enjoy your baby. You learn much faster when you are enjoying yourself rather than fretting anxiously. When you are learning your baby's unique language you are like a sailor learning to predict the weather after being at sea for a long time. Many sailors find their own forecasts are more accurate than those of the weather bureau, even without all the gizmos, techno-gadgetry and satellite imagery. Sailors aren't clairvoyant; they predict the weather by reading the clouds, the sea, the wind and feelings in their own bodies. They learn to read the weather better than anyone by being intimate with it, day after day, by watching the elements with fascination. The same works with your baby. Your hours and days together make learning inevitable. Relax and trust yourself, knowing that you will always make mistakes (we all do), and that she can deal with the stress of waiting much better when you are with her, holding her and comforting her.

Babies can learn sign language before they can speak

Recently, a number of people have been developing the idea of sign language for babies as young as six months. Baby sign language classes are springing up around the world. Baby signing experts claim that long before they can speak, babies can learn to understand and make signs for their needs. This makes their communication easier for parents to understand and removes a lot of frustration for baby and parents. Using sign language even helps with speech development. This growing phenomenon is a very intriguing idea that I am sad to say, I have no personal experience with, so I cannot personally vouch for it, but I wish I had heard about this when my daughter was a baby. It does seem to hold a lot of promise, and I would encourage you to investigate it.

Check out a baby sign language class near you and see for yourself. Any tool that improves communication between parent and baby must surely be an advantage. What is particularly good about baby signing is that it's showing even the most skeptical parents that babies know very clearly what they need and that they deserve to be taken seriously. My only concern would be that we don't rely on sign language at the expense of learning all of the other cues our baby uses. They are talking to us all along, whether or not they use hand signals. The sign language is for our benefit, to make up for our own lack of literacy about our babies' natural body language and vocal language.

Talk to your baby

Hold your baby face-to-face and speak with her, make wordless sounds or actually talk, tell your baby how you feel. She understands, because your feelings show on your face, in your eyes and in your tone of voice. Watch how she turns her face away in order to rest after a few moments, then turns back to you for another round. As long as you respect the rhythm of her dialogue and let her take the lead, she will not be over stimulated. If you wait patiently, she will turn back. Say something to welcome her back when she does. Indulge in plenty of these special, adoring one-on-one moments each day. They help your baby enormously to be more communicative and to feel deep contentment and security. These little conversations can bring oodles of joy into both your lives.

Who does not want a child who is unafraid to express their needs and feelings? These lovely little one-on-one interactions, done daily with your baby, wire her brain for more communicativeness and higher emotional intelligence.

Can we teach our babies literacy?

These days people seem much more concerned about literacy than ever before. Well, the essence of literacy is communication. If communication is rewarding right from the start, it encourages your child to be communicative. Literacy begins long before reading.

The first lesson in literacy is to listen to your baby and respond appropriately. When the baby can see that reaching out is met with a response, this conditions him to trust people, to be willing to speak his mind and speak his heart. No wonder researchers have found that emotionally secure babies who have enjoyed strong attachments to their parents can sometimes more fully develop their cognitive (mental and academic) abilities.

If a baby learns to give up on communication because her caregivers don't seem to be listening or responding to her reliably, this is no incentive for her to keep learning how to reach out. Many children learn to internalize their feelings and withdraw from relationships; they stop communicating, which can have a negative impact on many aspects of learning.

When interaction is too demanding

Too often, babies are treated like entertainment. It might go something like this: visitors crowd around, anxious to get a look at the little guy. Like a toy with buttons that make interesting noises when you press them, people poke at his belly to get a reaction—it's amazing just how many people awkwardly greet a baby by poking him in the belly, as they would an avocado to see if it's ripe. Invariably, someone then pushes their face within inches of the baby's and says, "Smile for Aunt Betty," or "Smile for Uncle Fred. Where's my smile? Oh, come on, gimme a little smile." Meanwhile, the baby's probably thinking: "Geez, lady (or Geez, guy), get a life!" One day, I may have to poke everyone I meet in their stomachs and beg them to smile at me, as a way of striking up a conversation. I wonder what this would do for my social status.

A smile may be what you need, but not necessarily what the baby wants to do. How about letting him be who he is and just enjoying him whether he smiles or not? Isn't that how you would want to be treated? How do you feel when people pressure you to cheer up, to make them happy?

Babies do not want to entertain us or make us feel good; it is not their job. They want to discover us, and they want to feel loved. Often, babies are deeply fascinated by just looking. The world is intensely wonderful to them.

Babies are delightful and it is natural for people to want to see them, but too often we grasp at them, demand they please us, we talk too much and too loudly at them, pass them around like toys and treat them like exhibits. Perfect recipe for an over stimulated, stressed-out baby. After a session of being peered and poked at by a procession of well-meaning but overwhelming guests, don't be surprised if your baby looks stunned for a while, then ends up screaming for an hour.

Give the little one some space. And respect his limits.

7

Science and Babies' Emotional Needs

Science has come to the aid of parents with a number of insights that can help make a huge difference to our babies' sense of security in ways that will benefit their emotional health for the rest of their lives. The following suggestions, the result of years of research, have received rave reviews from countless parents— and their babies.

Wear your baby on your body

A baby's need to be held is almost unending. Babies are genetically programmed to want to be close to you, and preferably, in direct physical contact with you for much of the day. When they are carried on their parents' bodies for much of the day, babies tend to cry a lot less, seem to enjoy themselves a lot more and are noticeably more peaceful. Parents who wear their babies in slings consistently report this, and researchers have verified it. Babies love quietly watching the world go by while feeling the warmth of your body, your rhythmic breathing and heartbeat right against them. You might be surprised by how many of your ordinary, day-to-day activities your baby will love to join you in, and so much of what you do can remain uninterrupted if you just bring your baby along. If you wear him in a sling, in front or on your back, your arms remain free to do many of the things you normally do.

The swaying and rocking they enjoy as you move, walk around and generally go about your business, can be profoundly calming for your baby. Knowing that you are right next to them at all times also contributes enormously to their sense of safety and tranquility. Breastfeeding mothers find it very convenient to have their babies right near their breast, in their sling, so they can latch on with minimal effort. This works well with the type of sling that goes over one shoulder, rather than the carrier that has the baby sitting upright and facing you. The over-shoulder, sarong-type of sling has many advantages. It hugs the natural curvature of your baby's back and supports her head. It enables your baby to turn her head and see you, as well as the world around her. Baby carriers that strap over both shoulders force babies to sit upright before their spines are naturally ready. Their legs dangle unsupported and their heads often flop around uncomfortably. They are forced to either look into your chest, or directly out in front of you, depending on which way you face them in the carrier, so they don't have the choice.

Babywearing can feel very sweet for the parents, too. Having your baby close helps to keep you in a state of delicious intimacy; both baby and parent seem to be enveloped in a peaceful and contented state.

A growing number of parents are noticing the benefits, and hence they are wearing their babies around for most of the day. Like little marsupials, their babies virtually live in their pouches, eyeing the world quietly and contentedly. Often, babies fall asleep and take a nap quite naturally while in your sling. This can be one of the most nurturing and satisfying ways to ease into sleep. You— and your baby—can decide if it is better to stay asleep in the sling or to be eased into the bassinette.

You might at this point start to have some questions, such as: How often should I wear my baby? How long should I wear him for? Is it ever OK to put him down? How long is it OK for a baby not to be directly on someone's body? If you have those kinds of questions, then ask your baby. That's what being watchful and responsive is all about. Better than all the experts in the world, babies tell us when they are enjoying what is happening to them. If you watch and listen, they tell you when they are happy to just lie on a warm and comfortable surface kicking their legs in the air, when they love to be set loose to move around, sit on the floor and play, practice crawling, and so on. If your baby seems content, babbling away while lying down separate from you, then trust that while it lasts. It probably means she is more than fine.

She may also love to sit in a rocker near you where she can watch you doing whatever you do. Advice about what to do with a baby should not be treated like a rigid rulebook or a millstone around your neck. Besides, there is a huge variance between babies. The main thing is that you are tuned in to what your baby is telling you, and that you are listening to your heart. By listening attentively and trusting yourself you will become your baby's parenting expert.

If ever you are feeling highly stressed or very upset, that is a time when your baby may not like to be on your body. Give yourself and your baby a break and ask someone else to hold him.

When your baby calls to you, respond as promptly as possible

Until the science on attachment reaches every corner of our society—and it may yet take a few years—someone will still occasionally advise you to ignore your baby's calls to you, usually as a method to train him to fall asleep on his own. Science is gradually making this kind of advice disappear, while, increasingly, parents are encouraged to listen to their hearts. Over the years a veritable legion of parents have told me how their hearts break when they stop themselves from going to their crying or calling babies because they were told by nurses or older family members not to comfort them. Deliberately denying your baby the contact he asks for is needless, painful for you as well as for him, and it harms his sense of secure attachment to you. When a baby is left to cry alone, she becomes immediately anxious; this soon turns to panic and the baby's levels of stress hormones become sharply elevated. If this happens repeatedly, it causes neurological changes in the baby's brain that can have a long-term negative effect on how she responds to stress (see Chapter 8, "How separation stress affects the child's brain'). So trust what your heart is telling you and act upon it: always respond to your baby's calls for you, whether she is crying or simply yelling.

You may have already heard a number of times that you cannot spoil a baby by promptly meeting his every need. This is perfectly true. In this regard, babyhood is a stage of childhood that stands well apart from the rest. If you give a toddler everything he asks for, you would be overindulging him and preventing him from growing up. With a baby, the very opposite is true. If you answer his every need, you are helping him to feel profoundly nurtured, safe, secure and connected to you, thereby giving him a reinforced-concrete foundation on which to build his emotional intelligence. Responsiveness is exactly what will give him a strong sense of autonomy and independence, and a caring and empathetic nature as he grows up. Responsiveness is the heart of attachment and your child's emotional health. It is the greatest investment you can possibly make in your child's future happiness.

Occasionally, there will be unavoidable delays in your response time—you have your own needs to attend to and you might be held up. That's OK. You can comfort your baby when you get to him. There is no need for you to be anxious and jumping at every sound he makes; just respond in a relaxed manner. Babies who are used to feeling well-connected tend to sooner develop their capacity to wait and are less likely to descend rapidly into despairing howls. Should your baby do so, it is far easier and less stressful for you if you are wearing your baby, or in some other way keeping him close to you.

Sleeping close together

Many years ago, I sat on a park bench while watching my three-year-old daughter playing in a local playground. Next to me was an Indonesian woman who, having married an Australian expatriate, was in Sydney for the first time to meet her in-laws. As our children played together, we struck up a conversation. In her broken English, she told me how astounded she was at how hard life seemed for Australian parents. When I asked her what she meant, she explained that she could not understand our struggles with sleep deprivation. Back home, she told me, babies sleep in bed with their parents, and night waking was limited to breastfeeding breaks, often while the mother still snoozed and without her having to get up. If the parents ever needed a break for an uninterrupted sleep, there would be a grandmother on hand to take a turn at sleeping with the child. The child's peaceful rest and emotional security did not come at the expense of the parents' need for sleep.

I felt self-conscious. This woman must have found our habit of making our babies sleep in a separate room quite bizarre, not to mention inconvenient.

In most Western cultures, sleep struggles are among the most frequent reasons why new parents seek professional help. This epidemic of nighttime agonies and wrung-out parents places us at odds with most of the rest of the world. So does the novel idea of putting a baby down to sleep, all alone, in a separate room.

Why babies should not sleep alone

Human babies have traveled a long evolutionary road and all along this road they have slept right next to their parents. Humans have always felt instinctively more vulnerable at night, and for good reason. It is harder to defend ourselves in the dark, especially when we are asleep. At night, any baby or child feels the need for protection more keenly. No separation is more terrifying for a baby than nighttime separation. Sleeping alone threatens the baby's security of attachment to his parents.

Nature usually ensures that any behavior that has been honed down through millions of years of evolution provides us with not just one, but a whole array of health advantages, for both mother and baby. Sleeping next to or near your baby (co-sleeping) has the following advantages:

- ♱ Babies' breathing is very irregular for the first few weeks of their lives; by having you near them or right next to them at night, their breathing is measurably improved. For this to work, your baby needs to be at least close enough to hear you breathing.
- ♱ Babies can only feel connected to you if they can detect your presence directly through their senses. As your baby can smell you from 12–15 feet away, she should be at least this close.
- ♱ It makes a huge difference to babies' and toddlers' emotional security to hear your breathing at night and to see you right there next to them each time they awake. This has long-term psychological benefits.
- ♱ Babies' body temperatures are better regulated if they co-sleep.
- ♱ If safety guidelines are observed, co-sleeping can protect your baby from sudden infant death syndrome (SIDS).
- ♱ When sleeping next to you, babies tend to spend more time quietly sleeping.

⸸   Co-sleeping facilitates nighttime breastfeeding, with its massive health benefits.

⸸   Babies who feel secure tend to be far more placid through the day and night, which makes the parents' work a lot easier. Everyone wins.

⸸   A University of California study found that children who co-sleep are more self-reliant, more likely to initiate friendships and more likely to independently work out problems with their relationships in preschool.

⸸   Mothers who co-sleep swear by the convenience of being able to simply roll over and breastfeed their baby at night.

⸸   A study of mothers who co-sleep found that, even if they may sometimes wake more frequently, overall they get more sleep.

James McKenna, PhD, director of the Mother-Baby Behavioral Sleep Laboratory at the University of Notre Dame is the world's leading expert on baby sleep. His research has found that babies who sleep away from their parents tend to wake more often and show more signs of stress.

Decades of cross-cultural and laboratory research led Dr McKenna to conclude that babies must be biologically designed to sleep next to their parents. In fact, according to him, we should be asking if it is safe for babies not to sleep right near their parents since co-sleeping can protect your baby from SIDS. Some research suggests co-sleeping can reduce the risk to half, even as much as one-fifth of the average SIDS rate. As a result of these findings, the UK Foundation for the Study of Infant Deaths launched an awareness campaign called "Sleep safe, sleep sound, share a room with me" (see References).

If it feels too uncomfortable to have your baby in bed with you at night, and no matter how you try you can't seem to get used to it, don't worry. Your baby still feels you nearby if you have her right next to your bed in a co-sleeper. A rocking crib right next to your bed, or a bouncing hammock suspended from the ceiling just above you are also both excellent ideas. They enable you to flop your hand over the side (or lift it in the hammock case), without sitting up, and gently rock her back to sleep if she awakes. You can reach out and, with minimal effort, just touch, caress or rock her back to sleep when she awakes and whimpers, if hunger is not the issue. Many parents are able to comfort their baby in this way without waking fully, and they doze off quickly, having lost only a minute of sleep.

As I said earlier, there are few things more comforting and more natural than having your baby fall asleep on your body, in a sling. Wearing a peacefully napping baby, you can keep an eye on him while you go about your business.

SLEEPING NEXT TO BABY

Human parents across the world have always slept next to their babies. Separate sleeping for babies is a recent eccentricity among a minority of the world's societies. In seventeenth and eighteenth century Europe, Catholic priests were alarmed at the number of parents who, under the protection of the confessional, admitted deliberately smothering their unwanted babies at night after they were baptized. The command for parents to make separate sleeping arrangements was a measure to curb epidemic rates of infanticide. Separate sleeping soon became the unquestioned norm in many parts of Europe, which has influenced our nighttime parenting customs to this day.

How much can we expect babies to sleep?

James McKenna says that infants rarely have sleep problems, it's the parents who have the sleep problems. By this he means we have all been led to have some very unrealistic expectations of what a baby should do for us. There is a simple explanation for this. Until recently, accepted notions of babies' sleep patterns came from studies conducted in the US during the 1960s, when almost every baby was bottle-fed. Artificial formulas are harder to digest, and so they plunge the baby into an unnaturally long sleep phase. Most people began to expect all babies to sleep for longer than they are biologically designed to. In other words, our understanding about healthy baby sleep patterns needs to be revised.

Sleep patterns vary a lot from baby to baby, so ideas about averages are only very rough guides. Generally, during their first few weeks, babies can spend around 15–16 hours asleep every day. By 3 months this is down to 14 hours, but you should not be surprised or alarmed if your baby strays from this norm. Infant sleep studies define sleeping all night as five hours. A long-term sleep study conducted by Bristol University found that at 6 to 8 months, only 16% of babies were sleeping for those 5-hour stints. Nearly all babies wake at least once a night, and more than 5% wake up at least 5 times. Even though occasionally you hear of a baby that sleeps through the night quite naturally, the vast majority won't, and it is unreasonable to expect a baby to do so.

Is co-sleeping safe?

There is a lot of scare mongering about the risk of parents accidentally rolling over and suffocating their baby if they co-sleep. This fear probably dates back to the days of nighttime infanticide in Europe, and reflects how alienated we have become from natural practices. The vast majority of babies around the world sleep right next to their parents, and this has been true since our ancestors first climbed out of the trees. You'd think that over millions of years of evolution, our bodies would have learned something about safe co-sleeping. In fact, video studies of co-sleeping mothers show that, without even waking up, they make constant adjustments to their babies' positions to make sure the baby is able to breathe freely and not get overheated. In their sleep, they even adjust the covers on the baby.

IMPORTANT PRECAUTIONS FOR SAFE CO-SLEEPING

There are some conditions in which co-sleeping—more specifically, bed-sharing—is not safe. In order to make bedsharing safe a number of precautions need to be taken.

- Don't put your baby in bed with you when:
  - you have been drinking
  - you have been smoking
  - you have taken medications or drugs
  - you are overtired.
- If you want to have your baby in bed with you, make sure you:
  - have a firm mattress
  - keep the baby on her back
  - keep pillows and covers away from her head.
- If you have long hair, keep it bunched up; it could be a choking hazard.

This is not an exhaustive list of precautions but they are the main and most common safety tips mentioned in co-sleeping literature. Every list seems to have a slightly different emphasis, so it is worth taking the time to read a few of them (see References).

How do we help our baby fall asleep?

If you understand that healthy and happy sleep is a reflex that takes over the baby when his physical needs are met and when he feels emotionally secure (seen, heard, responded to and not alone), then you will see that helping your baby to sleep is not necessarily about finding some fandangled technique. You don't have to become a technician, and certainly not a magician. Helping your baby to sleep is about helping him to feel well connected. Most of the natural impulses that come directly from your heart are the best ones, and you already have them inside you: cuddling, rocking, singing, keeping lights dim, noise levels down and keeping your baby close to you, at least until he dozes off. Also, breastfeeding your baby to sleep is one of the many things that work beautifully, Nature has carefully designed this to happen, as you will see in the breastfeeding section coming up.

If you feel stuck and need more help, there are now many excellent books entirely devoted to the subject of baby sleep (see References).

Dispelling the cultural hang-ups

There are many scary myths circulating about how ruinous co-sleeping will be to the whole family. If you tell enough people about your choice to co-sleep, sooner or later you are likely to hear some grim warning about how you are teaching your child bad habits and now you will never get them out of your bed. The misery won't stop there: sexual intimacy with your partner will go out the window and you won't get a good night's sleep for years. Usually, these dire scenarios are painted by people who have never co-slept with their children. Certainly, there are practical issues to solve, not the least of which is how to preserve the parents' sexual intimacy, but with the help of a little imagination, solutions abound for the specific circumstances and preferences of each family. There are countless ways to combine co-sleeping with privacy for the parents—for starters, co-sleeping doesn't necessarily have to mean bed-sharing, and babies can feel secure *next* to your bed. Ask others for helpful tips, but make sure you ask people who have successfully co-slept with their babies and toddlers (see References).

So many parents co-sleep in secret that I think there must be a growing underground network of clandestine co-sleepers. One of them told me she kept her blinds drawn so the neighbors wouldn't see their baby in bed with them. Although these days co-sleeping is very quickly gaining mainstream acceptance, there are still many parents who are subjected to criticism and ridicule by friends or family.

So far, every co-sleeping family I have spoken with has largely enjoyed the experience, as has my own. Most speak of it in glowing terms, about how beautiful it can be to wake up to your baby's smiling face. And if the child is not pressured or hurried out of the parent's room or bed, as toddlers they quite easily and gradually adapt to—and love—their own beds. The many myths about the disadvantages of co-sleeping are easily dispelled.

I have no way of proving this, as I don't know of any research to back it up, but based on anecdotal evidence (and my own experience) co-sleeping can protect children from the night fears that affect so many children. Co-sleeping children seem less afraid of the dark and have less trouble falling asleep at night. It makes sense—for a baby and a toddler, being close to and connected with her parents is the most important thing.

When is a child ready to sleep in his or her own room?

Anxiety is, by definition, about loss of control. We all tend to get frightened when we are helpless and unable to influence our environment. Just like us adults, children feel more secure when we don't take away their control, particularly around important times of transition. If we let them make the move to their own bedroom gradually, and at their own pace, the transition is far more likely to be painless. Rather than pressuring them to move out of your room, you can make their own bed seem attractive by associating it with happy experiences. You could, for instance, regularly read their favorite books to them in their own bed. Tell them early on it is their own, special bed. To begin with, start them off just having naps there. Leave a soft night light on for them, and tell them they can come into your room if they want to should they wake up at night. It may take time, but the number of hours you have your bed to yourselves will steadily grow.

A special note on sleep training
This widely used but controversial technique, used to train babies to go to sleep alone, is a typical example of the fact that we live in a time of transition, when old parenting styles are gradually being replaced. Practitioners who understand the workings of the mother-infant bond would never recommend this technique. Sleep training, which has been spoken out against by an ever-growing chorus of health professionals, is falling out of favor.

Basically, sleep training (sometimes called "crying-it-out" or "Ferberizing") involves denying your baby a response when she cries at night. You begin by making her wait for a few moments, then keep making the periods of refusal longer and longer, until, supposedly, she "learns" how to fall asleep all by herself without bothering you. Sometimes babies might spontaneously fall asleep without you having to rock them, breastfeed them to sleep or lie next to them, but there are serious problems with this technique.

First of all, it is based on the expectation that babies need to learn to fall asleep all alone, all the time—the very opposite of what babies have, over millions of years, evolved to expect. This enforced self-reliance comes long before the child is biologically ready for it and ignores her most important attachment needs. For the sake of retraining the baby's behavior, this technique ignores the fear, helplessness and betrayal the baby feels while crying out for a parent who won't come. As we learned earlier, when you are gone, babies cannot understand that you will come back. They cannot reassure themselves by imagining your return, which makes your absence all the more devastating.

For many thousands of desperate parents suffering the worst agonies of sleep deprivation, this has been the only solution offered. For many years, it was the default mode, even recommended for parents who were managing well and not asking for any assistance with nighttime parenting.

Sleep training and other techniques that are based on ignoring babies set parents against babies in a battle of wills to see who gives up first: will you, the parent, cave in and comfort the baby? A sleep-training coach will invariably admonish you to stay strong and wait out your baby's howls until he goes quiet, no matter how agonizing that feels.

If you succeed in this, you have won the battle—your baby blinked first. It might be tempting to think, if your baby finally goes quiet in his crib, that all is OK and he is now skilled at putting himself to sleep without your help, but this is not a happy sleep for the baby; it is nothing like falling asleep contentedly, feeling connected to you. By the time a baby gives up on calling you, he has gone through what developmental neuropsychologists call the "defeat response." On the surface it might look like peaceful slumber, but it is more like a state of shock or numbing out—a collapse of all the healthy efforts to reach out for human contact, with none of the pleasure associated with the sleep that comes through emotional security. Once your baby's brain becomes habituated to producing the defeat response, this practice becomes neurologically set. The child's brain is then more likely to use resignation as a strategy to face stresses later in life. The risk with these techniques is that they program the child's brain to give up on reaching out to others. Ignoring a baby undermines his trust, his sense of safety and emotional security, which can have adverse effects on his later behavior and relationships.

Some babies become so frantic after a period of crying alone that they throw up. Imagine how distressed you would have to be in order to vomit. I have seen contemporary literature compelling parents to clean up the baby's vomit in a matter-of-fact way and continue with the procedure. I don't understand how anyone can ask a parent to remain so indifferent to his or her baby's obvious trauma—this is heartless and damaging advice.

The Australian Association of Infant Mental Health (AAIMHI) was so concerned about sleep training practices (called "controlled crying" in Australia) that it produced a position paper (see References), literally crying out against the use of this technique. Among other things, the paper says that:

> AAIMHI is concerned that the widely practiced technique of controlled crying is not consistent with what infants need for their optimal emotional and psychological health, and may have unintended emotional consequences.

Some surveys have found that sleep training is "successful" for less than half of the people who attempt it. The high failure rates are not the main problem with sleep training—what we should be particularly worried about is when it "works."

Full-term breastfeeding

Breastfeeding would have to be one of Nature's most wondrous accomplishments. Every year medical research discovers more about the benefits of breastfeeding for the mother, the child and all of society. There is probably no other single act of mothering that can better prepare your child for a lifetime of physical and emotional health. It is hard to imagine one biologically driven act of generosity that offers more benefits than breastfeeding does.

THE INCREDIBLE HISTORY OF BREASTFEEDING

Throughout most ancient civilizations, including Rome, Greece, Egypt, Babylon, China, Japan, India and the Middle East, mothers who could afford to, offloaded their babies to be breastfed by wet nurses, strangers who would breastfeed for a fee, or slaves belonging to the family. Over the centuries this practice became increasingly popular—in direct contravention to all the world's great religions, and peaked in Europe in the late eighteenth century. Babies were farmed out to wet nurses living in faraway villages, and the parents would not see the child again until he or she was returned at 2 to 4 years of age. Wet nursing became embraced by all social classes, and parents were quite open about their reasons: babies were thought of as burdensome, their cries obnoxious. A survey conducted as late as 1780 by the police chief of Paris found that over 80% of parents sent their babies to live with out-of-town wet nurses. Throughout Europe, babies who weren't wet nursed were often fed meal pap—a mixture of flour and water—or diluted animal milk through teats fashioned from clay, metal, leather, animal horns or cow udders (the rubber teat was eventually developed in 1850). In some areas infant mortality rates reached 50%.

Over the eighteenth century, when doctors such as William Cadogan of Britain began to notice that babies who were breastfed by their mothers were much healthier, normal feeding began to make a comeback, though very slowly. All progress was thwarted during the twentieth century, when baby formula manufacturers orchestrated an aggressive worldwide campaign to boost their sales. Women the world over were strongly persuaded to abandon breastfeeding in favor of formula, which was dishonestly touted as equivalent if not superior to breastmilk. These campaigns of deception were unimaginably successful, and the skills involved in breastfeeding were almost completely forgotten throughout affluent and developing nations. Child health deteriorated, while infant mortality skyrocketed. In some places, in order to suppress lactation, mothers were given injections or had their breasts tightly bandaged.

Until the 1990s, mothers were told to breastfeed every three or four hours (scheduled feeding). This archaic practice of parenting by the clock has undermined maternal milk supply and caused many problems with breastfeeding. It has also caused much anguish to babies as their needs went unheard. The quirky idea of scheduled feeding was advocated by the likes of Dr Cadogan at a time of ignorance, when strict control over children was the ideal parenting style.

In the 1940s, Dr Spock endorsed the idea of scheduled feeding without so much as a hint of a scientific rationale. The desire of hospital staff to have predictable routines kept the scheduled feed alive, at a time when newborn babies were senselessly separated from their mothers and brought to them at regular intervals for feeding. Scheduled feeding existed before health professionals understood that babies give clear signals of their hunger, and that feeding on demand is far better for milk supply and for the baby's emotional security. Feeding by the clock is now widely recognized as an anachronism, as risky to the baby's health, and must never be advised.

Breastfeeding is instinctive, but there are specific skills involved that must be learned from more experienced women, without which a number of things can go wrong with supply or painful injuries can occur to the breast or nipple. It may take generations for this global damage to be repaired, as mothers around the world painstakingly relearn a lost art. Were it not for the tireless efforts of volunteer organizations such as La Leche League International, formed to combat the might of profiteering formula makers, breastfeeding today might have been a quaint traditional practice seen mainly among tribal peoples.

WHO has also weighed into the ring by issuing its strongly worded International Code of Marketing of Breastmilk Substitutes. This Code heavily restricts the advertising and promotion of infant formulas, stating that, "There should be no advertising or other form of promotion to the general public of products within the scope of this Code (infant formulas)" (see References). The Code also requires all packaging of breastmilk substitutes to be marked with "a clear statement of the superiority of breastfeeding." Worldwide, the loss of breastfeeding has been damaging to public health. The WHO Code reflects international alarm about the extent and severity of this damage and a great sense of urgency about the need to return to breastfeeding. It has required intense lobbying to persuade marketers to abide by this ethical code, and still not all of them do.

The natural role of grandmothers, who once taught mothers the skills of breastfeeding, has had to be replaced by professional lactation specialists, since today's grandmothers themselves have scarcely breastfed. During the trough of the 1960s and early 1970s, almost four in five mothers did not breastfeed, and those that did, usually abandoned the practice within about three months, which is less than an eighth of the minimal optimal duration. Moreover, breastfeeding happened behind closed doors. This was a catastrophic near eradication.

Incredibly, by the 1960s and 1970s, the art of breastfeeding was almost lost to humanity and had to be rescued from oblivion. It is making a steady comeback, thanks to the efforts of medical science, volunteer pro-breastfeeding organizations and mothers around the world. For a while, authorities took the softly-softly approach to recommending breastfeeding, perhaps they did not want to offend the vast majority of mothers who, over the last half-century, had been cynically duped into becoming consumers of artificial formula. But as the nature of breastfeeding becomes more clearly understood, authorities are becoming more assertive and, increasingly, we see artificial feeding described as a health hazard. There are clear medical and psychological risks posed to the baby, and vast healthcare costs to the community. The overuse of artificial feeding has been identified as a significant public health problem, worldwide.

You might wonder what all the fuss is about. Many readers might be thinking: "But I wasn't breastfed, and I'm fine," or, "If bottle-feeding is so bad for our health, then how did we ever survive as a nation when, in the last generation, hardly anyone was breastfed for more than a few weeks?" People would have been dropping like flies, wouldn't they? With most public health issues there are plenty of exceptions to the rule, such as the proverbial uncle who smoked a pack a day and lived till he was 96 (most people know one of those; I actually had one). It took medical science decades to suspect, and then establish, the links between cigarette smoking and some common diseases that were previously thought unavoidable. Even today, there is no perfect proof that smoking causes lung cancer, but the smart thing is to bet on the side of not smoking.

The story of artificial feeding is similar. Medical science has only recently begun to uncover the links between many public health problems and insufficient breastfeeding, and more of these health consequences are revealed every year. If we want perfect proof that bottle-feeding can contribute to diabetes, we may never get it. Many people appear—at least on the surface—to grow up symptom-free, but overall, there is little doubt that if all babies were fully breastfed to full-term, the rates and severity of many diseases and psychological problems would fall dramatically. As the list of health risks acknowledged by medical authorities keeps getting longer, the urgings to return to natural breastfeeding become more strident.

Baby formula is a very poor substitute. It can't hope to imitate a mother's milk, which has delicately orchestrated changes in composition from day to day, and from beginning to end of feeding ("fore milk" and "aft milk"). Breastfeeding carries vital information and protection (antibodies) borrowed from the mother's immune system, which help the baby to build a strong immune system. Baby formula is a one-size-fits-all solution that neglects a huge array of the baby's developmental needs.

Here are just some of the diseases and dysfunctions that full-term breastfeeding can protect your child from:
- a range of infectious diseases, including bacterial meningitis, respiratory tract infections, urinary tract infection
- Type 1 and Type 2 diabetes
- asthma
- diarrhea
- high cholesterol
- overweight and obesity
- some cancers (lymphoma, leukemia)
- a range of behavioral problems and mental health problems.

By breastfeeding, mothers also strengthen their own bodies against:
- breast cancer
- ovarian cancer
- osteoporosis.

Breastfeeding can save lives. Postneonatal infant mortality rates in the US are reduced by 21% in breastfed infants, and there is a lower rate of SIDS among breastfed babies.

Some studies have suggested that breastfeeding offers children an intellectual advantage. Breastfed children have mentally outperformed others, and they may even have, on average, a higher IQ.

You can see that the avoidance of breastfeeding has come at a huge cost to society. Looking only at the economic costs, here is a conservative calculation: prematurely weaned babies are four to five times more likely to end up in the hospital. The cost of this hospitalization and other health problems associated with bottle-feeding is around $3.6 billion annually. That said, these are big underestimates because there are so many intangible costs, such as the loss of the intimacy and emotional security that only breastfeeding engenders for the baby, which cannot be given a dollar value.

Breastfeeding is more than just for physical health

The massive benefits to physical health are only a part of the picture. More and more people are beginning to realize that breastfeeding offers huge psychological benefits, for the mother as well as the child. The sucking action of the baby's or toddler's mouth directly on the mother's breast stimulates the secretion of oxytocin in the mother's body. Remember oxytocin, the love hormone? If the mother is reasonably relaxed and contented, feeling supported and loved by people in her life, this oxytocin rush can make her feel enveloped in a peaceful, pleasurable and loving state. Beta-endorphins are naturally occurring opiates that reach a peak in the mother's body during breastfeeding, inducing a state of pleasurable connection with her baby. These and other hormones, directly passed to the baby through the breastmilk, lull her into a similar, blissful trance. A mother's milk literally contains the biochemical messengers of her love. This is one of several reasons why no baby formula in the world can ever hope to do what breastfeeding can do.

Many mothers are embarrassed by the physical pleasure of breastfeeding, fearing it might have inappropriate sexual overtones. Yes, breastfeeding can be an intensely sensual and physically pleasurable experience. Far from being an inappropriate pleasure, this is Nature's way to encourage breastfeeding since our health so depends on it. The best thing any mother can do is to surrender to this pleasure, enjoy the connection with her baby and relax. For starters, shouldn't mothering be as rewarding as possible? Secondly, the more delicious the experience, the more the happy hormones are secreted. A fulfilling connection at the breast brings immeasurable love into your baby's life; it is a central building block of the emotional fitness that will give him a lifetime of psychological strength. And, as always, if this lovely experience is repeated often enough, it becomes etched into neural pathways in the child's brain. Her brain is growing rapidly, taking instruction from the love she receives. Loving impulses, strength of character and resilience are being hardwired into your baby's brain for life, as the two of you just sit and enjoy the most natural act of maternal love.

Don't fall into the trap of thinking about breastfeeding as simply a healthy form of nutrition. It is, but it is also fundamental emotional nourishment, and when you are feeling restful and connected to your baby, breastfeeding nourishes your child's heart and will make a lifetime of difference to her relationships.

Breastfeeding your baby to sleep

You might have been given advice to avoid breastfeeding your baby or child to sleep lest your baby becomes addicted to this and will never again fall asleep without your breast in her mouth. Again, this is advice that belongs to an antiquated style of thinking. Here is what the Australian Breastfeeding Association has to say:

> We mothers have, at our disposal, the perfect sleep inducers. They are called breasts. Breastmilk contains a wonderful hormone called cholecystokinin (CCK). CCK induces sleepiness, both in the baby and the mother. When the baby sucks, CCK is released within the mother to help her rest and relax. Many mothers say that breastfeeding tires them out. Certainly caring for a new baby is tiring for all mothers, but the sleepiness caused by breastfeeding is to ensure that the mother gets the rest she needs.
>
> In the baby, CCK release is caused by sucking and when food, especially fat, enters the stomach. There are actually two CCK peaks, one at the end of a feed, and the other higher peak between 30 and 60 minutes after the feed. The baby sucks, gets sleepy, dozes off for a while then wakes again for a top-up feed. That higher-fat feed causes the second peak and the baby goes into deeper sleep. Top-up feeds are also great for the mother's milk supply. [Breast]feeding a baby to sleep… is helping sleep to come in the most natural way possible. The baby feels satisfied and secure and learns to trust.

Most difficulties associated with parenting arise when cultural forces lead us to ignore the most helpful, natural processes that have taken millions of years to evolve and fine-tune.

A lifetime protector of psychological wellness

The rhythmic sucking that happens during breastfeeding can result in orgasm-like, blissful sensations in the baby's body—another one of the human body's avenues to bliss. The more of these experiences a child has had, the easier it is for his nervous system to find its way back to bliss when lost. People who don't have this kind of experience recorded anywhere in their emotional memory end up looking for it later in life; too often through unhealthy and addictive activities (see Chapter 8).

Inevitably, there will be many times when breastfeeding happens in less than optimal conditions, simply because everyone's life has normal ups and downs. Sometimes, mothers need to breastfeed even though they are in a bad mood, or while they are busy talking on the phone, typing on a computer, attending a meeting—the earth does not have to stop turning every time she feeds her child. Babies learn a lot about the natural rhythms of life in this way, and if the baby is worn in a sling, she can feed with little interference to her routines. A growing number of mothers run a business from home, and sometimes do a little of their work while their baby or toddler is attached at her breast. I see no reason why our workplaces can't be more breastfeeding-friendly, so mothers can wear their babies and feed them while conducting some of their work.

But for the fullest effects on your child's emotional intelligence, when you can, let breastfeeding be a conscious act of connection, so that you are relaxed, and your attention can be exclusively for you and your baby. Think of it this way: the greatest nutrient for your child comes from the way you feel while breastfeeding, so, the more pleasurable and enjoyable you make the experience for yourself, the more joy you transmit to your baby. Make your environment just right for yourself—create a safe space, gently rock on a rocking chair, play your favorite music, seek a private and quiet space or, if you prefer, surround yourself with people you trust and love.

Every so often, treat breastfeeding as a special occasion. Have direct, skin-on-skin contact with your child as you feed, and every so often, gaze at her eyes. Without overdoing it, have some eye talk; it is not by accident that newborns' eyes have been designed to focus at precisely the distance to the mother's eyes from the breast. As your whims take you, talk to your baby, converse through your eyes, or just sit quietly and meditatively. Let yourself slide into the trance of love. These are the conditions that turn on the tap of blissful hormones for mother and child, triggering a cascade of the neurochemicals of love. Your connection will feel deepest when you take care to prepare your environment in the way that makes you feel most at ease, most contented—and you and your child will be immensely rewarded.

Now you know why the mother-baby connection is the basic unit of human love. In the most practical terms, mutually enjoyable breastfeeding can change the world.

General recommendations for healthy mothers

The norms of breastfeeding had largely been lost to Western cultures (see "The incredible history of breastfeeding," page 119) and are having to be painstakingly rediscovered through extensive research and practice. For this reason, authorities keep updating recommendations every time new information comes to light. It seems both sad and unfair that families living just ten or twenty years ago may not have received the most appropriate advice, and families living fifty years ago in the developed world would have received woefully inadequate guidance. The best approach is to empower yourself: look for the most up-to-date information—if you are connected to the internet, it will take just minutes (see References, "Breastfeeding").

The following basic guidelines are gleaned from recent publications of lactation textbooks, WHO and the latest update to a policy statement from the American Academy of Pediatrics (AAP). Note that these guidelines are basic and must not replace more in-depth advice from qualified breastfeeding counselors and lactation consultants.

- ♱ Breastfeed exclusively (avoiding other foods) for the first six months.
- ♱ Breastfeed at the time of your baby's hunger cues, as often as your baby wants, not on a time schedule. Familiarize yourself with—and do your best to respond to—your baby's early signs of hunger, such as the rooting reflex. Crying is usually a late indicator of hunger.
- ♱ Child-led weaning is best. The AAP recommends aged at least one year, and agrees that two years, three years or more can be good. Breastfeeding for at least two years is the recommendation of lactation texts and WHO (interestingly, a two-year term is recommended in Judaism and Islam; all the world's great religions have very positive breastfeeding policy statements, though as we've seen, they have often gone unheeded).
- ♱ You can breastfeed your toddler and young child occasionally; it is up to both of you to decide when to stop.
- ♱ Co-sleeping is recommended since nighttime breastfeeding is so important.

The AAP states: "Mother and infant should sleep in proximity to each other to facilitate breastfeeding."

You need to consider breastfeeding as a skill that can be honed; it doesn't always go spontaneously according to plan.

All mothers can learn to breastfeed, it doesn't require special talents—however, some helpful tips need to be taught. As each mother and baby are different in one way or another, sometimes the advice of a specialist may be needed. When you begin breastfeeding, there might be many unexpected questions that arise. The more you know about breastfeeding, the better chance you have of enjoying the process and of having it last for as long as you and your child desire. So, definitely read more about breastfeeding and seek the support of a lactation consultant in advance, so that if any difficulties arise you have access as soon as possible. There is also plenty of good-quality, easy-to-read literature on the subject (see References).

Breastfeeding can heal emotional wounds

It is now widely accepted that breastfeeding offers huge immunological advantages to the baby, powerfully protecting him from disease for the long term. But there are also great benefits to the child's emotional health. Suckling offers not only food for the body, but it is also food for the soul. In earlier chapters we saw how stressful experiences at birth or afterward can linger in the baby's nervous system, manifesting behaviorally in many ways, such as emotional distress, difficulty in settling or sleep disturbances. Breastfeeding can be a powerful healer. The hormonal contents of breastmilk add to the positive effects of skin-to-skin contact, the affection, the holding and the bodily pleasure of suckling to soothe the child's nervous system and restore a healthy balance to his brain.

Why breastfeeding can be difficult sometimes

Almost all problems encountered by mothers attempting to breastfeed can be remedied by a skilled counselor or consultant, as most problems arise simply because of the disconnection from the knowledge of our ancestors. Breastfeeding had, until recently, vanished into the shadows. Role models were almost extinct, and many mothers do not have any of their own pleasurable body memories of being breastfed themselves. No wonder so many mothers struggle with it. In societies where breastfeeding is the way of life, all girls grow up watching women breastfeeding all around them. Their own bodies are totally familiar with its pleasures, recorded as emotional memory. The breastfeeding problems that abound in the Western world are largely unheard of in such societies.

While support for nursing mothers is being rebuilt, there is still much social damage left to repair. Mothers have fought hard against social stigmatization to win the right to breastfed their babies in public places, but would still endure horrified stares if they breastfeed a toddler. It takes a thick skin to be openly nurturing against a tide of judgment and prejudice. The body's capacity to lactate can be directly hurt by social anxiety.

Breastmilk supply can, as we saw earlier, also suffer as a result of drugs used during labor, and this can be an unnatural but common cause of breastfeeding problems.

There may be a host of other factors that make breastfeeding uncomfortable. Women who come from families that were not physically demonstrative or openly warm might feel confronted by the physical intimacy of nursing a child.

Others, who have experienced physical or sexual abuse, may also feel disturbed by the passionate physicality of a hungry and loving baby. The refusal—or inability—to breastfeed often has its origins in a painful aspect of the mother's own history. If she never knew the fulfillment of being at her own mother's breast, she is being asked to give something she never received. Struggles with breastfeeding are a time for compassion and healing, not for judgment or blame.

You might like to ask your mother about your own attachment history as a baby. This might feel scary, and it could bring some painful emotions to the surface, but it may also help you to understand yourself better and to have more compassion for yourself if you do encounter any difficulties in mothering. Things that have hurt you as a child can leave you feeling guarded or averse to too much intimacy or dependence. If you find yourself experiencing bewildering emotions at the thought of breastfeeding your child, such as revulsion, resentment, exhaustion, even hatred, it's important for you not to keep these feelings bottled up.

If you succumb to guilt about your "negative" feelings as a mother, you deny your right to have natural reactions to your own childhood wounds, and you pass up opportunities for healing. Open up to someone you trust, share how you feel and reach out for understanding and compassion. At the very least, write down how you feel, which can help to release emotion. If you meet with insurmountable emotional blocks to intimacy with your child consider having counseling or psychotherapy.

What if breastfeeding is impossible?

There are many instances in which breastfeeding is impossible or weaning comes too early. There might be insurmountable psychological or medical reasons for this, or in countries that offer inadequate maternity leave provisions, such as the US and Australia, the reasons might be financial. Most adopted children are not breastfed although there are supplemental nursing systems available (see: medelabreastfeedingus.com) and there are a few known cases of adoptive mothers re-lactating.

If breastfeeding cannot happen, all is not lost. Neuroscientists have found that the hormones of love can flood the child's brain when he is lovingly held with direct skin-to-skin contact and when his eyes meet his mother's loving gaze. Knowing this can help you to make bottle-feeding an emotionally nourishing and loving ritual.

Nature has provided many different kinds of opportunities for deeply loving and transformative connection with your child, and breastfeeding is definitely not the last. If breastfeeding must be missed, there are boundless opportunities to restore a most intimate and loving connection with your child as she continues to grow. Many more avenues for healing and connection with your growing toddler and child will be described in later chapters.

When do I wean my child?

If I asked you to guess the global average age of weaning, what would you think it is? Six months? A year? Eighteen months? Well, the truth surprises, even shocks many of us in the modern world, so you might find the answer hard to believe.

According to WHO, the average age of complete cessation is 4.2 years, which means that somewhere in the world there are a lot of 5- or 6-year-olds, even older, who are having the occasional suckle. If you find that startling, it's only because you would never, in our anti-breastfeeding culture, have seen a toddler or small child at the breast. Yet this is perfectly natural, and even desirable.

We in the Western world have come to assume that weaning will be a painful, sometimes even traumatic struggle because we enforce weaning long before the child is emotionally mature enough to gracefully let go. Mothers who breastfeed to full-term, allowing their child to wean herself in her own time, tend to say it is a seamless and painless transition.

There is a huge variation in natural weaning ages. Some children have been known to self-wean before their second birthday, others prefer to have at least a few brief suckles every week well past their fourth or fifth birthdays. Leading health authorities would like to see mothers breastfeed for at least two years. It would be so wonderful and so life giving if all children could continue until they were ready to let go. The reality is that our modern world has not accommodated this need yet, which puts natural weaning out of reach for many mothers. With each generation, mothers do their best and breastfeeding rates and duration improve, little by little. Mothers need to find a midpoint between doing their best (which these days is usually longer than they were nursed themselves), and accepting their own limits. If you breastfeed too long past your comfort zone, you might feel irritable, angry, drained, and much of the joy of breastfeeding will be gone.

Breastfeeding over and over while gritting your teeth and wishing you were somewhere else is far less nurturing for your baby. Your baby ultimately prefers you to remain energized and affectionate, so a compromise may have to be reached. Make your own decision based on weighing up your baby's needs with the circumstances that best help you to come alive. Avoid making your decision on weaning time based on guilt, but look for the best possible compromise based on love for yourself as well as for your baby. Your connection with your child is much stronger when you are being authentic, rather than forced, in your giving.

When breastfeeding is unpleasant, too draining or difficult, this is a sign that you need more support—emotional or practical. Breastfeeding is such an important aspect of mothering that it deserves every chance to succeed and to be enjoyed; it is worth exhausting every possible solution in order to maintain this bond until your child is naturally ready to move on.

However, if nursing becomes too stressful for you, no matter what you do, no matter how your counselors help you, no matter how your partner and community support you, then you are probably better off gradually weaning sooner than intended. Every parent-child partnership, without exception, has its compromises. There are many ways to help your child to deal with the emotions that come up when he is disappointed. Nurturance takes many forms, and there is so much you can do to connect with—and even heal—your child through your voice, and your touch, holding and your eyes.

Touching, holding, eye contact

Human touch is like protein—it is an essential nutrient that forms part of a balanced diet of emotional nourishment. Deprived of human touch, infants have perished, children have been known to become withdrawn and emotionally empty. For a baby, the need to be touched and held is more urgent than it is at any other stage of life. They can become frantic if left untouched when they long to be held.

As we saw earlier, the hormones secreted in the body of a tenderly held baby are clear evidence of the power of a parents' touch. These hormones—such as oxytocin—are the gauges that indicate a baby's wellbeing. They make sense of why babies who are worn on their parents' bodies for most of the day are noticeably more contented and serene.

Let yourself explore and you will find your own unique ways of holding and caressing your baby. When you are enjoying the contact, your hands are faithful messengers of your heart; they bring your love directly to your baby's body through the quality of your touch. Simply to hold or gently caress your baby can bring her the most divine sensations.

You can develop the wonders of touch further by taking a baby massage class. Infant massage is rapidly gaining in popularity because mothers and fathers seem delighted with the results. It is a simple but enchanting art form that has helped parents to bond more closely with their babies and to tune in to their needs. Massage charges the baby's immune system, aids his digestion, helps him to release any build-up of stress and calms him beautifully (see References).

You will realize the uncontainable joy your gaze brings to your baby when he squeals and kicks in delight, each time he finds your loving eyes. The difference between touch and eye contact is that, whereas babies probably never tire of being touched, they cannot hold eye contact for too long at one time. Touch is a pool they could bathe in all day; eye contact is a puddle to jump in and out of. Both are rivers of love and joy, and both can help your baby and child to heal from any emotional wounds.

I have spoken to a number of people who are lucky enough to remember how they felt when they were babies and their mother or father would gaze smilingly at them. This memory is a bottomless source of joy and wellbeing for them. Your touch and your loving gaze will never be lost; it will warm your child for a lifetime.

Group cooperative parenting

Parenting is meant to be done in a group. This is the conclusion that anthropologists and evolutionary psychologists have come to after evaluating the success of myriad parenting customs from every era and from every continent. We have cut ourselves off into isolated nuclear families at great cost to our sanity and to our children's emotional health. Parents everywhere are hit by frustration and exhaustion like a bolt from the blue—and they berate themselves for not handling things better. Locked between four walls, mothering becomes monotony and tedium. Mothers—and fathers—starved for social connection are diagnosed as "depressed," and shamed for not being happy with their lot. When it comes to the mom and dad and the kids model of parenting, we have got it all wrong. A large slice of the typical everyday problems faced by parents can be done away with when we have a trusted, loving group of others nearby to share the load (see Chapter 15).

At times you will feel overwhelmed by the demands of having a baby or child. This is natural; we were never meant to do it alone. That's why it is so important to have your own parents or other family members nearby. If your extended family is not available, gather other parents to yourself so together you can share the nurturing and entertaining of the children. Isolation and social disconnection are possibly the greatest risk factors for postnatal depression.

There are so many mothers and, increasingly, fathers, who suffer from being alone at home with their baby all day. What is crazy about this is that there are millions of parents, all alone with their babies, inside their house all day, wishing they weren't alone.

See anything wrong with this picture? Please don't let yourself be alone, except in those times when you want to be. Your life with your baby is supposed to be a time to enjoy, so make it enjoyable for yourself and share this time with others. Your joy is the energy that feeds your baby's joy.

Every parent needs their baby and child to have a small number of additional close relationships. We all need what anthropologists call "alloparents." Alloparents are others who can form intimate and special bonds with our babies. Your child's alloparents—or secondary attachments, as psychologists call them—can be your own parents, your siblings, or your close friends or neighbors. If we expect ourselves to be the sole source of the enormous love and attention our baby needs, we are on a one-way street to fatigue and resentment. Every parent needs to have an alloparent around sometimes, to hold your baby while you catch up on some sleep, for instance. There are countless ways in which members of a cooperative parenting group can help each other. Every parent needs to balance the baby talk with some stimulating adult conversation. In company, we are stronger, happier, and we have more to give.

The benefits of cooperative parenting are endless. With more helping hands around, the task of parenting becomes less of a burden and more of a pleasure. When you feel securely held in a web of loving friends and family, you are better placed to help your child feel secure. When your social needs are met it shows in your demeanor, your mood, your tone of voice, your expression; even the way you hold your child is different. The good vibes you emanate are immediately picked up by your baby, and this helps him to feel contented.

A friendly group of parents who share your values can be an asset, particularly when you are trying to raise your children in more recently developed ways—co-sleeping or full-term breastfeeding, for instance—that might not yet be fully accepted in your community.

In a cozy, small-group environment, babies and children can become attached to people other than Mom and Dad, which helps them to develop a more well-rounded social self. Groups also provide your child opportunities to learn how to relate to other children in the safest possible way: with at least one of their parents or another attachment figure—Grandma perhaps—close at hand.

What makes a good alloparent? A good alloparent is someone who is:

- warm
- demonstrative
- responsive to your child's needs
- available fairly regularly.

In short, anyone who loves your child and can fulfill your child's attachment needs can be a good alloparent. Ideally, this is something you should start thinking carefully about and talking to others about well before the birth of your baby. Who will be your child's alloparents?

Join—or start—a parenting group with like-minded individuals (see Chapter 15). Meet as often as you like—why not a few times each week? If it seems too hard to gather your own group, then join a local community group or, preferably, a group set up around these new, scientifically based parenting styles.

Emotionally supported parents

Have you ever noticed how when you are feeling tense, stressed out, when there is conflict between you and your partner or if you have been feeling depressed for a while, your baby appears more distressed and has more difficulty in settling?

Sometimes, it is not enough to do all the right things recommended in the parenting books (the co-sleeping, the breastfeeding, the babywearing). You might think you are pressing all the right buttons, and yet your baby doesn't seem to respond well to you. There are times this can happen because your baby is picking up that you are emotionally distressed and she is reacting with anxiety. If, for instance, you are holding your baby to comfort her but you are grinding your teeth in resentment because you are tired and cranky, it is quite possible that your personal torment is undermining your efforts to calm your baby—this is a good time for your partner or an alloparent to take over and give you a break. Your connection with your baby rides on the quality of your presence. If you are enjoying yourself and enjoying your baby this is the energy you radiate and your baby is more likely to dance to this tune. It is often the case that the parents' emotions, like the loudest instrument in a band, set the key that the children play to.

It's not that your baby is utterly at the mercy of your shifting moods all of the time. Sometimes your baby can be so absorbed in her own experience that she might be shielded from your emotional state. I remember one day, when I was poring over the annual misery of my income tax calculations. I thumped my fist on my desk in frustration and yelled out, "Damned taxes!" I had momentarily forgotten that my six-month-old daughter was perched in her sling, carried by my wife, just a few feet away. I turned to her immediately, concerned about how she had fared through my outburst. She was giggling at me, as if to say, "Do that again, Dad." It doesn't always go so well. There have been other times of more pervasive stress in our household when our daughter has soaked up our stress and become unusually fragile.

So, when you find yourself doing the "right thing" but feeling cranky or distracted, as if you are miles away, that is a signal that you need rest and support. It is time to pass the baton, to share the parenting with your partner, your child's grandparents or a trusted friend. As well as becoming physically fatigued, it is also possible to be emotionally depleted. Always check your fuel gauge—renew and replenish.

It is important for us parents to feel loved and supported, and that there is always someone there for us to talk to. This does not mean that your every upset is going to cause damage to your baby. It does mean that frequently the best way to help your baby to be calm and content is for you to feel that way too, and you will, by making sure that you are taking good care of your own emotional needs. In other words, you need to indulge yourself in open and caring friendships.

What to do about anger

One of the times we most need the support as parents is when the travails of caring for a baby incite us to anger. Doesn't your baby drive you mad sometimes? Are you sure? Come on, let's not romanticize: sometimes parenting can feel like a right royal pain in the behind. If you're wondering why, then let's have a quick reality check about some of the downsides of this venture.

Your baby asks more and more from you each day, without saying thank you, not even once. She makes you feel useless when she cries endlessly. He makes you wonder if you are really a bad parent. She has ruined your svelte figure. He has thrown a monkey wrench in your sex life. She wakes you up at night—often. He has snuffed out your nighttime social life. You have never seen so much excrement in your entire life. You have never done so much wiping, and for your trouble, he pisses in your eye when you are changing his diaper. You feel drained, tired, unappreciated. And you are not angry? Tell me where you went to saint school, I want to sign up.

Meanwhile, the rest of us who are less holy get pretty annoyed sometimes. But we hide it from each other and smile out from under our pile of diapers and dirty laundry. It horrifies us to notice that we are feeling angry with our baby. It frightens us—makes us ashamed. Most parents bottle up quite a bit of anger. The internal guilt police blow the whistle: "How could I be angry at such a beautiful and helpless little creature?" "What kind of a monster am I? We bury our anger under six feet of syrupy denial. This suppression is not good for our health and it contributes to our exhaustion. What's more, it takes a lot of energy to suppress anger. The worst thing about suppressed anger is that it can often come out later, explosively, inappropriately and even dangerously.

Suppressed anger is like a vicious circle. Since we all feel so guilty and ashamed about the anger we feel as parents, we sometimes hide it from each other, and so we all think that everyone else is coping better than we are. It makes us feel even more ashamed when we look around and see how well all the other parents seem to be doing—and so we bury our true feelings even deeper.

Be assured—some frustration and anger is a completely normal part of the parenting adventure. It is fine and healthy to feel angry. What is not OK is to think that your frustration is your baby's fault. Anger can be safely and gracefully managed, whereas blaming a child is unjustified, injurious to the child and harmful to your relationship.

So, what do we do with anger? The first thing we have to do is acknowledge it, at least to ourselves. It is impossible to do anything helpful with anger if we pretend it isn't there. What's more, when we deny our anger, it often comes out later, inappropriately and hurtfully. Denial places us out of control of our emotions.

The next thing to do with anger is to find a safe place, preferably away from your baby, in which to express it. Go for a walk or a run; any vigorous physical exercise can dissipate anger. Every parent needs a "padded cell," a place where we can kick a garbage can, break a plate, hit a punching bag or scream into a pillow, in other words, a safe place to let ourselves unload the weight of our anger so that nobody, or nothing of value, will be hurt. Make a pact with a friend that you will give each other permission to talk to each other about your anger. Choose a friend who can listen without judging or guilt tripping you, a friend who doesn't butt in with advice—someone who cares about how you feel. Turn to someone you trust and whose shoulder you can cry on—and some day down the track, return the favor.

Anger can be a force for healing; it is very life giving when you express it. Anger is not about blame, and it is certainly not about violence. Anger only turns to blame or violence as a result of its suppression. If you understand that whatever frustration you encounter as a parent is never your baby's fault, you can give yourself freedom to express your anger safely. And you will know when you have given your anger full vent because once you have, you will feel emotionally renewed.

By allowing your anger to come forward safely, you liberate your love from its clutches. Unexpressed or suppressed anger dulls your love. Like bird poop on your windshield, it muddies your vision of your child's beauty and innocence. When you have fully expressed your anger and received whatever emotional support you need, don't be surprised if you find yourself returning to your baby with all your love blazing.

There may be times when the anger triggered in you through parenting springs from unresolved issues from your own childhood. We saw earlier how your child can re-awaken old, unhealed emotional wounds. With some help from a counselor or psychotherapist, you could find some healing for yourself while unburdening your relationship with your child.

Your wellbeing nourishes your child

What your baby wants from you is your presence. When you are centered and emotionally available, your baby experiences you quite differently. It is as if your baby is nourished by your essence. Think of it this way: when you are feeling supported, connected to the people you love and connected to your own heart, it is as if you radiate a positive energy; your baby basks in your aura and feels nourished and safe. It keeps your baby contented and emotionally secure. There is nothing magical or mysterious about this—if you think about it, you also immediately feel the effects when you are near someone who feels calm and happy.

Now, I don't believe we can become suddenly calm and happy just by deciding to—by flicking a switch. Calmness and happiness come from self-care and from good relationships, which is why it is so important that mothers and fathers feel well connected to each other and to other supportive friends and family.

8

Helping Parents to Connect

Keeping it pleasurable for Mom and Dad

"My God! I have to respond immediately to every little noise my baby makes? Thanks a lot. Now I feel totally freaked out!"

Did all this stuff about responding promptly make you anxious? I wouldn't blame you. At first it looks pretty daunting. There's no point lying to ourselves: looking after a baby is an awesome responsibility. We do hold their future in the palms of our hands. But I would like for your time with your baby to be incredibly precious and enjoyable—and it can be, so here are some things to help you feel relaxed:

First and foremost, although a mother is unquestionably *numero uno* for baby, babies benefit from attachment to more than just one or two special people. When you start to tire, remember to think about having others near you who can take over for a little while (see Chapters 7 and 15 for more about cooperative parenting).

If you wear your baby on your body for much of the day, he is likely to cry a lot less, it will take far less effort for you to respond immediately before your baby slides into inconsolable howls and your baby will feel constantly connected to you. Often, a brief look and a little hello is all it takes to keep your baby connected and contented. The benefits of babywearing are many (see Chapter 7).

"But, what if I am in the shower while my baby is asleep, and I don't hear him awaken and cry out for me? Will he be psychologically damaged?" This kind of thing will happen often, in every family, to every baby. Yes, it might upset and frighten your baby when he calls you and you don't come, but if you comfort him afterward, until he settles, he can take it. What babies can't handle is when this is done routinely and repeatedly, which leads many of them to give up on reaching out for comfort. It's when a baby gives up on calling out that we should be concerned.

The Australian Association for Infant Mental Health, Position Paper #2 has this to say about it:

> Parents can be reassured that babies are resilient enough to cope with
> incidental or accidental lapses in responsiveness (for example, when a parent

is caught in traffic while the baby is crying). This resilience increases with age, and normal delays such as these can be healed if followed up by soothing and comforting. Babies bounce back when their feelings are heard and validated.

OLD WAYS VERSUS NEW

I have lost count of the number of women who have said to me that when they move to pick up their crying baby, their own mothers and many of their friends pounce on them with dire warnings about not spoiling their baby. Many mothers are made to feel ashamed for wanting to be responsive. They are accused of being overanxious; ultimately, this negative social pressure leads many to ignore their own maternal instincts. This is a typical example of what I mean when I say that old beliefs are clashing with the new. Mothers and fathers really need to be allowed to follow their hearts. Babies want to feel connected, not controlled.

Does being responsive sound like a lot of work? It is, but it soon ends up saving a lot of work. When you are closely tuned in to your baby, your connection can at times feel like a dance, it can be delicious. The fact that your baby feels emotionally secure will actually save you an enormous amount of effort in the later years of childhood, and a healthy attachment between you and your baby will make a lifetime of difference. You can count on it (see "Lifelong consequences of healthy attachment," page 152).

Why a baby's dependency can sometimes seem yucky

Most of us can feel annoyed by a baby's cries from time to time, but the urge to care and protect usually overwhelms the aversion. The fact that our baby's cry can feel heartbreaking, as if their pain is our own, is a sign that our connection is deep. But for some people the helpless and dependent cry of a baby is so irritating, it is almost repulsive.

The way we feel toward our babies has a lot to do with how we were treated when we were babies. When most of us were babies our parents were told that it's good to let a baby cry uncomforted, as crying exercises their lungs, and that babies can't remember anything so their feelings don't matter much anyway.

Many in our culture who are adults today would have experienced some painful, perhaps even traumatic, moments when we were babies. When it's our turn to be parents, our babies' cries can press our buttons, stir up some of our earliest emotional memories of despair, loneliness and anger.

Yes, babies can feel angry at their parents when they feel rejected and abandoned. At times this anger can turn to absolute rage, they scream until they are red in the face. Sometimes being a parent is like being stuck between a rock and a hard place. Perhaps without knowing it, we carry deep-seated anger toward those who made us feel abandoned or rejected as babies or as children. Suddenly, our own child sits before us, screaming at us for the comforting and attention that we ourselves did not receive. Women who have felt emotionally deprived as children can find the demands of a baby particularly taxing, and this places them at risk of postnatal depression (PND).

It is never too late to learn how to have our feelings listened to, how to connect emotionally with caring friends, how to be comforted when we are hurt. We all need to have received this before we can give it.

Some parents can barely offer any genuine empathy or comfort. This has nothing to do with them being inherently bad parents. They are struggling, because no one has shown them comfort, or because a loving connection was broken early in their lives. Judgment is unwarranted. When we lose our way as parents, what we all need is an understanding of how we grew up, we need compassion and healing.

HEALING IS POSSIBLE

Women who are more bothered by the sound of a baby crying are more prone to PND once their own baby arrives. But healing is possible once we connect with our feelings. Mothers who seemed insensitive toward their babies were given a safe environment in which to talk about their own childhoods and to connect with how they had felt as children. Many spoke about experiences of loss or neglect. As they spoke, many of them wept for the grief and loss they had been carrying inside. Researchers who conducted this exercise found that afterward, the mothers tended to become more empathetic, tuned in and warm toward their babies.

It can be immensely liberating to allow our childhood feelings to come forth in a safe environment, in the presence of caring others. Grieving openly can free our hearts to love ourselves and our children more.

GUSTAV—AN ANECDOTE

A father, Gustav, regretfully told how angry he felt toward his breastfed baby, when sometimes he would see him "pawing" at his wife's breasts. Gustav felt like shouting: "Stop that! How dare you!" While talking with his mother Gustav learned that she had felt somewhat invaded by his passion for her breast as a baby, and as a consequence he was weaned quite early.

As a toddler, Gustav recalled, he was once enjoying touching his mother's breasts and giggling. His father, who was watching nearby, sternly snapped at him to stop this. Gustav immediately recoiled in shame. As an adult, he had sometimes felt inhibited with his sexual partners, but thought nothing of it. When his baby came, he became worried about the strength of his hostility toward the little one's unbridled ardor for his wife's breast. Gustav was otherwise a warm, loving, devoted dad. It was a sign of his love that he took responsibility for these feelings and sought his own healing rather than impose his own childhood wounds on his son.

EXERCISE

Pay attention to how you feel when you are with your baby. Really listen to your feelings. Without doing anything to change, dismiss or judge any feeling that comes up, note whatever feeling passes through you. Even if you feel nothing, totally blank or numb, take note of that. Perhaps you feel loving, restful, peaceful, or you might feel tired, irritable or anxious. No matter what you feel, just notice the feeling, welcome the feeling—it is a messenger.

At first, don't do anything in particular with these feelings other than taking note for yourself. Do this noticing exercise a few times over several days, and in particular take heed of any feelings that seem to come to you persistently, any patterns of emotion when you are close to your baby.

If there are any persistent, difficult feelings when you are with your baby, or if you find that you often feel detached or distant from your baby, then ask yourself these questions.

- What was going on around me when I was a baby?
- How was I treated?
- How were my emotional needs attended to?
- Was I hugged a lot? Was I picked up and comforted when I cried?
- Was I breastfed?
- Was I allowed to sleep near my parents or caregivers?
- Were my parents or caregivers happy to have me, or were they stressed or anxious, going through difficult times?

Although you may not have access to clear memories, your feelings may tell you much about your time as a baby. When you think of yourself as a baby, how do you feel inside? These feelings may be telling you much about how you felt back then. Stories told by your parents or other family members might give you some clues.

If there are sad, scary or angry memories for you, it may be important for you to find someone you trust and share your feelings, bring your feelings into the sunlight. Find whatever environment helps you to feel safe enough to grieve or be angry if you need to. Give yourself emotional release, but also seek the comfort of friends, family or anyone you trust. Remember, the more supported you feel, the more likely you are to enjoy your connection with your baby.

Last, you might like to ask yourself the same questions about your babyhood or childhood in relation to the loving and happy feelings you feel when you are with your baby. It is possible that these feelings are made available to you from earlier experiences of feeling loved, held and welcome. If you let the joyous feelings evoked by your baby connect you with your past, you might find yourself recapturing some of the most wonderful childhood feelings. If you allow these earlier feelings to come flooding back it can enrich your life and your connection with your baby.

CAROLYN—AN ANECDOTE

A mother—Carolyn—found that sometimes, when her baby cried and clung to her, she would feel angry and want to peel her off. It distressed Carolyn immensely to notice that at the worst of these moments, she felt like shouting "Get off me, you parasite!" Even though she could easily hold this impulse back, she felt great anguish about feeling this way.

When Carolyn was little, her mother was quite standoffish, caring and protective in many ways, but unable to be physically demonstrative. As an adult, Carolyn shunned physical demonstrations of affection. She was a loyal friend and a successful businessperson, but people in her life found her somewhat armored and unyielding. Carolyn's healing journey involved learning to accept her own emotional vulnerability and increasingly letting herself be held and hugged when she needed it. She found that over time, the more she was able to receive affection, the more she had room for her daughter's occasional need to cling.

Cultivating the capacity for attachment

Childhood has been a mixture of joy and sorrow, in varying amounts, throughout the evolution of human societies. In some form or another, all of us parents were, as children, once emotionally wounded. For each of us, our ability to have empathy for our children, our capacity to create a well-attached relationship with our babies, bears the hallmarks of our childhood histories. Knowing how we felt as children, talking openly about this with trusted others and bringing loving and healing experiences to our lives are essential steps that help us forge strong and loving connections with our children.

Before we can nurture our children, though, we need to ensure that we ourselves feel supported and nurtured. When people say, "It takes a village to raise a child," the village should be there to nurture and support the parent as much as the child.

Even if your emotional memories of childhood remain entirely unconscious, they affect how you relate to your child. If you can consciously contact the feeling of what it was like to be a baby, even if only fleetingly, this can help you to connect more deeply and more consciously with your child.

A bill of rights for mothers and fathers

Caring for a baby might be the greatest feat of love in action that you have ever done and will ever do again. You owe it to yourself—and to your baby—to remember that you also have needs. If you are to nourish a baby emotionally, you need emotional nourishment. I am going to propose a list of fundamental needs that I believe all parents have. Of course, you might see this Parents' Bill of Rights a little differently and may like to alter it—add a few, subtract a few—to fit how you feel. The main thing is that you pay attention to your emotional

EXERCISE

Here is an exercise that may help you to touch upon some of your earliest emotional memories: To begin, lie on your back on a comfortable mat or bed. Close your eyes and breathe gently but deeply, not through your nose, but through your mouth. As you breathe, extend your lips upward and literally breathe in by sucking in air. Slowly raise your arms up toward the ceiling and reach upward, stretch with your fingers, hands and arms toward the sky—as if you are trying to touch something or someone way above you. Keep breathing in this way, sucking in air through your lips, while you continue to reach upward for a minute or so, but stay lying down. As you reach up, notice if any images or words come to you about what or who you might be reaching for.

After a minute or so, relax your arms and mouth, let your arms drop gently by your sides and notice any feelings or sensations in your body. Are you aware of any emotion that arose during the exercise? Did any images or sounds or words come into your mind?

When you feel ready, begin again by breathing in through sucking lips and reaching upward. This time imagine yourself reaching up and crying out for someone to come to you, pick you up and hold you. Imagine that nobody comes—in your mind's eye look up and see no one. What do you feel? If some painful feelings arise for you, you may need to roll over onto your left-hand side, curl up and envelop yourself in your arms. If you feel teary, let yourself weep; you may even like to rock yourself. Make sure you rest, and don't proceed to the next section of the exercise unless you feel ready. There is always time to do this on another day.

As variations, you could repeat the exercise, this time imagining a time when someone (your mother, your father, someone else—you choose) did come to you and hovered above you looking coldly, impassively, expressionlessly at you. What does that feel like?

Later, repeat the exercise, this time imagining that as you cry out, an adult comes to you looking angrily at you, shushing you to be quiet. What does this feel like?

If there are painful or scary feelings whenever you do these exercises, always make sure that you finish with this: imagine that soon after you begin crying out, a warm, smiling face comes to you, talking tenderly to you, touching you softly, holding you and perhaps picking you up and cuddling you. What does this feel like?

You might like to do these exercises in private or you might, if you need comforting, like to have a trusted person nearby who could hold you or talk with you afterward. If you feel comfortable enough for you and your partner to do this together, it can be wonderful to take turns supporting each other as each of you does the exercise.

It is important to know that, if at any stage in these exercises the feelings that come up are too scary or too overwhelming, you can bring yourself out of this experience by standing upright, breathing normally and walking around. This adult posture brings the feeling of being adult and in control back into your body. If you are worried that the emotional memory will be too intense for you, make sure you do not do this by yourself but with someone you trust on standby. You may need a reassuring presence with you.

Consider seeking the support of a counselor if you have any lingering painful or disturbing emotions.

You might prefer to do this kind of exercise with professional assistance. Psychotherapists who work somatically or in a body-oriented way sometimes assist their clients through this or similar experiences. Many people have found this process to be life-changing, healing and heart-opening.

If you try this exercise and draw a blank, feel nothing, try the same exercise differently. Imagine you have lost the power of speech completely. You can't even remember what words sounded like, or what they meant—as if you had never known words existed. Imagine that you cannot sit up, cannot control your limbs very well, especially your legs. Imagine further that you have lost the ability to imagine your loved ones coming back to you once they leave you alone, even if only for minutes, so that you cannot think in terms of the future or the past.

And now, imagine that you are lying in your bed, hungry, and longing for a hug with someone you love. Imagine you cannot switch off this feeling and it spreads through your whole body. You cannot call out this person's name; all you can do is wordlessly cry out. You are physically unable to get up and you don't know where everyone has gone. If you can imagine yourself in this position just briefly, with just a little vividness, you can understand how babies often feel when they call out for connection, and you will remember, at least in part, how you yourself once felt. If you follow this up with an image of the person you longed for coming to you and taking you in their arms, you will also taste some of the joy that babies can feel.

needs and make a place for them in your life as a parent.

Here are my suggestions:

✝ Emotional support from a partner (and if no partner is available, get a double dose of the next point).

✝ Emotional support from family or friends.

✝ Some space to yourself, some time to be alone, even if only a few minutes each day.

✝ Some regular quality time with other adults (for conversation, and so on).

✝ Have fun in whatever way you can fit it in to your life.

✝ Some pleasurable activities, such as sunbathing, having a massage, listening to music, walking in nature, and so forth, as often as possible.

✝ Do some (at least a little) activity that is creative or personally meaningful, such as some paid or volunteer work, study, learning a new skill or a creative hobby such as gardening, reading or yoga.

I am aware that at this point many readers will be thinking, "Get real. I'm up to my earlobes in diapers, the house is a mess and we don't even know how we'll make the rent (or mortgage) this month. You think I've got time for fun?" If at first glance my Parents" Bill of Rights seems unrealistic, it is only because of our bizarre modern ideas of isolated parenting. It is a far more unrealistic proposition to think that, if we hope to find the joy that is our birthright, we can go on parenting in separate and lonely little clumps. Go back to what I said earlier: parenting is meant to be done in a group and when it is, when parents, families and communities help each other, all the items in my list, and more, are eminently possible.

Parents' emotional transformation

When a new baby arrives, most mothers and fathers notice themselves undergoing some profound emotional changes. One pair of parents told me they could not bear to watch the news on television for a long time after their first baby was born. All of a sudden, images of tragedy had become a lot more upsetting. Both of them were surprised at how much more sensitive they had become.

I can imagine it would seem bewildering to find all your emotions amplified once your child is born if you had not known to expect this. This pronounced sensitivity probably won't last longer than the first few months, but it is a natural and healthy part of parents' development. When a new child arrives, Mother and Father undergo intense hormonal changes. You might find yourselves feeling more vulnerable, teary, elated, and more tender and affectionate than you have ever known yourself to be. You might also find yourself feeling more protective, tense, watchful and reactive. At the core, this is a wonderful transformation that is taking place and you should welcome it, surrender to it. It is precisely this emotional aliveness that helps you to be protective and helps you to tune in and connect to your baby. Many mothers and fathers have cried together and laughed together at the birth of their child, and for days afterward. This is not a time for being logical and composed. It is a time to give in to the power of irrational and senseless love. We do a great injustice to parents—and worse, to their baby—if we interfere with or judge this beautiful and natural process.

One father told me how he spontaneously burst into tears the moment his daughter was born. The nurses clumsily told him to "Get over it, your wife and baby are healthy." What a pathetic misreading of the ineffable joy and wonder behind his tears. Another man I know was so ecstatic he ran into every single shop in our local community shouting about the birth of his son to everyone who happened to be there, friend or stranger. Startled bystanders clapped and cheered him; his boundless joy became everyone's joy and he lit up our community like a sun. When my daughter was a few days old I tried to sing a love song to her, but broke down and wept. So many fathers and mothers become misty eyed when they recall the birth of their child.

Although the emotional changes are not so immediately visible for everyone, most parents will experience some kind of softening around their hearts—and the effects are stronger if we welcome them. These changes are more than just a natural mechanism imposed by Nature to help us to be more nurturing and sensitive as parents. We should all give thanks to our children for bringing us back to our hearts so irresistibly, for helping us to be more human.

Living in this task-oriented culture, we seem to be achieving material wonders while we starve for connection and a heart-centered life. Families are disintegrating and depression is at epidemic levels. Our unbalanced focus on productivity has made us successful, yet empty and alone. If we are to bring spirit, passion and a sense of belonging into our lives, we need to wholeheartedly embrace this return to our feeling natures, to make room in our lives for the swell of emotion brought to us by our children. Feeling is what connects us, and connection brings harmony to our families, our community and our world.

The psychology of bliss, revisited

Sitting with your baby when all is well, you might find yourself being lulled into a deep tranquility, a sense of peace and satisfaction that envelops you. It can be like a spontaneous meditation, a trance-like state in which your mental chatter dies down and you simply enjoy being there. Let yourself sink into this experience, let your baby take you there. Hang out idly together, looking at each other sometimes, humming a tune or just sitting quietly with your eyes closed. Mothers and fathers can both do this, whether you are feeding your baby or just sitting together enjoying each other's presence. You might find this particularly relaxing if you are in a rocking chair. Just enjoy the feel of your baby's little body against yours, and take the time to do... absolutely nothing.

If you give in to these quiet moments with your baby, you might find that a deliciously peaceful feeling sweeps over you. If you make a special time to enter into this meditative space together, this can be one of the most nourishing acts for you and for your baby.

We saw earlier how breastfeeding generates streams of blissful hormones. Sitting quietly together as mentioned here, especially if you have direct skin-to-skin contact with your baby, will also generate this hormonal infusion for both of you. Early childhood seems to provide repeated opportunities for you and your baby to feel more than just contented. It is as if Nature is doing its best to take you and your baby into states of bliss.

If that is the case, then what has happened to this human capacity for bliss? Has it been lost to us? Is it something reserved for mystics, monks and those who practice yoga and meditate for hours every day? As we saw earlier, natural birth, breastfeeding and healthy attachment, those generous purveyors of ecstatic hormonal flows, have been quite badly interfered with on a global scale and have all but been eliminated from childhood. Is it any wonder that we have lost touch with so much of the pleasure and the joy that comes from bodily life? Our brain's pleasure centers have not been given the chance to grow enough neural connections, which leaves us feeling empty and needy. By the millions, people around the world spend their lives searching for this missing link to inner fulfillment. We look desperately for the lost bliss in artificial substitutes such as drugs, alcohol, food, fame or compulsive sexuality. All the mechanisms to produce these feelings exist in our nervous systems, but it is as if the bliss centers remain unplugged or the wiring has been cut.

The common problem of substance addiction would be dramatically reduced if we, as a society, did more to support the parent-baby connection at its fullest. This is not just speculation. Scandinavian researchers have linked substance abuse to the use of painkilling drugs at labor. The evidence showing that insecure attachment can lead to substance abuse is even clearer. This evidence has convinced many psychologists to redefine addiction to drugs or alcohol as an attachment disorder.

Psychotherapists have known for a long time that obsession with power, fame or fortune is also a desperate compensation for the empty space inside where parental love and blissful connection should have been.

The bliss connection can be worked at and learned in adulthood; we don't need to see ourselves as irreparably damaged. Psychological healing involves experiences that stimulate the growth of new neural pathways in the brain, much like forging new tracks through a forest to a clearing that is bright and sunny. Healing is about connection—stronger connection to our selves (our feelings, needs and limits), and enriched connections with others. But doesn't it make more sense to take advantage of the opportunities offered so generously by Nature during early childhood? The human brain grows fastest during the first three years, and it can be quite a bit harder for a mature nervous system to relearn its reactions.

The human body is designed for sublime pleasure. I don't just mean transient, genital pleasure. I'm not just talking about shallow hedonism here, but the physically perceptible pleasure that appears in our hearts when we love, or when we stand before something of great beauty. I am talking about the all over pleasure that is the pleasure of the soul. Life provides all of us with ample opportunities for following our bliss as adults. If we choose a line of work that has a lot of meaning for us, it can bring us profound satisfaction.

Immersing ourselves in Nature can restore our emotional wellbeing, if we let it. We can be enraptured by listening to a piece of music, looking at an exquisite work of art, reading poetry or literature—or creating any of these ourselves. Dancing, intense exercise or a thrilling sport can also be avenues to ecstatic experiences. Meditation is a well-accepted doorway to blissful depths. When you add these things together, it looks like bodily life teems with abundant fonts of joy—and the best are free of charge. Of all life's pleasures, it seems like relationships may be the most rewarding. When we connect with people we care about, oxytocin levels go up—and when we are making love, it rains oxytocin.

Our nervous systems are innately capable of peak moments of bliss and profound states of peace. If enough children are given the fulfilling connection that is evolution's design, we could create the most loving and peaceful societies that ever graced the earth. I am not suggesting that human suffering and human conflict can be entirely eliminated, but I do mean that our potential for human love, enjoyable living and social harmony has so far only been superficially tapped. Our progress toward more natural styles of parenting is a key to reclaiming humanity's emotional health.

A word about discipline

You might be wondering why I am talking about discipline in a chapter about babies. If you protest that babies cannot possibly misbehave, you'd be absolutely right. It would be absurd to think of a baby as misbehaving, since babies are utterly unable to calculatingly manipulate others, to understand the consequences of their actions or to deliberate over a course of action.

But there is a good reason to begin thinking quite early about how your child will learn to be empathetic and considerate. Pretty soon, as your baby grows, you are going to want your toddler and child to listen to you and to listen to others. If she is to be a good listener, she needs to be listened to as a baby. The single most powerful influence on the behavior of toddlers, children, adolescents and even adults is how their attachment needs were addressed. You can prepare the groundwork for good behavior during the baby months. Your empathy and your responsiveness are the most effective tools at your disposal for raising a genuinely helpful and considerate child.

Research on this issue has been churned out in great quantities, from all corners of the globe—it confirms that children who have had their attachment needs fulfilled thoroughly are far better learners of interpersonal boundaries and are far less likely to be compulsively defiant or to have behavior problems. Other research shows that babies who spend more time away from their parents are more likely to have behavioral difficulties later.

It might seem a lot easier to take a casual approach to a baby's attachment needs, but this can set the parents up for a lot of headaches as the child gets older (not to mention how painful this is for the baby). Taking care of your baby's attachment needs as closely as possible will be the greatest investment you can make toward good behavior in later years.

Lifelong consequences of secure attachment

When you hold your baby and give her your affection, your love actually alters her brain chemistry; as was said earlier her brain is steeped in the hormones that produce tranquility and joy. The most obvious and intuitive acts of love offer a double dose of rewards throughout your child's life. There is almost no end to the riches discovered by attachment researchers.

HOW LOVE GROWS THE CHILD'S BRAIN

World leaders in neuropsychology, such as Allan Schore, PhD, and Daniel Siegel, PhD, explain how the hormones of loving connection—such as are copiously generated during birth, breastfeeding, affectionate holding and eye contact—do more than just create good vibes—they literally nourish the child's brain and stimulate the growth of new networks of connections in the precise regions of the brain concerned with regulating emotions. All of the loving and intimate interactions from birth onwards mentioned so far, biologically help the child to become a more considerate, loving and confident individual from the beginning. Without these daily interactions with reliable attachment figures, the emotional centers of the brain fail to develop properly. These effects are most powerful during the first three years, when the child's brain grows at the fastest rate.

The effects of loving connection on the growing brain explain why children who have benefited from secure attachment are given so many advantages in just about every dimension of their emotional health. They tend to be more independent, assertive and self-confident, more enthusiastic, more resilient in the face of adversities, more empathetic and more caring. They have a better shot at forming trusting and enduring relationships as they grow. While secure attachment is not the only building block of emotional intelligence and loving relationships, it is the most important. Secure attachment is not a panacea to the world's ills—but it seems to be the next best thing.

Non-responsiveness can cause many problems

How separation stress affects the child's brain

When a child experiences something very scary or painful, she gets a surge of cortisol. For a baby, separation from the people she has bonded with is the greatest stressor, and it causes cortisol levels to spike. Fortunately, the child's body re-absorbs excess cortisol when she is comforted, so she can handle going through moments of stress if a warm and loving person comforts her soon afterward. But if a child is in a scary situation, separated from the people she loves and trusts, and is not soothed by a trusted adult, the cortisol levels remain high. After a time the high cortisol levels are neurotoxic, in other words, destructive to brain cells. Cortisol can cause erosion in the emotional centers of the brain. If this happens repeatedly, children can become more prone to anxiety, anger or depression.

Most of the common emotional or behavior problems that were once blamed on children's genetic makeup are now understood to come from insecure attachment. Researchers have traced a huge array of emotional problems and behavioral idiosyncrasies to unmet attachment needs during the baby months. If they were not consistently helped to feel safe and secure as babies, toddlers can be moody, clingy, excessively attention seeking or anxious and mistrustful. Many react by being less compliant with their parents or teachers, hostile or bullying toward their peers. All these vexing behaviors are, without the child realizing it, protests about feeling neglected, abandoned or ignored. They are belated cries for help, attempts to somehow make their world a safer place.

Gaps in secure attachment don't affect all children in exactly the same way, but they are wounding to all children. Some tend to react by becoming more aggressive, some lean more toward shyness or withdrawal as a defense, and others might get depressed. Others react by becoming overly driven, competitive and ambitious, so that winning takes the place of love.

In more severe cases, insecure attachment has been identified as a major mental health culprit. Insecure attachment is one of the main factors at the root of depression, bipolar disorder, attention deficit and hyperactivity disorder (ADHD), anxiety disorders, panic attacks, phobias, eating disorders and substance abuse.

The more we move toward ensuring that all babies have their attachment needs met, the healthier our society will be. The way children's emotional needs are addressed in early childhood is probably the single most important factor for deciding the overall health, harmony and happiness of any society. Every effort we make to be attuned to our babies will save ten times more effort later.

But I thought it was all in the genes

Our genes do have some influence on our emotional makeup, but only indirectly. There are no genes ruling our personalities: no angry gene, no shy gene, no anxiety gene. Certainly, we all come in various shades of temperament. Some of us are, say, naturally more introverted while others are more extraverted. But the presence of emotional or behavioral problems is not determined by the genes we were born with. Until recently, people used to think our genes were in the driver's seat but new information has come to light that explodes the idea that our personalities are trapped by genes. The following recent discoveries shed new light on the importance of parenting:

- Genes can be switched on or off, in other words activated or deactivated, as a result of our early life experiences.
- Brain growth in childhood is shaped by a child's experiences.
- Emotional intelligence is not static; it can change through life, but it changes fastest in early childhood because that's when the brain grows fastest.

Our relationships script our personalities by interacting with our inherited, genetic strengths and weaknesses. Genes influence some aspects of our temperament but our emotional or behavioral problems and strengths reflect how we were related to as children.

NATURE VERSUS NURTURE

Internationally renowned psychiatrist and childhood development expert Daniel Siegel throws light on the nature versus nurture debate in this way: "Environmental factors play a crucial role in the establishment of synaptic [neural] connections after birth. Genetic potential is expressed within the setting of social experiences, which directly influence how neurons connect to one another. Human connections create neuronal connections" (Siegel 1999: 85)

We have a lot of freedom to influence our own and our children's emotional intelligence, and early childhood, a time of super-accelerated brain growth, is when the iron is hot. The baby's brain watches, feels, takes notes and builds itself according to how human relationships appear to her. Childhood shapes the child, and parents—and those who look after and support the parents—are the main authors of the child's emotional makeup. In this, the genes play only a humble role.

The question of daycare for babies

By now you may have heard or read a lot of talk in the media about the pros and cons of childcare for babies and children under three. There is, in fact, a controversy raging, with passionately opposed camps. Mostly, the debate seems to focus on the huge amount of research that has been done to find out how babies and toddlers cope with outsourced childcare. Thousands of children who have attended daycare centers in many parts of the world have been followed up for several years in order to see how they grow up. In other studies, toddlers in childcare centers have been given non-invasive tests (of their saliva) to measure levels of stress hormones.

Do we really need to leave our decisions about childcare entirely up to the results of these research studies, many of which take several years to complete? Even without any of them, we already have so much information—from developmental science and from mothers and fathers consulting their hearts—about how to help babies feel securely attached.

There are so many models for non-parental care, ranging from cooperative parenting or extended family care, and alloparental care (discussed earlier) to employing a nanny at home, family daycare, community daycare, daycare at your place of employment or the big daycare corporations. There is also a huge variation in the number of hours that children remain in daycare.

So much of the debate seems to be based on your child's academic future. Since this is a book about emotional development, I want to look at considerations about your child's emotional wellbeing. During your child's first three years, emotional development is a far more important issue, with much bigger ramifications for your child's future. So many parents today fret about their child's literacy and numeracy when they are barely one or two years old, while the child's social skills, capacity to love and to manage her emotions rate as a mere afterthought. Our priorities are way out of kilter.

To help you arrive at your own decision about whether to use daycare or how to use daycare, here are some questions for your consideration. Of course, your decision needs to be based on weighing up your needs and your child's needs together. This varies a lot from one family to another. Since I cannot know your circumstances as a parent; your access to social support networks, your need to work, your financial situation, and so on, the questions I am posing will be one-sided: purely about your baby's developmental needs. I leave the rest of the balancing act up to you.

What will happen to breastfeeding?
Breastmilk supply is dependent on regular, on-demand nursing. The more hours your baby spends away from you, the less likely it is that you will continue to lactate normally. It is also less likely that your baby will want to return to your breast since milk is so much easier to suck out of a bottle. You can of course express milk, which is better than the artificial substitute, but the psychological benefits of holding your baby close will be missed.

Who will provide the vital, one-on-one, face-to-face interactions?
Who will hold your baby, rock her, sing to her and look lovingly into her eyes? The quality of sustained, face-to-face interaction that a parent provides is impossible in a daycare center. In Australia, the minimum required ratio of caregiver to babies is 1:5. The most affectionate caregiver in the world can't possibly meet five babies' needs for loving, face-to-face conversation. Investigations have found that toddlers in these centers receive very little individualized attention, very little intimacy, affection or physical touch, and that often their attempts to reach out for contact are simply ignored. Italian researchers reported that even in centers with staff to child ratios at 1:3, babies appeared to be disengaged or in despair.

How well can your baby bond to a daycare worker?

So far, I have never met a childcare worker who was not a sweet, lovely and caring person. But can a worker offer what a parent, family member or close friend can offer? As a parent, your love is perfectly visible to your baby: your pupils involuntarily dilate, your skin tone may flush, the tone of your voice changes when you are suffused with loving feelings. You have no control over the evidence of love being painted all across your face. It is not possible to fake a look of love this profound. Babies know the difference straight away. Babies become distressed when we look at them dispassionately.

Remember also that from the day she is born, your baby becomes attached to your face, to the unique contours of your body and to your smell. She feels quite differently when she is not with you for extended periods. Even the most loving daycare caregiver cannot replicate the feel of you, the smell of you.

Until a child is about 18 months old, when she is parted from those she loves she cannot soothe herself with the image of their return. When you are gone, you are gone—full stop. This can feel immeasurably sad to a baby.

Childcare workers cannot imitate the natural production of extra doses of oxytocin and prolactin that breastfeeding mothers do to make them naturally more affectionate. Many of them are not mothers themselves and cannot hope to access these deep feelings for your baby. Caregivers are often quite young; they have not had their own children and have not undergone the powerful maternal hormonal changes. Caregivers are mostly casual staff who come and go before a baby can form a bond with them. Any attachment that forms will be soon followed by a painful loss. For this reason, caregivers are actively discouraged from letting themselves become emotionally attached to any baby in their care. Tragically, this is precisely the most important thing a baby needs—to spend her days with people she is emotionally attached to, not separated from them. In daycare, your baby will receive a small fraction of the attention she needs from an individual who has been instructed to not become emotionally attached to her.

Since your baby's need for sustained and frequent affirmations of attachment will almost certainly go out the window while she is in a daycare center, your decision, should you opt for daycare, is how often and how long can she stay there without changes to her emotional health?

Gender equality and secure attachment for babies are both non-negotiable hallmarks of a civilized society. The fact that affluent nations force mothers to choose between their own happiness or that of their children is a disgrace and puts at risk the health of the nation. Modern, civilized societies must provide generous maternity leave entitlements as well as guaranteed career security for mothers. The US and Australia lag far behind the rest of the developed world on support for parents—no wonder we are still paying strangers to mind our babies for us.

RESEARCH ON CHILDCARE—SOME RESULTS

What does the research about childcare generally say? The National Institute of Child Health and Development (NICHD) followed up the progress of 1100 children in childcare around ten US cities. It found that the longer the hours a child spends in daycare, the more disharmonious the mother-child relationship becomes. At 4.5 years, children in long daycare (more than thirty hours per week) were three times as likely to show aggressive behavior than children who had attended less than ten hours per week. Similar observations have been made in Australian and UK studies. One study involving 1200 children in the UK concluded that children in childcare perform worse in developmental tests and they tend to be more withdrawn, compliant or sad—as well as showing higher levels of aggression. As little as twelve hours per week of daycare for infants was sufficient to be associated with significant increases in difficult behavior.

A Cambridge University study showed that, without their mothers present, children's cortisol levels doubled during the first nine days of childcare. Even five months later, cortisol levels remained comparatively high. Many more studies have found elevated cortisol levels in the afternoon for full-day, center-based care. This effect holds true even in the most high-quality centers. It is important to note that abnormally elevated cortisol levels have been detected in daycare children even if they show no obvious outward sign of distress.

When given the choice between extended maternity leave with decent pay and placing a baby in daycare, very few mothers choose the latter. In Sweden, where mothers receive generous paid maternity leave, hardly anyone uses daycare facilities. Meanwhile, in the US and Australia, mothers are given miserly assistance. This is hurting their relationships with their babies and children, and damaging children's emotional health. We must all pressure our governments to modernize our family support provisions. Well-paid maternity and paternity leave is an obvious policy that needs to be implemented without delay (see References for further reading on the research related to the impact of daycare for under threes).

MATERNITY LEAVE ENTITLEMENTS AROUND THE WORLD

US: 12 weeks, no pay.
Australia: 18 weeks at minimum wage.
UK: 39 weeks of well-paid ordinary maternity leave and a further 26 weeks of additional maternity leave if mothers meet certain criteria, but the latter may be unpaid.
Canada: 50 weeks divided between the two parents, at 55% of their wages.
Cuba: 18 weeks at 100% of wages.
Sweden: 16 months leave per child, most of which is paid at 82% of wages. A minimum of 3 months out of the 18 is required to be used by the minority parent, which is usually the father. Norway has similarly generous leave.
Bulgaria: 1 year at 100% of wages, plus one year at minimum salary.

What your baby can teach you

I have often suspected that our babies give to us more than we give them. When my daughter was a baby, we would sometimes look at each other and laugh, uncontrollably, for no reason at all. By simply being herself, she showed me that life can often be intrinsically delightful and uproariously funny. Connection produces senseless joy. Babies liberate us.

As a parent, you might discover for the first time that giving—for its own sake, without anticipated return—is intrinsically pleasurable. You might find that love is senseless, it overwhelms you and that you have no reason or particular characteristic to pin it on. It's not "I love you because..." It's not always a response to a particular quality we see in our child. It is helpless love, felt simply because our baby is here. What a gift it is to be shown that we can have those feelings. Our babies make us better people.

As we grow older, the stress and disappointments of life can tend to color our vision so that the world we see seems to lose some of its magic and vibrancy. We look out and see the same, tired old images that remind us of obligation, hard work, sadness, loss and ordinariness. But when you look into your baby's eyes and see the way she views the world—her awe, her wonder, her complete lack of interpretation and judgment—you are shown a fresh view of the world in all its natural beauty. Babies are remarkable mystics who have come to visit us. They teach us, if we let them, how to be in the present moment, unconcerned with the past or the future. They teach us how to clear from our eyes the decades of accumulated jadedness and see the world anew. This is one of the most powerful forms of meditation.

Our baby's birth can be our own rebirth.

Part 4
The Toddler Connection

9

Creating a Joyous Connection with Your Toddler

Months have passed, and your little baby has grown into a toddler. He is standing up, starting to walk, talk and assert his presence in the world in a whole new way. Being a toddler is exhilarating. The world is starting to look like a huge playground. Suddenly, he can propel himself toward all the marvelous things he sees and grab them, hold them, put them in his mouth and throw them. The whole universe has opened up to him—and what's even more exciting, he is discovering that he can go places and get things all by himself. What a thrill that is.

A healthy baby brings so much power to this new stage of life. He is discovering his freedom as well as his personal strength. But when we marvel at our toddler's newfound self-assurance, we mustn't kid ourselves that he no longer needs a safe pair of arms to hold him. Despite all his bravado, he is still emotionally fragile and dependent. With each new sortie into the world, he needs to see that a loving and familiar person is nearby when he looks over his shoulder.

Now, the circle of exploration gets wider, little by little. It begins with one short crawl out into the great beyond and a furtive glance over his shoulder to check that we are still there, close by. He picks up and holds a new object, and turns around again to read our face, "Is this safe? Will this thing hurt me? Can I put it in my mouth?" When encountering another person along the way, the look back to us might be saying, "Is this other person a safe person? If something scary happens, how far is it to crawl, walk or even run back to the safety of a loving and protective adult?" Over and over, the toddler will come running back to us and fall into our warm embrace. His orbit is growing and he keeps coming back to refuel. But this growing self-assurance depends on one thing—his ability to control the rhythm of separation from us.

Our developing toddler spontaneously stays longer and further away from our reach, as she learns to trust her own knowledge—gained with the help of our feedback—about what is safe and what is not safe in the world. She is learning to enjoy her own company and is putting other relationships to the test. As she learns to enjoy the company of other children and other adults, her circle of security expands. Her capacity for attachment to others is growing, as are her skills to relate to a diverse range of people. Whereas before, nourishment was dependent on the primary caregivers, life is now offering nourishment in many more forms—and this includes the growing enjoyment of playing alone. The world beyond Mom and Dad seems both perilous and magical. In it, toddlers' emotional repertoire plumbs the depths of awe, mystery, profound curiosity, fear, frustration and rage, and unlimited joy.

If toddlers could somehow speak their deepest, evolutionary and unconscious longings, they might say this to you:

- ♱ Be my safe home base, be my support team at headquarters and say "Yes" to my pioneering spirit.
- ♱ Please be available to me, but let me go and make mistakes, let me fall over and skin my knees and let me have fun.
- ♱ Watch over me and protect me, but don't smother me. Let me run.
- ♱ Please be patient with me: let me wander from your side at my own pace, but don't leave me until I can really trust others to be my safe home base.
- ♱ And please, remember how to play—and play with me.

What is the best guarantee of toddlers growing to be self-confident, autonomous and independent? If they can control the rate at which they separate from you, without having separation thrust suddenly upon them, and without being held back, as we will see later in this chapter.

Your toddler wants to get to know you

Toddlers have strong attachment needs, but these don't always manifest the same as babies' attachment needs. Whereas a baby needs you (or another familiar and loving person) to be there for every need, it works differently with a toddler.

From your child's point of view, up until now you were a magical being who was there to pleasurably indulge her every need. You were an extension of her—in fact, a baby's brain cannot compute that you are an individual, separate from her. Now she is a toddler, it is time for you to begin showing up as a person, not just a caregiver. The time of symbiosis (when you and the baby were joined at the hip) is waning, and two differentiated, separate individuals are starting to emerge. Your toddler increasingly wants to get to know you, how you are different to her. Getting to know you as a person with thoughts and feelings all of your own gives her a lot of information about herself as a person, and it teaches her how to relate to others.

A toddler embarks on a remarkable, consciousness-changing journey that is crucial for being able to have healthy, loving relationships as she grows up.

Over many years she'll be learning to see that other people are other people—not extensions of herself, there for her consumption. The apparatus in the brain that enables this level of perception is just now beginning to develop.

EARLY SENSE OF SELF

By 18 months, babies have begun to develop a sense of themselves as separate from the world, with a mental image of what they look like. From around this age onward, a child can recognize herself in a mirror and know that it is her standing in front of it.

So, what does getting to know you mean? A child only begins to recognize that you are a person when you begin showing him your feelings, that you have some of your own needs and some healthy, interpersonal boundaries.

Of course, showing your child that you have your own feelings doesn't mean pouring out your difficulties from your day at the office. I mean letting her see, in a way that is not too overwhelming or threatening for her age, how she affects you. The reality of your emotions needs to be disclosed to her gently, little by little, as she grows more robust over the years. But she needs to know how she affects others. Without this knowledge, others do not seem real to her, so she cannot fully develop empathy, considerateness and respect. For all of us, it takes many years for the reality that other people are other people to fully sink in—and for many people it never really does. How many self-centered or self-obsessed adults do you know, who talk as if everything is about them ("Enough about you, let's talk about me")? Don't they remind you of toddlers who never grew up? In the sense of emotional intelligence, this is precisely what has happened to them.

Parenting is always about connection—but whereas to a baby connection comes from you saying yes to all his needs, to a toddler connection comes from getting a sense of self. Sometimes you will agree with each other, sometimes not. Over time, you will want to make more and more demands on him. Sometimes, you will have to say "no" to something he wants. Sometimes what he does will upset you, irritate you, hurt you or disappoint you. And sometimes, you will be overcome with affection and will want to sweep him off the floor and cuddle him. If he is to mature, he needs you to openly show him all these feelings. Conflict and disagreement, if sensitively managed, are now important opportunities for connection, just as much as affection and indulgence.

Seeing that you have feelings and that she has an impact on your feelings is a kind of essential nourishment for your toddler. She thrives and grows from seeing that sometimes you get tired, sometimes you want your own space, sometimes you are delighted by her, sometimes you are cranky when she does something to trouble you (such as throwing food, or hitting another child), that sometimes you are sad when she breaks something that was special to you, that she can make you laugh, be angry, be sad, and melt into tenderness. Your feelings, expressed with transparency, are what make you appear real and human and your child feels connected to you when she is shown the effects she has on you, both positive and negative.

Some people might feel surprised at my suggestion that showing all your feelings, even your so-called negative feelings, is important so that your child can feel connected to you. But that's what a real person is: someone who feels all kinds of feelings. Your child senses when you hide your feelings, and this can make her uncomfortable. But revealing your feelings appropriately is what makes you feel closer to each other. We will be looking more deeply at emotionally authentic parenting later.

Toddlers need freedom to play and explore

Your toddler has an almost boundless energy for exploring her world. Her appetite for fun, discovery and engagement is almost insatiable. The world is her oyster, and she wants to climb it, tear it up, throw it, taste it, bite it, push it, grab it and squeeze it. It is a sensual bonanza.

The drive to play is genetically programmed, having evolved over millions of years. It serves a vital survival purpose, as play, believe it or not, is the most efficient instrument for learning. Nature has filled us with a burning curiosity so we can learn everything we need to know for our survival and wellbeing. Nature has made learning so exciting and intriguing, to the point that we take personal risks in order to explore.

Through play, the toddler learns to coordinate his body movements, learns how things work, that hard things can hurt, that delicate things can break, that sharp things can cut or stab, that rubber things can bounce. Discomfort and disappointment are his teachers; they show him where the limits are. But delight is the greatest teacher of all—it motivates us to want to learn more. Humans are in relentless pursuit of knowledge. As if it wasn't enough to learn everything about our own planet, we invented rockets so we could go to the moon. Now we want to go to Mars. And it's just as well we are innately thirsty for discovery and invention. Without this thirst, we would still be hunting with pointed sticks and huddling in caves. This impulse to playfully explore begins in earnest during toddlerhood and if it is not punished, shamed or squashed, it forms the basis of a lifetime of zest for learning, creating, inventing and problem solving. Child's play can be the greatest ally of teachers and parents.

In my work as a counselor and psychotherapist, I have often noticed something unique in individuals whose parents were playful and supported their playfulness as children. They seem more radiant and they maintain a generally playful and adventurous approach to life. They seem more fulfilled in their work, they laugh and smile more, and tend to enjoy a positive attitude. I have also noticed they tend to be more tolerant of others' quirks and idiosyncrasies. Individuals whose parents were controlling and pushed them to be serious and prematurely responsible, tend to reflect that in their demeanor. They are more likely to seem formal, even humorless. They can lack creativity and ingeniousness, plodding dutifully through life's obligations.

So, I could not recommend this more enthusiastically: parents, get on the ground with your children and play. Play with their dolls, their toy soldiers, their teddy bears, their train sets and their toy cars—enter their world of imagination. Every so often, let yourself be a child with your children. These simple moments of playing together are incredibly special for your child and give both of you memories you will treasure forever. Playing together is marvelous for your relationship—and good for your health.

Why toddlers and children need to play and play and play and play

Free play serves a critical developmental function that is a central human need. Without it, we shrivel up emotionally and become humorless, hopeless and angry. To the toddler, every moment of unrestrained free and imaginative play brings her immense joy and feeds her spirit.

When play is unstructured and child-led, it serves a further, vital purpose. Have you ever seen infantile animals at play, such as two puppies chasing each other and pretend fighting? Play is a rehearsal for an important life skill. Young puppies play tussle as a way to cement friendships, but all the while they are honing skills for hunting and self-defense. Left to their own devices, children create some incredibly elaborate fantasies, employing increasingly sophisticated communication skills, such as negotiation, self-assertion, teamwork, leadership and mutual care. Their imaginations are groomed and sharpened and they become more inventive and good problem solvers. Imaginative, self-directed play is a formidable educator.

TURNING GOOD IDEAS INTO REALITIES

The lower brain contains a seeking system that drives our curiosity, our thirst for discovery and exploration. Whenever we come up with a new idea, its roots are generated in the brain's seeking system. When this part of the brain is well connected to the brain's frontal lobes, this enables us to have a good idea and to follow through with action until we turn our good ideas into realities.

When toddlers are absorbed in the explorative games that they make up for themselves, this seeking system is activated and connections are enhanced between it and the frontal lobes. Free play with friends in a stimulating environment builds children's abilities to manage emotions and stress, while training their brains for creativity and good problem-solving skills.

Like any one of our muscles, the faculty of imagination falls into the "use it or lose it" category. A child who is given freedom and support to play for hours each day strongly develops this faculty. It is obvious that a well-developed play consciousness is what every artist, writer, musician, humorist, designer and architect draw upon. But the energy of play and creativity can also greatly assist people in the health professions, in business and in the sciences. Play is the mother of creative problem solving and critical thinking. Further, playfulness makes our relationships alive, spontaneous and delightful—it is a cornerstone of emotional intelligence. How limiting to our lives, our relationships and our careers to have allowed our imagination to dull, and our playfulness to be suppressed.

Because play is an activity that can be shared, and it is a source of pleasure and joy, play is the glue of comradeship and community. It enables human friendship to be associated with pleasure and joy.

Television—the play killer

Violence on television, videos, and computer games makes viewers more aggressive, and it contributes to bullying behavior and a general increase in social violence. The more hours children spend witnessing violence, the more violently they are likely to behave. So many studies now confirm that link that the American Psychological Association has declared the debate on the subject to be "essentially over."

But there are further compelling reasons to switch off the TV. A child who sits passively watching a screen is not activating the seeking mechanism of the brain. The long hours that many children spend glued to the set these days lead to wasting of this vital brain area and distort emotional development. Certainly, television can offer delightful stories, beautiful fantasies and fascinating educational features, but as a medium it makes the child's mind so passive. For children three and over, I would personally restrict watching to no more than a couple of hours per week—with zero exposure to advertising. Under-threes are better off without any screen time.

BREAKING FREE OF THE BOX

In the US, children spend an average of 4 hours in front of television each day. Australian toddlers spend an average of 2.3 hours, and British children 3 hours per day. Most children today have more eye contact with television characters each day than with their own parents. Letting our children vegetate in front of the box to this degree is wasting their childhood, and it is developmentally ruinous. Here are some of the other damaging effects of television that have been established by research:

- The rapid-fire editing and totally unnatural audiovisual images damage attention centers in the child's brain. Increasingly, evidence points to television as a major culprit in the soaring rates of ADHD.
- Within thirty seconds of switching on the television, our brains become neurologically less able to make judgments and think rationally. This induced passivity makes children acutely vulnerable to advertising images. The frontal lobes of the brain, a critical area responsible for self-control and rational thought, are deactivated by television viewing, and over time their development is stunted.
- Television damages future learning abilities, including numeracy and reading comprehension.
- Television is strongly associated with sleep difficulties in toddlers.

Play is healing

Research shows that when children play freely, physically and imaginatively in an enriched environment, such as when wrestling on the ground or when inventing pretend games (cops and robbers, mock-rescue operations, moms, dads and babies, superheroes) this kind of play can heal emotional wounds. Hours spent in this kind of unstructured and creative play can actually regenerate and restore damaged parts of the emotional centers of the brain. Structured games such as organized sports and board games are also quite wonderful and they offer unique benefits, but the physically engaging games that children invent for themselves seem to have the most powerfully healing effects. All they need is free time to play in a stimulating environment rich with opportunity and possibility: out in nature, in a room with a few simple toys, in a yard with things to climb, and things they can pick up and use as props. If a child has gone through emotionally painful experiences, free and creative play with trusted others can be very therapeutic.

Drawing upon your own childhood memories of play

Do you sometimes find it difficult to let yourself go, to get down on your kid's level and be a little silly and spontaneous? Do you find your child's games unstimulating and hard to stay with? Do you find yourself often protesting how busy you are when your child wants you to play? I assure you, you are not alone.

It's rarely the case that we can play endlessly for as long as our children want us to. It is true that as parents we are often busy. It is also true that what is entertaining for adults is different to what is entertaining for children, and we don't always like playing the same games. And how many of us can keep up with a toddler's boundless energy? But it can be wonderful and enriching for parents to let themselves enter the child's fantasy world and meet the toddler on her level, play her games, at least from time to time, at least a little bit each day. So if this feels like a drag, there is something that can help you relate more naturally, from the inside, to your child's games.

There are many of us as adults who have lost our own play connection. Early demands for us to be serious have led us to be over-focused, obsessed with goals and outcomes, even somber. Our children provoke us; they alert us that we need to loosen up. The more serious ones among us need to hang around people who know how to be playful. Let them help us to be more comfortable with that dormant part of ourselves.

If we let them, our own children can teach us—they are naturals. They produce more play ideas per minute than most adult creative geniuses. That's not a pencil—it's a small man. That's not a shoe—it's a car the pencil-man can drive around in. When you feel up to it, see if you can let your child lead the game, and follow her. You are the troupe of actors (let yourself be cast in roles) who enable her grand design to come to life. Think of it as a voyage of discovery, because when you do you are going to learn so much about your child's inner world. And there is a further pay-off for you: loosening up and playing with your child can be good for your health, your emotional wellbeing, even your immune system.

EXERCISE

Take a few minutes to remember your fondest memory of playing as a child—if possible from a time when you were similar in age to your child. Relive those moments in your mind, what you saw, what things smelled like, how your body felt and what it was like emotionally. Let those feelings come back to you—the excitement, the awe, the magic, even the frustration when things did not go like you wanted them. What happened to that part of you? Can you be sure it is not still there? Your natural desire to be playful with your child and immerse yourself in her games flows more freely when you can tap into your own inner playful child.

What if there are painful memories for you about not being allowed to play as a child? What if your parents or caregivers were unsympathetic toward natural childishness, or there were other stressful factors at home that made child's play difficult? If this is how it was for you, then pause for a few moments and ask yourself: How do I feel about this? There may be a range of emotions wanting to surface (do you feel sad, perhaps, or angry?). If you can give these emotions some expression by talking with someone you trust or perhaps by writing them down, you may experience a sense of release and renewal that makes room for your natural playfulness to come through.

Literacy begins with pleasure

Learning can and should be pleasurable and joyous. Read to your toddler, even to your baby. Read to them regularly, often and, if you both like reading, do it nightly. Reading a story to your child can be part of a bedtime ritual that quickly gets associated with falling asleep peacefully and contentedly. You can start even before your baby or toddler can understand that books have stories in them. It cements an early association in your child's mind between books and pleasure, and may well make reading attractive to your child for years to come.

So, let her handle the book, put it in her mouth if she insists, and toss it around. Let go of any expectation that your toddler has to immediately sit passively and wait for the story to begin—let alone listen patiently through the whole tale and clap obligingly at the end. Your child has her own way of relating to a book; let her discover that. Just enjoy your time together and have a sense of humor about it if she wants to play with the book so much that reading more than one page at a time proves impossible. Show her the letters. Trace them with your finger. Let her trace the letters too; a letter can be a sensual experience. Choose stories that both of you can enjoy, so she feels that you are also having fun. These days there are so many books around that are funny and delightful for the parents as well as for the child. Remember, the greatest incentive to learn comes from pleasure and love. If you surround the act of reading with an experience of humor, fun, warmth and closeness, your child may well fall in love with books—and of course, with reading. She is more likely then to become an avid reader and learner of everything.

What is healthy separation?

We saw earlier that for a baby, extended separation from the ones she loves can be the most painful and even traumatic experience. A toddler, on the other hand, brings new resources to the experience of separation. In fact, the toddler years are the appropriate time when a child begins the gradual uncoupling from her exclusive attachment to her caregivers. In order to gain in self-confidence and emotional security, toddlers will, little by little, dare to venture into having time alone, time away from parents, and time with others. This is the beginning of the child's journey toward differentiating themselves from parents: "I am not my mom, she is not me. I can be more of myself."

Now, what is it about a toddler that helps her to manage separation for longer periods than a baby, and sometimes even enjoy some time away from you?

ᚦ At around 18 months, the child's brain becomes mature enough to make a mental image of you, and to be able to anticipate your return. Just because you are not visible doesn't mean you don't exist any more. Your child now begins to be able to soothe himself with a memory of you if you are absent for a little while.

ᚦ Control is the key. Trauma is, by definition, about enduring a painful experience that we cannot control, a situation we are totally powerless to influence. When a toddler masters standing up all by herself, walking and even trotting, she realizes that she can propel herself toward you or another safe person. This makes separation increasingly less scary. As she learns to speak, language becomes another empowering tool that gives the toddler more control. The more she feels able to communicate her wants and needs, the more she trusts that she will be OK when she is momentarily out of range from her main caregivers, and the more you can rely on her to tell you where and when she feels safe.

With these brand new tools in the toddler's tool belt, no wonder she feels safer to be separate from you. But it is very important that this process of individuation be gradual, as toddlers can still feel separation anxiety quite acutely. The key to making separation non-traumatic, is to let it be, as much as possible, child-led. Let your toddler explore her new frontiers away from you at her own pace. She will show you, through her behavior, her words or her facial expressions, when she is ready to let you go. Remember, trauma for a child is about loss of control, so if she is allowed to have some control over how fast to let you go, her separation from you will be painless.

There is a large variation in toddler's rates of separation. Some may dash off very quickly and feel very comfortable in a new environment with new people, while others may need to touch base for reassurance far more often. The main thing is to allow each toddler to set the pace and to feel a measure of control over the process.

In this way individuation can be better than just "not scary" and "not traumatic" and it can be an exhilarating experience. In fact, as your toddler gets a little more self-assured, you will find that sometimes she pushes you away.

First day at preschool, kindergarten or childcare

There are many people who recall their first day at school as a uniquely frightening ordeal, in which they could not possibly understand why their parents were suddenly leaving them alone with strangers for hours on end. No amount of crying attracted a comforting stranger, let alone brought back their mother or father. They felt bewildered and devastated as they watched their parent's back, purposefully disappearing into the distance. This kind of sudden and lengthy separation can be traumatic, and the pain involved for the child has been largely dismissed. Folk beliefs hold that children get over it and it won't have lasting effects. This is not true. Many people remember this first day rite for the rest of their lives with much sadness. The fear and the betrayal they felt has a long-term impact on how they view themselves, and the importance they place on their own feelings and needs.

The first day at school can be a sudden separation that comes as a shock to the child. They are dropped off and left in the care of strangers, without being given a chance to learn to feel at home in their new environment and to see if they feel safe with the staff and the other children. There is no reason for this to happen.

In all preschools, kindergartens and childcare facilities, parents should be allowed to remain in the background, quietly available while giving their children the space to roam around and bond with others. The common closed-door policy to parents is unjustifiable and hurtful to children and parents. This policy runs foul of all that is now clearly understood about children's developmental needs and should be changed as soon as possible.

If your toddler becomes distressed, let him come to you for comfort. Don't go checking in on him too much; let him come to you under his own steam. It might surprise you to find that although sometimes he needs you, at other times he might self-soothe, or find solace in the company of others. Knowing that you are there might be enough. Parents and teachers should wait and let toddlers show them when they are ready to be left. Parents can then begin to leave their child behind, for short periods initially, gradually increasing their absence, and allowing their toddler to be comforted by others if they do become distressed. For this to work well, teachers and caregivers need to be responsive to the children's emotions and willing to be comforting toward them. It also makes all the difference, of course, if it's fun for your child to be there.

Today, there are few preschools offering this kind of open-door policy to parents. In contrast, Swedish preschools are, as a rule, open to parents. Separation trauma need never happen in a child's life.

Insist on your rights as a parent in being allowed into preschool with your toddler or shop around for one that allows you to come in and graduate your exit. If your preschool won't allow you to come inside with your child, don't take no for an answer too readily. Explain to them that you do not intend to shadow your child and interfere with her need to get out in the world and learn to forge her own relationships with teachers, caregivers and other kids. Let them know you simply wish to be quietly available, in the background, for decreasing periods of time so your child has a chance to regulate the process of separating from you.

When small children feel very anxious but they are not with someone that they feel safe with, they don't necessarily let their feelings show. That is why teachers and busy childcare workers do not always notice that a child is in distress. Only someone very familiar with that child might detect a difference. The cortisol studies mentioned in the previous chapter are alerting us to the fact that many toddlers endure a length of time separate from loved ones before they are ready. This should concern us, since high levels of cortisol for extended periods can be corrosive, as we saw earlier, and have a detrimental impact on the emotional centers of the brain. Cortisol damage can lead to long-term emotional and behavioral problems.

Can others care for your toddler?

We said earlier that babies can and should be allowed to form attachments to alloparents. This is even more true of toddlers. Toddlers are growing in their ability to connect with many different kinds of people. In fact, children benefit enormously from having several safe and caring people in their lives who they can bond with. All parents need and deserve at least a few hours each week to refresh themselves, to spend a little time alone, with their partners or friends, and to catch up on the tasks that are difficult to accomplish with a toddler around.

Many people choose alternatives to childcare or preschool. Some invite family members to join them in looking after their child (alloparents), increasingly parents gather into support groups where trusted mothers and fathers help each other care for the children, and others employ a caregiver to come to their home. How do we know if these alloparents are appropriate for our child?

What if you decide to employ a nanny to come to your home on a regular basis, or ask another family member, such as one of your parents, to join in the care of your child? The main thing you can do to reassure yourself, is to let your toddler vote with her heart. Your child does the interview. Ask her directly how she likes being with the caregiver. Sometimes, toddlers can be very up-front and honest. But since toddlers cannot always be clear about their feelings—do you know many adults who are?—watch closely how she behaves around the caregiver. Does she run to them? Does she reach out to them to be held or picked up? Does she laugh and giggle with them? Does she climb all over them? These are some of the signs that your toddler feels safe to be herself with the caregiver you are testing.

Look for someone for your toddler to bond with who is warm, responsive to her feelings, and who is able to be playful. Imagine yourself as a child and ask yourself: Would I feel safe with this person? How would I feel about being left with this person?

When you find someone or some place for your toddler to be cared by, then—take some time out. Enjoy your time to yourself and with other adults. Intimacy with a child requires intense focus and energy from you. Recharge your batteries by having some of your adult needs met. You are a much better caregiver when you also care for yourself. And allow your child to learn to relate to others who are different to you; she will thrive from this, and gain many new relating skills.

10
The Passionate Toddler

Why toddlers can be oppositional (and exasperating)

Have you noticed that your toddler, on becoming more self-confident and mature, has begun to push you away sometimes, to tell you to go away, to defy and oppose you? Have you noticed that sometimes your toddler shouts out "No!," even when you are offering him something he loves? Does that bewilder you? Do you find yourself asking where your cute, friendly little baby went?

Your toddler needs to differentiate; that's how he starts to develop a strong sense of self. Differentiation comes in many forms. For one, he is likely to physically separate from you by running off on his own to discover what the world has to offer.

Another kind of separation takes place, an emotional separation, when your toddler discovers that he can feel differently to you—and that he is still OK. This is a life-changing moment, and your toddler can feel tremendously empowered by it, even if at first he finds it a little scary.

As he becomes more self-confident, when you and he disagree, he will not be so afraid. He will assert himself more forcefully. At times this will mean outright defiance, which feels like a big challenge to many parents. How do you face the might of your assertive little toddler without collapsing and giving in, but also without punishing him or otherwise crushing his spirit?

Sometimes, toddlers even act as if they don't like you, which might make you feel rejected. But consider this: to a healthy, emotionally secure toddler, pushing you away can feel wonderful.

Why does your toddler do these things? Partly because you are the one who sets most of the boundaries in his life, you say "No," or "Don't" more often, you get in his way. Toddlers need to safely express their frustration, which is important for their emotional health. Remember, toddlers are enormously passionate about everything they feel and want. This means they feel their disappointment intensely when told they can't have or do what they desire. Your toddler, like every one of us, has every right to express his frustration. It is by being allowed to express their feelings that toddlers gradually develop a healthy self-containment. If we respond to our toddlers' emotionality with shaming and guilt tripping (see Chapters 11 and 14), they learn to suppress their feelings, and this comes at a great cost to their self-confidence.

Toddlers are ready to begin flirting with the awareness that they are separate individuals, no longer merged with you as one. They are ready to become their distinct selves more fully. It begins as an experiment: they practice autonomy by pushing you away, defying you. When toddlers begin to discover their inner strength and autonomy, it gives them a thrill. There is great pleasure in saying "No!" so they say it again and again. Do you remember what this was like for you when you were a toddler?

These early rehearsals of self-assertion are among the most important developmental milestones for emotional intelligence. The toddler's assertion, however clumsy and raw, is the foundation that helps to build an individual who can stand up for himself and his beliefs. Self-assurance is what enables us to respect others who are different and see the world differently. It is what enables us to accept rather than avoid conflict, without resorting to violence or belittling others. To own and express our uniqueness while appreciating others' is one of our most important social skills; if more people had been given the kind of parenting that helps them to master this interpersonal skill, the whole world would be a happier place.

So this is the challenge we each face as parents: can we let our children stand up for themselves, even when it means they are standing up to us? Is it possible to actually enjoy this stage and to take pleasure in our children's growing strength?

The challenge for parents

"You want me to actually enjoy my toddler's willfulness? Are you kidding?"

When you think about it, it's not surprising that this stage can be so confronting for parents. How many of us were supported by our parents and our teachers to speak up for ourselves and to strongly voice our feelings, both positive and negative, when we were toddlers? How many of us can honestly say we were not punished, shamed, put down or powered over if we were strongly self-assertive at that age? Almost all of us were raised at a time when children were expected to do as they were told, no questions asked. There were dire consequences for daring to question our parents' authority. Those of recent generations who were allowed our personal power as toddlers are a rare breed.

Is it any surprise, then, that our toddler's power makes us uncomfortable? It is so hard to give freedoms to our children that we did not receive. We tend to view our toddlers through glasses that reflect what we were told about ourselves as children.

Some parents feel a great sense of indignation when their toddlers begin to be demanding, which they label as misbehavior because as children they were punished for doing the same thing. The very idea that a toddler would like to have choices strikes this parent as outrageous, a personal affront. Other parents who were never allowed to be assertive are so bowled over by their strong-willed child, that they can't set strong boundaries with them. They are afraid of conflict with their child, and find it hard to say "no" with any conviction.

How do we meet powerful toddlers without crumbling, without letting them dominate us, but without punishing or shaming them and crushing their spirit, as happens in so many homes? How do we give them their freedom to be strong without giving them license to hurt themselves or others? There is most definitely a way through these dilemmas and, as we will see, it involves connection, in other words, making contact with our child by means of our own emotional realness, or authenticity.

As parents we have our own needs, limits and rights. If we fail to assert ourselves and meet our potent little toddler eye to eye, she feels as if we are not being ourselves, we are not really there with her. This frustrates her, causing her to feel lost and rudderless. By being strong and showing our feelings to our toddlers, they receive a rich experience of us, our essence. Even when we say "no" or curtail something they want to do, they feel us with them as a solid presence. To our toddlers, this is very nourishing. Our strong and assertive presence is what helps them feel emotionally secure at this stage. Being assertive with our toddlers has nothing to do with punishing, shaming, or in any way squashing their will power. It never means crushing their spirit.

Love, not pain or domination, has the true power in any relationship because love is what connects us, and the meaning of connection is this: I am strongly myself, with all my feelings, and I allow you to be strongly yourself with me. This is how we connect with our toddlers in a way that is most alive and satisfying. It is what prepares us for a lifelong relationship that is rich, trusting, respectful and mutually enhancing.

A word about anger

The toddler stage asks both parents and toddlers to come to terms with the energy of anger. Over and over, you will feel frustrated, irritated and angry and your healthy toddler will, many times over, feel angry with you.

Your toddler is trying to understand and master the energy of anger. He feels it so wholeheartedly, and over the next few years he will be trying to learn how to channel this potent and life-giving emotional charge. You are his helper in this regard.

The greatest thing that the toddler can learn here is that we can disagree, we can have conflict, we can even be angry with each other—and this does not mean loss of love. In fact, when we express our anger toward each other (in a responsible manner, without blame or shame) this builds love, deepens our connection with each other and helps us to understand each other better. In its pure form, anger is a passionate face of love. It is the way we burst forth and insist on being seen, heard and understood. It is the force with which we seek to heal a rift, a disconnection that we feel from each other. It redresses relationships and returns us to harmony.

This is probably the most important lesson for humanity right now: to stop confusing anger with violence or domination, since the two are opposites. Violence destroys and domination suffocates, whereas anger connects.

Although it is very tempting to blame our toddlers, our personal difficulties with anger stem from the way anger was handled in our homes, schools and playgrounds as we grew up. For most of us, any show of anger, whether it was our own or the anger of our caregivers, was immediately followed by some kind of punishment or a distancing in relationships, a break or a rejection. Most of us have learned to fear and despise anger because it has been so closely married to violence. The sound or look of anger in ourselves or in our children rings alarm bells and, as a matter of reflex, we hose it down, repress it, punish it, try to overcome it. This can actually disconnect us from each other and block out loving feelings.

JACOB—AN ANECDOTE

One morning, a battle of wills erupted over breakfast when Lucy kept insisting that her boy, Jacob, eat his cereal. When Jacob shouted, "No! I don't like it!" Lucy was indignant. How dare Jacob raise his voice. She took all his breakfast away and sent him to his room to think about what he had done. Jacob cried bitterly. He could not understand why his mom was so mad at him since he couldn't help disliking his cereal that day—it was yucky. He could not understand why he was being punished for showing his feelings to her with all of his heart.

BETTINA—AN ANECDOTE

When 5-year-old Bettina had her girlfriend Tula over to play one afternoon, Bettina grew weary of sharing her toys, and in anger she pushed Tula down. Bettina's mother Cindy feared a brewing tantrum and was afraid to confront her too strongly lest she trigger Bettina's rage. In the sweetest voice she could muster, Cindy said, "Now Bettina, it's not nice to push your friend. Why don't you say sorry to Tula?" Irritated by her mother's contrived, syrupy voice, Bettina lunged at Cindy and hit her.

ARMANDO—AN ANECDOTE

As a father, Armando felt it was his unquestionable right to lay down the law in his home. Often, when he would forbid his son Joaquin from doing something he longed to do, Joaquin would simmer with hurt and anger. One day, Joaquin dared to challenge his father. Loudly and with indignation, he demanded to know, "Why?" Glaring at Joaquin, Armando screamed at the top of his voice "Because I'm your father! Now you watch that tone, boy!"

To Joaquin, his father's red, frowning face and his glaring eyes were very intimidating. As he turned to stomp away, Armando thought to himself, I'm the one that does the shouting around here!

Joaquin became sullen and withdrawn and sat alone for a long time, hunched in his chair.

EXERCISE

Next time you witness your child's anger or willful self-assertion, pay attention to the first feelings and thoughts that come to you. Write the thoughts and feelings down. You might feel all kinds of things: anger, outrage, indignation, irritability, fear, embarrassment, pride or compassion. You might have fleeting thoughts about your child, and fleeting impulses about things you want to do and say in response to your child's outburst. Write down all of these things you think, feel and want to say.

- Now take a few minutes to ask yourself these questions, and write down your answers.
- Do any of these impulses, thoughts and feelings sound familiar to me?
- Do any of these impulses, thoughts and feelings remind me of someone I know (or once knew)?
- Was anger ever openly expressed in my family, when I was growing up?
- How was anger dealt with in my family? How did my parents express their anger?
- How was I treated when I got angry?
- How did my other family members (siblings, etc.) express their anger?
- How did all this make me feel as a child?

Do I see any links between how anger was managed around me when I was a child, and how I react to my child's anger now? Make sure you take plenty of time to connect with the feelings that each of these questions brings up, as clearly and honestly as possible.

Share and discuss what this exercise has helped you to discover with your partner or a close friend. You will gain more compassion and understanding for yourself and for each other if you share your discoveries together. And perhaps you will be better able to support each other in your efforts to grow and develop, and deepen your connection with your child.

In these three anecdotes we saw three diverse parents encountering great difficulty in relating to their child's expressions of anger. None could allow their child to be, and to express themselves. Each of these parents felt threatened by their child's personal power, and each of them had distinct ways of compensating for how threatened they felt. Lucy punished, Armando dominated and crushed, and Cindy bent over backward to placate with her softly-softly approach. In all three scenarios, the child suffered emotionally and none of the parents created a boundary that connected with their child.

Anger: a force for healing

Our relationship with our toddlers can actually be a source of healing for us, if we let it. If we can, in our own minds, separate anger from violence or abuse, if we can learn to express our anger appropriately and to listen open-heartedly to our child's anger, this can deepen the love between us, bring us emotional healing and enhance all our relationships.

Learning how to express our feelings self-responsibly, and how to listen to our children openly are fundamental skills of relationships and keystones of emotional intelligence.

Why toddlers' willpower and independence can be so difficult

Toddlers are naturally narcissistic. Learning that others can actually get hurt is a reality that takes years to fully sink in (look around—there are many adults who have never fully taken this fact into their hearts). When it comes to human empathy, toddlers are barely beginners. How could they not be? They are only slowly emerging from a state of awareness in which the whole world appears to belong to them. This world of no boundaries is absolutely appropriate for babies. The idea of interpersonal boundaries dawns on toddlers very gradually as their growing brains enable them to realize that they are in fact separate individuals. That's why toddlers sometimes trample on others; they can be aggressive and take things that don't belong to them. It takes years to reorganize their baby-like perception of the world.

Understandably, toddlers can be quite frustrating at times. They push each other, they even hit each other, they help themselves to things that don't belong to them and refuse to share. We have a long-term task ahead of us: to help our toddlers to learn respect for others' boundaries.

Toddlers press our personal buttons

There are also deeper reasons why we find our toddlers so trying. As we saw earlier, this has a lot to do with the way we were ourselves treated as toddlers. Most of us have difficulty offering what we haven't been given ourselves. It is hard to relate to a toddler's power, to the pleasure and exhilaration it gives them, when this same exuberance was punished or shamed in us. Our toddlers trigger our own childhood frustrations. Many parents react to this by becoming controlling and authoritarian, or by withdrawing affection and approval. Until we understand how our own childhoods have affected us, we tend to mimic our own parents' mistakes.

When parents get separation anxiety

With every month that passes, toddlers become more independent. They no longer constantly want to be in that one-on-one, private love bubble with their mother, they run free and seek the company of others, which causes many parents to feel some sadness and a sense of loss. They feel rejected, as if their child no longer loves them. The baby has left the building. You've heard of empty nest syndrome? Perhaps a name should be given to this unique phase, such as empty cradle syndrome, or empty sling syndrome.

The baby phase was a special time of intimacy, at times even exquisite, so it is a common experience for parents to miss their baby. Do let yourself say goodbye to your baby and let your tears come if they want to. As with any goodbye, some grief is natural. The passing of this relationship brings feelings that deserve your respect: honor them and share them with your partner. The more open you are to your emotions, the more your heart can open to the new joys that await you as your baby metamorphs into a toddler.

For many parents the toddler's flight to independence can be scary. Some find themselves feeling empty, as if they are no longer wanted or needed. Others find themselves constantly fretting about their child's safety (Will he fall over and hurt himself? Will another child hurt her?). If you are unable to let your child go, if you can't help clinging on and being overprotective, do not judge yourself. Think about how your transition to toddlerhood was managed by your parents or caregivers. If your mother or father were overprotective when you became a toddler and if they were anxious about your growing independence, fearing too much that you would be hurt, holding you back from running, climbing, exploring, discovering, making mistakes and occasionally getting a little bruised—you may have absorbed strong messages about your own frailty, and about a perilous and unfriendly world. Initially, you may have felt smothered and frustrated, you would have railed against the restraints placed upon you. Over time your parents' anxiety may have become your own.

Alternatively, what if your parents or caregivers were inattentive, and you had to fend for yourself too much and too soon? Was this a time of fear for you? Perhaps you did get hurt or bullied and felt bereft of a safe person to run to. There are so many reasons why, for many of us, entering toddlerhood was a time of fear and hurt.

When your toddler declares her independence and ventures out of your parental safe haven, it is possible for this to bring up anxieties that you once felt at the same age. We agonize about our child ever feeling the same pains or fears we felt at their age. How often we act from these fears without knowing it. It is important that you talk about these feelings with your partner or someone you trust to be non-judgmental and empathetic. Don't leave yourself alone with these feelings; reach out for reassurance—you deserve it. This can be an opportunity to heal old wounds and to grow, so use this opportunity and have some counseling if you feel the need to. If you can connect with supportive and reassuring individuals, your past is less likely to impose itself on your present. Emotional support and receiving comfort for old childhood fears can liberate you to better enjoy this wonderful stage of parenting. The more supported you feel emotionally, the easier it is to take pleasure in your child's self-discovery and her adventures into the greater world.

Things we do to control our toddlers
We punish them, we hit them.
- ✝ We shame them.
- ✝ We dispense approval manipulatively—rewarding obedience or compliance.
- ✝ We use guilt tripping—How could you do this to me?
- ✝ We ignore them, turn away from them, withdraw affection.

Authoritarian methods such as these have been used by parents since the dawn of civilization. They have enabled parents to control their children, though these methods give little more than an illusion of control. Authoritarian behavior control methods come at a grave cost to your child's emotional intelligence and place a barrier between you and your child. In the following chapters we will look at why the above methods backfire so badly, and how they impoverish your connection with your child. We will also look at approaches to setting strong boundaries with your child in ways that empower both of you, and deepen the connection between you.

Freedom does not mean license
I have been talking a lot about your toddler's needs and rights. So, what about your needs and rights? In order to connect well with your child, you need to be connected with yourself. Denying your own feelings, your needs and your limits, does not connect you to yourself. The more we deny our own feelings, needs and limits, the more inauthentic we appear to others—and our children are the first to detect this. A toddler can hardly mature if, when they do things that hurt or impinge on others, they are not told to stop, and shown why. Nor can they mature if they are shielded from the demands of relationships, in other words, if they are never asked to be helpful.

Our generation is living in a time of hiatus—suspended between a desire to turn away from old-fashioned and damaging authoritarian parenting styles, and trying to find new ways. Unfortunately, in trying to reject the punishment they got as children, many parents overcompensated by becoming permissive. Afraid to hurt their child like they were themselves hurt as children, the permissive parent tries never to raise their voice at a child, never say "no", never expect them to change their behavior and learn to respect others. Effectively, this has meant a swing from abuse of power to having no personal power at all. While saving children the humiliation, pain and fear that authoritarian methods caused, permissive parenting creates a whole new set of problems.

Have you ever been in a café or cinema where some children are running wild, screaming and bumping into you and the other patrons? Sure, the kids are having fun—but what about everyone else? Doesn't it drive you nuts when you look around and find that their parents are setting no boundaries? Have you ever seen a toddler deliberately hit a parent, break things and receive no response at all, or only a very sweet-scented and limp rebuke? This is permissive parenting and it is as neglectful of the parent as it is of the child.

Why are boundaries important?
To begin with the obvious, toddlers need our guidance for the sake of their safety. They cannot possibly understand many of the dangers that present themselves and it is our responsibility to restrain any behavior that places them in danger. The example of a child running out onto the street is probably the most commonly invoked.

But there are deeper reasons for strong and clear interpersonal boundaries, reasons that have to do with the quality of your connection with your child. When your child does something to upset or hurt you, if you don't say, "Hey! I don't like this, stop it!" you do not seem real to your toddler. Unless you demand respect, he does not see a reason to respect you. Unless he is shown your needs and your limits, there is no reason for him to see you differently from the person you appeared to be when he was a baby—when (hopefully) he saw you as one who would give, be endlessly patient, and ask for nothing in return. He is a toddler now, and only if you are assertive can you role model self-respect and teach him the art and skill of considering others' feelings.

Meeting babies' attachment needs, as we saw in earlier chapters, is the best guarantee of considerate behavior as they grow into children, but by itself, healthy attachment is not enough. Empathy, consideration and respect are learned by your toddler to the degree that you show them your feelings and strongly ask for their respect.

What is a boundary?

Simply put, a boundary means saying no—either refusing to do something that is being asked of you or asking your child to stop doing something. Clear interpersonal boundaries are like our social skin—they are absolutely essential for any relationship to function. As anyone who finds it difficult to say "no" can tell you, without boundaries we feel invaded, violated, and we soon get exhausted by others' demands and end up feeling resentful. About half of all the things that go wrong in relationships involve boundary issues: failure to set adequate interpersonal boundaries, unclear or fuzzy boundaries, lack of respect for each other's boundaries and confusion about what is your responsibility and what is mine.

Several times a day you will need to say "no" to your toddler: "No, don't push your little brother," "No, don't run away where I can't see you (in a crowded mall)," "No, don't throw your food around in this restaurant," or "No, don't poke the dog with a stick."

A toddler is all passion, which sometimes gets him and everyone around him into trouble. Toddlers do not comprehend the consequences that you and I worry about: the broken vase, the soiled carpet, the injured dog and so on. They don't comprehend the world's dangers—the cars, the electric outlets, the pot full of boiling water—in the way adults do.

Until your toddler starts to see you having an emotionally charged response to her risky or harmful behaviors, she cannot understand. Unless you actually look and sound annoyed when she does something hurtful, or worried when she does something dangerous, the boundaries you set don't make any sense to her. You can tell her not to do this or that, or not to go here or there, or to stop that all you like, but all she understands is that you don't approve of something. She does not get why. For her to understand the why, to truly internalize this understanding so that it is her own, your toddler needs to see your emotions. How have her actions caused you to feel? Your feelings, appropriately but openly expressed, are her teachers.

Arguably, the question most frequently asked by parents with little children is this: How do we get our toddler to listen to us? When you help your toddler to see clearly how you feel boundaries get set in a way that sticks. Are you angry at something she has done? Are you hurt or sad or frightened? Show her that. Let it be visible in your eyes, your face and body, and let it be audible in the tone of your voice. Your emotional authenticity is what makes the connection with her. The old ways of punishment do not work—they backfire mainly because they do not create any real connection between you and your child. As always, connection is the key.

Emotionally authentic parenting

Your toddler now hungers to get to know you as a real person. What is a real person but someone who can be warm, affectionate and tender, but also can be sad, worried, hurt, and can get cranky?

If you want your toddler to listen to you, simply let yourself be the person you are: be emotionally real, authentic. It is important that we communicate our feelings to our children in ways that are effective yet safe, and not too overwhelming for the child (see Chapter 14).

When you allow your feelings to show, your child experiences you as a solid presence. This is a new source of emotional security for your child. It helps them to trust you.

BARNARD TODDLER CENTER FINDINGS

A study conducted at the Barnard College Toddler Center in New York confirmed that mothers who openly—but appropriately—expressed anger had children who were more emotionally secure.

Why some toddlers deliberately provoke their parents

If you hide your feelings from your child your presence seems incomplete somehow, as if something were missing. It is uncanny how sharply our children detect our emotional state—often before we do. They even become unsettled or chaotic in their behavior as a response to the unexpressed emotional tension they pick up in us. Since they are so tuned in to how we feel our children may get confused when we hold back our feelings.

It is very reassuring to our children when we are emotionally real, whereas when we are emotionally detached, remote or incongruent, our children can feel alone, anxious and irritable. Our true essence is missing, which can be tremendously unsatisfying and frustrating to our children. They become restless, and without any idea why they do so, they begin to poke and prod. They torment us. They find the things that most drive us mad and do them. This is a desperate plea for connection. Children don't have a better way to say "Hey! Where are you? Come out from in there. You look like you're here, but you're not. What are you really feeling? Wake up, and respond to me!" Our children call for our strength; they need us to be solid. Only a strong, emotionally real response—how you feel when your toddler acts this way, what you want your toddler to do—will meet the toddler's hunger for connection and help him to settle down.

There are more reasons why toddlers can sometimes be provocative. If there were painful lapses in healthy attachment during the baby months, toddlers often act out in anger and hurt. This is how they cry out for help, reaching out to have their pain recognized. Though their behavior seems unpleasant, the only thing that heals them is to feel heard. There are always genuine reasons underlying children's emotional outbursts. Fortunately, it is possible even for the most troubled and neglected little children to calm down considerably when they feel validated. In Chapter 13 we will look at how to listen to children so they feel heard, understood and comforted.

Whatever the reason children may goad you, they aren't helped in any way if you allow yourself to be trampled. Children come to peace when they are with adults who know how to say "no" with conviction, who dependably listen and validate their feelings, and who are warm and affectionate.

RETHINKING MISBEHAVIOR

Science is forcing us to rethink the meaning of misbehavior. There is an emerging, research-driven consensus that difficult behavior in toddlers often comes from unmet attachment needs. There is also mounting evidence that the more time babies and under threes spend in childcare in the care of strangers, the more disruptive their behavior is likely to be.

Many behavioral problems can be remedied if toddlers are held and listened to empathetically, if they are shown patience and warmth and if they are given support to play freely. But if children's need for empathy and affection is not met in the toddler years, their behavioral problems are likely to persist into later childhood, adolescence and adulthood.

Conversely, a number of studies show that babies who have been consistently and warmly responded to grow to be more cooperative with their parents and develop a stronger conscience. They tend to be less oppositional, less angry, less fearful and more capable of empathy. As was said earlier, good discipline always begins with responsiveness and affection, starting at the baby stage.

The tantrum thing

The majority of toddlers will have tantrums from time to time. There are endless advice columns telling you how to get control over your child's tantrums. Many of them have involved some kind of punishment, such as time out or ignoring the child. The old-fashioned shortcut was to give the child a whack. Over recent years, there has been an evolution toward trying to be more understanding toward toddlers' emotionality, and this is increasingly reflected in the parenting literature.

Why toddlers have tantrums

As adults when we become frustrated, we have a muscular system that helps us to contain a strong emotional charge so we can measure our outbursts. We can, for instance, say to another, "I am disappointed," or "I am angry," and we can accept disappointment without exploding into rage. We also have a neural system in the front part of our brains that helps us to regulate strong emotional charges so we can feel frustrated or angry yet choose not to strike out and instead channel our angry energies constructively. Most of us are able to modulate how we express our feelings so as not to hurt or overwhelm those we care about.

For a toddler, those body systems are still very immature. When anger swells inside them, it bursts its banks and runs out of control. Toddlers simply cannot contain the emotional charge, their musculature is not developed enough, and the part of the brain that can contain powerful emotions is not fully developed and won't be until they are at least four years of age.

This can be frightening for toddlers, so during a tantrum they need our help and support so they won't feel alone, frightened and fragmented—and of course so they won't accidentally hurt themselves. Our support and calming presence is vital so they won't grow up feeling afraid or ashamed of their emotions.

COMFORT = REASSURANCE = FEWER TANTRUMS

In a young toddler's brain, the areas of the cortex most concerned with regulating emotion are still relatively disorganized. Until this mechanism matures, they are not organically able to regulate strong emotions, which is why they have tantrums. Neuroscientists say that when you comfort and reassure a distressed toddler, the memory of your comforting is stored in their brain. It is these memories that help them to learn how to modulate their emotions later—and the more memories of being comforted, the better. You can think of it this way: every time you patiently soothe your child, it is an invaluable long-term investment that adds to his ability to manage emotions as he grows. Our children end up treating themselves in the same way as we treat them.

Understanding ourselves, understanding our toddlers

Why do we parents have such difficulty with our children's tantrums? Some parents are frightened of their children's tantrums, others infuriated by them, and many deeply embarrassed if it happens in public—the child on the supermarket floor scenario.

In order to find in ourselves the emotional strength to face our child's tantrums calmly and supportively, we need first to address our own relationship to strong emotion. The feelings triggered in us by our child's tantrum have a lot to do with the way our own tantrums were treated when we were toddlers.

EXERCISE

Take a few minutes to sit quietly on your own, somewhere where you are least likely to be interrupted. When you have relaxed into your quiet and private space, take a few moments to remember a time when you, as a child, had a tantrum. If you cannot recall any of these, then just try to remember any moments that spring to mind, when you might have felt very angry as a child, when you had an angry outburst in one way or another.

At each of these episodes, who was there with you?

Thinking of the person or people who were with you at the time, what did they say to you?

What did these people do for you, do to you, or fail to do?

Thinking of the way in which your angry feelings were treated in your home, or at school, how did this make you feel at the time?

If you were not happy with the way your anger was treated, can you think of what you might have wished to be different?

Imagine for a few moments what you would have preferred others to say and do for you.

Now, look closely at how you feel inside whenever your child has a tantrum.

Does it make you angry? Afraid? Ashamed? Disgusted? Compassionate?

Do you see any links between the way your tantrums were dealt with and the way you feel toward your own child's outbursts?

When you feel angry, how do you feel if someone tells you to calm down and to stop being so emotional? This may give you a clue about how your child feels if you try to diminish her anger.

When you feel angry, what is the best thing that others can do to help calm you?

Does this give you any ideas about what your child might want from you when he is angry?

I encourage you and your partner both to do this exercise and share your discoveries together. This will help you understand each other more deeply and enable you to work better as a team, helping each other to support your child.

Why do I find my child's anger so upsetting?

If you were punished, shamed or humiliated for getting angry as a child, you are likely to find it difficult to cope with your child's anger. You might feel embarrassed if she has a tantrum in public, as if you have failed as a parent and people all around are judging or mocking you. You might feel outraged that your child has the nerve to express herself in ways you were never allowed to.

If someone in your family was violent or they used their anger to intimidate, you might feel hostile toward your child's anger, since anger has been manifested as an ugly emotion. Alternatively, if anger led to violence, separation or alienation in your family, you might feel frightened when your child gets angry. Many people come from families in which no one ever expressed anger, no one ever raised their voice. Anger seems alien, or pointless, so when confronted by their child's anger they tend to feel helpless.

The reactions that are triggered in you by your child reflect real experiences that have left their mark on you. Give yourself limitless compassion and understanding. Anything you do to tend to your emotional wounds helps you to have more space, more patience and understanding for your child.

If anger tended to be expressed openly and responsibly in your family and led to resolution of conflicts and renewed affection, then you are likely to feel far more comfortable with your child's anger, even his tantrums.

Healing your own history with anger

Anger becomes problematic when it is denied ("I'm not angry, I'm a nice person") or repressed. When it is denied, anger can lead to distance in relationships and ill health; it can even erupt into violence. When expressed responsibly, the emotional honesty can lead to greater aliveness and to closer, warmer relationships.

The more you learn how to express your own anger freely (and responsibly), the more comfortable you will feel around your children's anger and the less you will feel like punishing them.

The following exercise is borrowed from Bioenergetic Analysis, a therapeutic system developed by psychiatrist Alexander Lowen. It is a body-oriented psychological healing method used by many psychotherapists around the world. This exercise can be wonderfully enlivening and stress-relieving, while at the same time helping you to feel more comfortable and less perturbed around your child's tantrums.

It is a noisy exercise, so you might prefer to try it someplace where you are least likely to frighten your neighbors. You can use the exercise whenever you feel an accumulation of anger or frustration or if you feel tense from a stressful day; it is a powerful and safe technique for emotional release. Don't be surprised if you find this exercise enjoyable, empowering, even exhilarating.

EXERCISE

Lie on your back on a mat or mattress so that you can extend your arms overhead as far as possible. While breathing in, lift both arms straight, as far back as they will go, and as you exhale bring them down hard beside you, slapping with both hands open on the mat.

Repeat the exercise, reaching as far behind as you can, but this time as you slap your hands down onto the mat as hard as you can, yell out, "Ha!" sharply and loudly. Repeat the downward slap several times, in sync with your "Ha!"

Now, lift one leg up quite straight, as far up as it will go, and bring the heel down hard on the mat while again yelling out, "Ha!" Do the same with the other leg. Alternating legs, repeat this two or three times, then take a few breaths to rest.

How is this exercise making you feel?

Now you are going to be moving both your arms and legs. Make fists, and begin by lifting opposite limbs (right arm and left leg, or vice versa). Hit them down on the mat, alternating sides. Start off slowly and then go faster and faster. As you speed up, let your movements become spontaneous and natural—forgetting the order in which the limbs should thrash.

Try to let your limbs do all the work, so your head remains resting on the mat. As you thrash your arms and legs down, yell out "Ha!" or let yourself yell any words that come to you. Yell "No!" for instance, over and over, or your favorite swear words, or just plain old "Aaaaaaaaargghh!"

You might find your head wants to move from side to side; if so, let it. Let yourself go completely. Enjoy the release and revel in the emotional power that is in your body.

When you have had enough, rest, breathing naturally.

You have just had a tantrum, just as wild as your child's. How did it feel? How do you feel now? The movements in this exercise are carefully designed to tap into the muscle groups that retain most pent-up emotional tension, such as your diaphragm, tummy muscles, hips, shoulders and upper back. Not surprisingly, the exercise mimics much of what children do spontaneously and naturally to relieve emotional stress. Tantrums are a well-orchestrated natural movement, a total-body emotive explosion designed to release the greatest amount of pent-up tension.

You might prefer to do your tantrum exercise in private so you are not preoccupied with frightening your child or with feeling observed. But if you and your partner feel comfortable enough with each other to support each other through this exercise, then take turns and do it together. Make sure you never belittle each other's efforts, and encourage each other to really let go and go for it.

If you have connected to your own tantrum, especially if you can let yourself enjoy it; then you will feel far more accepting of your child's tantrums. You will be able to relate to how she feels on the inside.

WARWICK—AN ANECDOTE

Warwick still remembers a tantrum he had on the carpet right in front of his mother when he was 4 years old. As he recalls, he was desperately trying to show her that he was very angry about something that was important to him. Warwick's mother responded by laughing at him, and when he stopped beating his fists on the floor, she gave him a small pill, presumably to calm him. Warwick does not remember ever having a tantrum again after that day. He remembers looking at the pill in his hand, feeling like there must be something shameful about him that needed fixing.

This was not the only time Warwick was shamed for becoming angry as a toddler. As an adult, Warwick continued to feel overcome with shame if he ever got angry. He found it very difficult to assert himself and struggled to react against injustices.

When his own son Michael began to have toddler tantrums, Warwick felt overwhelmed. He found it hard to accept Michael when he freely expressed what Warwick had never been allowed. Letting himself have a few mock tantrums, as in the bioenergetic exercise above, helped Warwick regain much of his self-confidence; it also helped him to feel far more comfortable around Michael's tantrums.

But tantrums are manipulative

Most of the time when a child is having a tantrum she is helpless and her emotions are beyond her control. She desperately needs a steady, reassuring presence with her. She needs to know that she will not be left and that you'll hold her and comfort her afterward. Far from being a calculated, manipulative ploy, tantrums can be quite scary for her.

Among older toddlers or young children, sometimes tantrums can be an effort to wear a parent down. But this does not mean that the emotion is not genuine and there is no point blaming a child. Rather than judge your child for being manipulative, just don't allow yourself to be manipulated. If, for instance, your child is challenging you for setting a boundary you feel is reasonable, then don't cave in. No child can be a manipulator unless he has this role modeled for him and unless others are open to being manipulated. Can you say "no" and mean it when you need to?

A helpful attitude

If we are to avoid being triggered into our own outburst, it can be very helpful to breathe deeply and slowly into our bellies as we support our child through a tantrum. By containing our emotions, we role model for our children how to do the same. Our children look to us to be the eye of the hurricane. If we can remain present, empathetic and calm, they sense this and, by osmosis, they gradually learn it for themselves.

When our children sense that we judge that their tantrum is bad, it makes them feel betrayed and alone, which only exacerbates their despair. On the other hand, each time we go all the way in supporting them to express their feelings, this saves us and our children more anguish in the future. The more supported a child feels, the sooner he learns to regulate his emotions, to express his feelings in a more grounded way, and the sooner the tantrum stage will pass.

This cannot possibly be overstated: to be willing to connect with your child's emotional world and remain openly present is the greatest investment you can make in their wellbeing and your relationship with them well into the future. It is a long-term investment that will even make the teenage years easier for both of you. Though you will often say "no" to many things your child wants, always say yes to your child's feelings.

Practical solutions to helping your child in a tantrum

The first thing to do for your toddler in a tantrum is to give her permission and space. There is no point in trying to hurry her through the maelstrom of emotion—doing so will only frustrate her and she will resist you. You will also find it a complete waste of time to try to reason with her during a tantrum.

When emotions are in full swing, the part of the brain concerned with reason is disengaged. She can't hear reason now. An attempt to reason with her will actually make her feel unheard and unseen. All she wants is her emotions to be seen, heard and understood and that is the only thing that can help her settle.

Speak to her but keep it simple. Just let her know in your own words that you understand why she is angry, that she can be as angry as she needs to be, and you are there for her.

If your child's arms and legs are flailing everywhere, place some pillows or cushions around him so he doesn't hurt himself. If he lets you hold him, do so, but don't overly restrict his movements. It is by moving his body that he discharges the emotion. Restraining your child tightly may frighten him, and it teaches his body to suppress emotion. Simply sitting near your child or holding him gently and placing your hand on his back, behind his heart, can be immensely reassuring.

If you absolutely cannot cope with the intensity of your child's emotion and you have to leave the room momentarily, check that he is not terrified when you go and that he is OK to keep on being angry on his own. Ideally, there should be another caring adult with you to take over if you feel exhausted or overwhelmed. It may be unsafe, as well as terrifying, for your child to be left alone during a tantrum.

Always provide soothing afterward. Hold your child and caress her, rock her or gently pat her back. Let her know that you love her and that you have heard and understood how she feels. You could say, for instance, "I know you're angry. It must have been so upsetting. It's OK, I've got you now." It can be quite scary to be so overcome with rage and despair, to be so tumbled about by emotions, so it may take quite some time, and lots of sobbing and sniffing, for your child to settle again. Often, she may fall into an exhausted sleep once you have comforted her.

If your toddler is hitting you or another child, quickly offer him other ways to show his anger. Let him know very firmly that it is OK to be angry, but not OK to hit.

What, then, are some ways to help your child channel his aggression and safely release his anger?

Helping your child express anger safely

There are many simple ways to help your child express anger without harming anyone. Begin by letting your child know in simple language that you want to show him a game that helps him to show his anger, but that it will not be OK to hurt himself or anyone else. You can show these exercises to your child purely as a game, helping him to rehearse them to use at a later time, when he is feeling angry or frustrated.

Put a big pillow or cushion in front of him, or against your shoulder, and invite him to punch it as hard as he likes. Set some ground rules, such as: "You can hit this pillow, but never my body." Encourage him to yell, even roar, as he strikes out. Let him keep going until he has had enough (or until you have). Alternatively, he could just place his hands against your pillow and push away with all his might. If you clearly reinforce the difference between hitting a person in order to hurt and hitting a pillow in order to release emotion, your child will not feel encouraged to be violent toward others by these exercises. In fact, the more comfortable he is with safe methods for venting frustration, the less likely he is to ever deliberately hit another person.

Anger wants to be expressed through the whole body, so provide some firm cushions for your child to kick, too. Alternatively, ask your child to lie on his back, and bring his knees up toward his chest. This will be a pushing away exercise, not a kicking one. Turn your back to him and help him place the soles of his feet firmly against your back and, on the count of three, push you away with a big, loud "Aaarrgh!" until his legs have stretched out all the way. Provide just enough resistance with your weight so your child has to expend some effort to shift you. Have fun. Pretend he has thrown you across the room. Repeat this exercise as many times as you both would like to.

Wrestle each other on the ground, or on a mat. Be noisy, growl. Roar together. Let your child win most of the time (but don't make it too easy for him!)—and don't overpower him and make him feel weak—this will only increase his frustration.

Don't be surprised if these exercises end in laughter for both of you. When your child feels that you wholeheartedly accept his anger, when he can express his frustration with all of his strength, with no one getting hurt, this can be incredibly liberating, even exhilarating. Your child is very likely to be absolutely delighted with these kinds of exercises and will increasingly turn to you for help to safely release his pent-up frustrations.

As your child develops more language, practice telling each other when you feel angry, even when you are angry with each other. You will find that anger can involve raised voices, but doesn't necessarily have to. The more you trust each other to hear, the less emotional charge comes up. In fact, it is true for all of us, adults and children, that the more we feel heard by others, the less likely we are to become angry. Nevertheless, when there is anger between you, you'll find that expressing it fully and responsibly leads back to warmth, affection and closeness.

If your child (and you too) learns that anger can be expressed safely and responsibly, that in this way no one gets hurt and a loving connection is created, it can be one of the most valuable lessons in emotional intelligence and relationship skills he will learn. Imagine what a difference this would make for all of your child's relationships. Imagine the kind of world we would have if everyone knew how to do that.

What your toddler can teach you

As adults we are so full of purpose, plans and responsibilities, so outcomes-oriented that we forget how to take pleasure from life. Our ability to make plans, to stay focused, set goals and implement strategies are, without a doubt, an essential recipe for success. But life is not only about success. To have balance in our lives, we also need to know how to let go of thinking about outcomes and being in the present moment. This requires us to tap into the kind of state of consciousness that children have.

To be absorbed in the here and now is essential to experiencing joy and bliss. Many of us have lost our connection to this state of mind. Our toddlers have not, and their exuberance, their sense of awe and magic are very contagious—if you let them be. When we are close to them, they remind us how to connect with those states. Let your toddler lead you back into playfulness, and from time to time, let yourself be a child. This will restore your connection with yourself as well as deepen the connection between you.

Your toddler will also challenge you to have resolve—to have strong boundaries. They teach us all what is probably the most important and urgent lesson for humanity today: that violence is not strength, and that the only boundaries that work are set with assertiveness, not with punishment. Punishing a child will sooner or later always backfire, and it always impoverishes the parent-child connection. We learn from our toddler that violence (such as hitting a child) might feel powerful, but it is in fact a weakness. Violence and domination only give us the temporary illusion of strength.

Having a toddler is like being in a school of assertiveness, and this is not an easily learned skill; we can all stand to hone it. With a toddler in the house, we are being challenged daily to learn how to assert without aggressing.

Your toddler confronts you, daring you to be real. You will feel stretched, incited to more love, more tiredness, more compassion, more frustration and more delight than you ever thought possible. You will feel pushed to express all of these feelings appropriately and caringly. Toddlers make us feel more alive.

And finally, one of the greatest lessons of love—our toddlers show us what it means to set the ones we love free. Our toddlers, just like our babies, help us to be better people.

Part 5

Talking and Listening So That We Connect

11

To Discipline or to Connect?

What do we do when our child runs toward a busy street without looking, when she runs away from us in a crowded shopping mall, pushes or hits another child, snatches something that doesn't belong to her? For parents of toddlers and young children, so many problems and questions seem to be about how to deal with our children's difficult and challenging behaviors.

Many popular books, advice columns and television series that talk about child discipline treat the child as the enemy, a beast to be tamed. We call kids oppositional and defiant, we talk about their misbehavior, without seeking to understand the emotions that drive the child's behavior and without trying to understand what made the child feel this way in the first place. The child is under a microscope, as if his behavior is disconnected from its context—and this context is always about the child's relationships. When we narrow our view of children to their behavior, we end up speaking about control, discipline or, if you like modern (but increasingly discredited) psychobabble, behavior modification.

To look at children's behavior without looking at how their relationships feel to them is like trying to understand the weather without understanding climate or like trying to understand surf without understanding currents and winds.

I wish I had a dollar for every parenting advice manual or video that offers a technique for controlling behavior in an adversarial way, based on this stance: "I'm the boss, don't defy me." They use the language of battle (of wills), winners and losers, dominators and submitters, pitching the parent against the child. It's not surprising. We come from a long history of authoritarian approaches to parenting. Authoritarian parents hold that since parents are older, they must be obeyed without question or explanation. It is the "Do as you're told, or else" style of parenting. Most of us had parents and teachers that leaned toward this approach, and they are the role models we most frequently learned from.

The moment we view the child as an adversary who is trying to overrun, manipulate or outsmart us, we have begun to contribute to the conflict. The perception of naughty child is in the eye of the beholder, and this perception sparks off much of the needless conflict we have with our children. If what you see is a contest, then there is no escape but through winning, and whenever there is a winner, there has to be a loser. For eons, human parents have thought in terms of disciplining their children.

Authoritarian parenting

Thinking of the child in terms of behavior, not so much in terms of feelings, is a hallmark of authoritarian parenting. The authoritarian parent rigidly divides behavior into right and wrong and invariably, the parent, by virtue of being a parent, is right while the child tends to be wrong. There is little room for discussion.

This parent demands obedience. Parenting is seen through the authoritarian lens as a behavior management strategy. Raising a well-behaved child depends on regulating the diet of reward and punishment. Simply, punish the child when he is bad, reward the child when he is good.

To progress beyond authoritarian parenting involves looking for connection with your child instead of limiting yourself to being a behavior manager. It means giving your child a say. It means realizing that your child's respect must be earned, not coerced.

Behavior control methods

Authoritarian approaches to parenting, from extreme to benign, have been the most dominant across a majority of the world's cultures for thousands of years. We seem to be the first generation that is boldly moving into new ways of guiding our children, based on connection rather than control. No wonder we all feel like learners; we are poised in a delicate moment in the history of parenting that involves pioneering new approaches and making mistakes as we go.

It can be useful, when moving forward, to define what we are moving away from.

There are four main methods of behavior control, all of which hark back to age-old authoritarian methods. The first of these authoritarian methods is corporal punishment, the whack or spanking, the wooden spoon or the belt that so many of us can painfully remember. The second authoritarian method of behavior control is shaming the child. The third involves guilt tripping the child, and the fourth, which is gaining popularity today, involves selectively rewarding good behavior.

It may surprise you that I have included rewarding as a potentially problematic and authoritarian method. These days punishment is on its way out, and we'll look at why in the pages to follow, but the use of rewards to control behavior is flourishing, backed by oodles of research and taught by countless psychologists and parenting educators. Am I swimming against the current by lumping it in with three more obviously unpleasant methods? Isn't reward the opposite of punishment? We will look at that more closely in later pages.

Why I don't use the word "discipline"

Discipline is something you do to children, to make them stop doing what you don't want them to do. The focus is on behavior, not connection. If all your child does is change course in order to get your approval, or to escape punishment, then your child has learned nothing about relationships. When you are a disciplinarian your child doesn't get to know you as a person, or learn about your feelings. He is good in order to win your approval, not because he feels empathy for you.

Truly considerate behavior, as we will see later, is more likely to be inspired through connectedness, by setting boundaries with children rather than by disciplining them.

The problem with behavior management

People keep saying the same thing over and over about discipline methods such as hitting or shaming: It works. Well, that's because these methods do work—*in a way*. Though very often discipline backfires—children rebel, or they opt for shallow conformism—children's behavior seems to change when you hit them or shame them. As a schoolchild in Australia, many times I watched other children become better behaved—if only temporarily—after getting caned by the teacher. On the way home from school one afternoon, I was being particularly rowdy on the school bus. My behavior, I am sure, would have been grating to the driver. He screeched to a halt, turned around and pummeled me around the head. I was never a bother to him again after that. Disciplinarians would take comfort from this tale: See? You beat a child once, and it really works. They are "good" afterward.

But when discipline works, what is it exactly that has worked? If all you want is *behavior* change, then you will feel satisfied with authoritarian discipline. But are you sure that's all you care about?

There is one thing that no punishment or reward can teach—and that's empathy. In that area, discipline methods fail miserably. The disciplined child is being good because she is afraid of your punishment, because she is afraid of your shaming, because she wants your approval or because she wants to get that gold star or whatever prize you have trained her to expect. In none of those examples is the child's behavior motivated by respect or care for you. Make a child busy protecting her own needs and there will be little space in her mind to consider your feelings. She will be looking out for herself, rather than looking toward you. From the moment he resorted to violence I lost all respect for the bus driver who thrashed me. It would have been naïve of him to mistake my good behavior as respect; it was fear, mixed with simmering resentment. When fear entered the relationship, it eclipsed any concern for how my own behavior may have upset him. Fear and shame blot out care. Ask yourself: Am I willing to settle for self-centered good behavior?

That is why I am not interested in teaching parents how to control and modify their children's behavior. What I am interested in is showing you how to connect with your child and, in so doing, how to help your child cultivate natural empathy for you and for others. But first, let's take a closer look at each of the four behavior control methods.

The slap

There are probably many readers who already find the idea of hitting children quite repugnant. But a majority of parents still hit their children from time to time. Perhaps you are a hitting refusenik, or perhaps you are still in two minds about the appropriateness of corporal punishment. Either way, I hope the following passages can add to your perspectives on the subject.

Here are some of the things parents typically say to justify hitting their children:

"A slap teaches the child respect"
Can you tell the difference between respect and fear? The beaten child fears you and the pain you inflict. The good behavior that follows has nothing to do with respect.

"A good whack is the way it's always been done—my dad gave me a whack, just like his dad hit him."
Well, this is absolutely true. We can't blame parents for thinking a whack is reasonable when almost everyone has been hit, and much worse, since time immemorial.

Attitudes toward punishment have been changing over the centuries. What we call child abuse today was not so long ago called "good parenting." The whip gave way to the wooden spoon, which was itself replaced by the old-fashioned, over-the-knee spanking. Although most parents have renounced the more severe methods, a sharp slap is still widely used. Around the world parents are resorting to ever-diminishing levels of violence. We cannot justify what we do today by appealing to bygone practices.

BATTERING CHILDREN

From the time of antiquity until the Middle Ages, images of schoolteachers depicted them holding a birch rod or some other instrument of punishment. Severe beatings were an integral part of education. Other tools of child punishment in regular use were the cat o'nine tails, the discipline (a whip made of small chains), or a goad (a knife made for pricking children on the head or hands). In the seventeenth century, American children were still being publicly flogged. Psychohistorians have found no European autobiography from the Middle Ages or earlier that failed to mention severe beatings in childhood. Well-to-do European parents would hire professional flagellants who came to their homes, where they would strap down and whip the children. Each year, in most Christian countries, children were ritually whipped on Innocents' Day, to help them remember the massacre of innocents by King Herod.

The old-fashioned whipping of children only began to go out of style in Europe and the US around the middle of the twentieth century. Until 1962, when American pediatrician, Dr Henry Kempe, published his milestone article, "The Battered Child Syndrome," almost nothing done to a child in the name of discipline attracted public scrutiny or outcry. Genuine efforts to protect children only emerged within, or just preceding, the lifetimes of many readers of this book. Non-violent parenting is quite a new social experiment.

CORPORAL PUNISHMENT LEGISLATION

Corporal punishment in education has been banned in 110 nations. In the "developed" world, only two countries have not implemented this ban nationally: the US and Australia. Civilized societies today are horrified at the idea of violence toward children in the name of education.

At the time of writing, 31 countries have made it illegal for parents to hit their children, and the list is quickly growing. Whereas in Australia, the US, Canada and the UK you can hit your child without attracting censure or disapproval, this is now considered abusive in most European nations, Israel, Iceland, New Zealand, and most recently several South American and African nations.

Under Article 19 of the United Nations Convention on the Rights of the Child, all signatory nations are expected to legislate against corporal punishment. The latest report on violence against children by the UN General Assembly (August 2006), based on international consultations and research, again urges that "States and civil society should strive to transform attitudes that condone or normalize violence against children, including… acceptance of corporal punishment" (see References). This means that at present, Australia, the US, Canada and the UK are in breach of their international obligations.

But attitudes are changing fast, and soon corporal punishment will be considered a relic of the past. In the US, a number of child-protective organizations have been passionately campaigning for a legislative end to corporal punishment in schools and in the home, and they have had impressive state-by-state successes in the education sector (see References).

"A good slap teaches children right from wrong"

"It keeps children in line," supporters of spanking say, and "It lets them know you mean business."

Research denies each of these beliefs any credibility. Punishment never leads children to absorb a lesson on ethics—except the ethics of might is right. An American psychologist, Elizabeth Gershoff (2002), reviewed 88 research studies that evaluated the outcomes of normal, culturally acceptable spanking. Overwhelmingly, these studies showed that spanking can temporarily change children's behavior, but it can never deliver a lesson in ethics. When it comes to changing the child's heart, hitting is totally impotent. Think about this: how can you teach love by inflicting pain?

You are your child's number one role model. If you hit your child, you model the idea that the bigger person can settle a dispute by threatening or physically overpowering the smaller. When a parent hits a child, the ethic of picking on someone your own size goes up in smoke. Like it or not, hitting sets the example of "might is right," reinforcing the very attitude we want our children to discard. Children learn by imitation. They do as we do, not as they are told. Research studies have clarified over and over that children who have been physically punished are more likely to become violent. Bullying and delinquency have been traced back to their source—harsh punishment in the home.

Punishment produces the opposite of what it was—ostensibly—intended for. In fact, some studies have revealed that you are more likely to escape the negative effects of your parents' punishment if you deny this treatment its legitimacy and reject the idea that you deserved it.

By the way, your version of right and wrong are no more than mental constructs to your child—a concept rather than a feeling. The rational mind has much less power to guide behavior than was previously thought. Our attitudes have their source in the emotional centers of the brain; words or good ideas have little power to influence us. New discoveries about the anatomy of the brain have revealed that the emotional centers of the brain (limbic brain) have always ruled the rational, thinking part (neocortex), and not the other way around. That's why rules and talk about good behavior have little effect. We do better to reach the child's heart directly through connectedness, rather than imposing concepts of morality through punishment.

"With some children, you have to hit them to keep them out of jail"

I am not kidding, I have heard this said a number of times. If this were true, then our jails would be filled with the unspanked. What surveys reveal is the exact opposite: jail inmates tend to be those who were beaten the most as children. When people are fixated on the idea that punishment is necessary, no amount of contrary evidence will shake their belief.

"I never hit a child in anger. It is only done with love—and I hug them afterward"

Do you really think that it feels any different to a child, to be hit "with love"? Psychologists have known for decades that learning comes through association. If you repeatedly associate love with physical pain, that is deeply confusing to a child. In that child's mind, the edges of love and pain become blurred, love and domination are melded. There are worrisome implications for intimate relationships later in life. In adult relationships, love withers the moment one person subdues another. Hitting is not love, and the two must never mix. Hugging a child to "make it better" after hitting her is, in my view, thoroughly creepy.

There are many books written by defenders of the rod professing that it's OK to hit your child—as long as it's not done in anger. These writers try to sanitize spankings by issuing health warnings with their product, much like the disclaimers on packets of cigarettes. Well, you can kid yourself, but it is hard to fool a child. Your composure is barely a fig leaf over your intent to cause pain. Anger is no less anger because you act cool and calm. A spanking delivered through a veneer of dispassionate detachment is all the more eerie.

I was 11 years old when I first heard an adult, one of my Sunday school teachers, trying to convince us that our parents hit us because they loved us. His statement was as bewildering as it was bizarre and it reeked of fraud. Its contradictions screamed out at me. How can anyone think of hitting a person as an expression of love?

"Surely there's nothing wrong with a little slap?"

Just a teensy-weensy tap on the wrist? A little sting? What could possibly be wrong with that?

If you're wondering what level of deliberately inflicted pain is acceptable, you can do better than asking me or any child development expert. Ask your child—and leave a space for an honest answer. Don't begin by asking a loaded question, such as, "Is it OK when I give you just a little itty-bitty slap when, and only when, you have been naughty?" Ask your child an open question, "How do you feel when I hit you?" and assure your child that a truthful answer will be appreciated, no matter what.

Then ask yourself if it is OK for your spouse, your partner or your boss at work to give you the same teensy-weensy, itty-bitty slap on the wrist or on the bottom when your performance is not up to par. "You have spent too much time on the phone, and your productivity has suffered," says your boss, as he hits you on the wrist. OK by you if he does that?

Go back to when your mom and dad gave you just a little slap. How did that make you feel? I know, I know, you did a bad thing. You agree that, as others told you, you were being a little brat so you had it coming to you. But that is not what I am asking here. How exactly did the slap cause you to feel at the moment you received it? Many adults recall the times they were hit with detachment, indifference, even peals of laughter. But can you try to remember how you felt, from the point of view of you as a child? What does that tell you about the value of a "little" slap?

Here is another way to investigate for yourself whether a little slap is OK. Ask yourself the following questions.

Would it be OK for your child to give you a little slap when you misbehave? Why not? Imagine yourself old and frail in a nursing home. Would it be OK for the nurse to give you exactly the same little slap if you refused to eat your pumpkin mash? Interesting how willing we are to give a green light to practices as long as they affect other people, especially children.

If you decide that you would not accept being slapped under any of these circumstances, then what is it about children that disqualifies them from the same protection you expect for yourself? How come children are the only people we are allowed to hit, without self-defense as the excuse?

CORPORAL PUNISHMENT AS A BEHAVIORIAL RISK FACTOR

Even culturally accepted corporal punishment is a risk factor for a broad range of social ills. Toddlers who have been hit by their parents are less likely to listen to them and more likely to become aggressive and defiant—the exact opposite of what the punishment hoped to achieve. In older children, slapping or spanking can lead to bullying, anxiety or depression—and in adults who were hit as children, it has been identified as a risk factor for alcoholism and domestic violence. People who have been spanked can lose their ability to feel empathy for others. The frequency and intensity of corporal punishment has much to do with these results. But all this means is that a little hitting can lead to a little more acceptance of violence later in life. Results such as these are universal. A comparative study of forty-eight diverse societies found that those societies with the highest levels of violent crime also had the highest levels of corporal punishment of boys.

In 2004, a Joint Statement on Physical Punishment of Children and Youth was developed in Canada. Here is what it had to say: "The evidence is clear and compelling—physical punishment of children and youth plays no useful role in their upbringing and poses only risks to their development. The conclusion is equally compelling—parents should be strongly encouraged to develop alternative and positive approaches to discipline."

The jury has returned a verdict on human violence: social and biological sciences have determined that it is passed down from generation to generation via childrearing practices. We can break the cycle of social violence by saying goodbye to child punishment.

"I was only hit when I deserved it, and it did me no harm"
Often, when I have spoken with adults who say that being hit as a child did them no harm, the conversation goes something like this:

Me "How did you feel when you were hit?"

The hit-ee: "Oh, you know, I deserved it, I was really being a little pest."

Me "OK, that's what your parents said to you. But what I am asking you is, how did the whack make you feel?"

The hit-ee: "Oh, I was fine, you know, I got over it" (usually said with a smile and a dismissive wave of the hand).

Me "You got over it? Got over what, exactly?"

The hit-ee: "Well, OK, I suppose I was a little upset, you know how kids are... but hey, I forgot all about it in a minute. Everyone gets a whack, right? It's just how it is."

You see, to connect with the inner child it is often not helpful to simply ask a few questions. The inner child hides, is vulnerable and does not like prying eyes. Probing questions may feel invasive, compromising the safety of the hideout. As adults we tend to go to great lengths to sequester our childhood feelings. We have moved on and left the inner child behind.

The inner child still speaks to us, but the signal is weak, there is static on the line. Sometimes, in order to really recapture how we felt, we need to sit still, breathe into the memory, bring our attention to our bodies and notice any sensations that appear. It is like patiently tuning a radio to a faraway station, making minute turns of the dial, listening with great patience. Emotional memory speaks through body sensations and impulses. The more you hear what your own body is saying to you, the more you will understand how your own child feels.

Remembering how you felt as a child helps you to disentangle your own self-image from the superimposed self-image that others gave you, through the things that were said to you as a child.

Meanwhile, it is true that many people who were spanked as children do not grow up to be overly aggressive, depressed or anxious. Being hit as a child can, over time, desensitize us to aggression, which can harden our personality and our attitudes without necessarily leading to major dysfunction. As we harden ourselves to withstand the blows, our threshold of tolerance to violence keeps getting higher. As a result, many people seem to have a high tolerance to violence in the community or in the media, or they might seem insensitive to others" feelings without necessarily engaging in violence themselves. They have hardened, driven personalities, and may even achieve great status and success through sometimes ruthless competitiveness. They tend to push others to work hard, and are intolerant of human vulnerability. Supporters of iron-fisted politics—such as slashing of welfare provisions, heavy penalties for offenders and belligerent foreign policy—are often drawn from the ranks of the punished. They are the ones who typically say, "It never did me any harm!" The impact of corporal punishment is very diverse, but never positive.

EXERCISE

Memories of love, security or joy announce themselves through pleasurable, warm or expansive feelings in your body. A pleasant tingling in the pit of your belly might accompany a memory of friendship, a leaping in your heart may herald a memory of love. Sensations of cold, tension or pain often reveal old fears, anger or grief. Notice what's going on as you wander through the landscape of your childhood. What is that tension in your shoulders? What is that tightness across your chest, that knot in your upper stomach? Do you notice a need to swallow, or is your jaw clenching? If you ask internally, your body can tell you what is going on emotionally. What do those sensations seem to be saying to you?

Here is an exercise you can do if you are not sure about how disciplining affected you as a child. You probably do not need to try this exercise if you are already clear about how you felt when you were punished. If your memories of punishment are traumatic, then please do not do this exercise without the assistance of a trained professional.

Close your eyes, and sit comfortably.

Think of a time when your parents, teachers or other caregivers spanked or otherwise hit you.

Who was the disciplinarian? Can you see the look on his or her face, hear the tone of voice?

What was being done to you? If you were hit, what did it sound like each time a blow struck your body?

When you have images of this memory as clearly as you can, ask yourself this question: How did this make me feel as a child?

You may have all manner of thoughts come to you at this point, such as, I deserved it, I had been a brat, and so on. You may also have thoughts rushing in about how good your parents were, how you never want to blame them or judge them. You needn't condemn your parents, that's not the point. This exercise is about recapturing how you felt, not about evaluating your parents.

Put all those thoughts to one side now and go back to the feeling. How did you feel when you were punished?

Pay attention to any sensations in your body. Ask these sensations what they are saying. What does this part of my body want to do right now?

Please make sure you do not continue with this exercise for longer than a couple of minutes. The object is not to relive a painful experience, but merely to touch upon it if you have become disconnected from how it felt. Your compassion for your child rests on your connection to how you once felt as a child.

Connecting with your inner child in this way will tell you more about the merits of discipline methods than any of my opinions or my reference to research studies.

"Sometimes you have to spank for the child's sake, like when a child runs onto a busy street"

When the American Automobile Association conducted a study of pedestrian safety it found that children who were spanked for running into the street would end up going onto the street more often. Spanking did not deliver the results expected by the parents. Yes, developing a road sense is a serious safety issue that demands strong boundaries, but it is not achieved through violence (see Chapters 13 and 14 for other ways).

"But surely you can't call a little whack violent?"

Hitting is more likely to feel violent when we are the ones receiving it. We don't think of it as violence when we are doing the hitting. Research shows that parents tend to underestimate the force of their hit. It is invariably more powerful against their child's delicate skin than they realize. Since children are the ones on the receiving end, they are the experts on whether a whack is violent.

HOW DOES IT FEEL?

In 1998 in the UK, the National Children's Bureau and Save the Children UK asked a large number of 5–7-year-old children for their views on hitting. Their heart-rending responses would make it difficult for anyone to downplay the effects of corporal punishment. Here are some of their answers (see References).

"It feels like someone banged you with a hammer."

"It hurts and it's painful inside."

"You feel like you don't like your parents any more."

"It feels… you feel sort of as though you want to run away because they're sort of like being mean to you and it hurts a lot."

Why parents find it difficult to replace discipline with boundaries

The history of childrearing is the history of corporal punishment. Western cultures have known virtually no alternatives for thousands of years. Our parents did it (to almost all of us), our grandparents did it and our teachers did it. How many of us can say that our elders guided us with strength and compassion, and without punishment? It is not easy to begin trusting a new approach that feels unfamiliar because it has been unseen in our lives. The familiar methods give us refuge from the anxieties of the unknown, even when the familiar is unhealthy—the devil we know. **Our empathy and our emotional authenticity can influence our children positively in ways that punishment could never hope to.**

Shaming

What is shame?

Have you ever felt, when you're in public, as if you want to hide your face, to disappear from view? Shame is the name we give to the overwhelming feeling that we need to crawl under a rock because we see ourselves as unworthy, unpleasant, dislikeable and reprehensible, and because we expect to be judged or rejected accordingly. It might just be one part of ourselves that we are ashamed of, such as when tears fill our eyes, when we feel attracted to someone, the way we look, or perhaps even the way we sing. Even our positive attributes can be a source of shame. We tend to hide whatever parts of ourselves we are ashamed of while displaying what we think others will find acceptable.

Shame is like a knife that sharply delineates the limits of love in every culture—the warning signal that something we are doing risks us being ostracized. Shame is a crushing emotion that arrives with a thump in the guts, leaving us feeling winded and doubled over. When we feel ashamed we avert our eyes, we go quiet, we withdraw, we hunch our shoulders, we make ourselves smaller so no one will see our inadequacies. Many of us have learned to hide our feelings of shame under a charismatic, bubbly or jocular personality.

Shame is hard to detect in others because it makes us want to hide. But its invisibility makes it no less painful or paralyzing for the person who is ashamed.

How does shame develop?

Toddlers begin to develop the capacity to feel shame as they approach their second birthday. With the beginnings of language and the beginnings of self-awareness, toddlers start to create an inner definition of themselves. Their self-identity is, to a large degree, an open book upon which the things we say to them are inscribed. What we say to our children colors their self-image. Toddlers are acutely vulnerable to shaming at this time.

Words are powerful, but they are not the only instruments of shame. Our eyes are rich with emotion and intent. The way we look at our children, when we glare at them, when we look at them in disgust, has the power to reduce them to shame without us uttering a single sound.

Shame comes through shaming

Nobody is born ashamed. We only start feeling ashamed when others shame us. Additionally, children sink into shame when they feel ignored or left behind. Children are naturally narcissistic, prone to thinking that the things that happen to them happen because of them. When they feel abandoned or ignored, children too often conclude it must be because of something bad or wrong about them.

How shame is stored in the brain

When a child is shamed, the audiovisual record of the shamer—his words, his tone of voice, his disapproving look—are stored together with all the accompanying feelings via the neural circuitry of the limbic brain, a part of the brain concerned with emotion. This archival "footage" is then replayed later, when a similar situation triggers the shame memory. It is as if the movie about the shamer replays in the child's mind and acts as a painful inhibitor. Even when we are not aware that these shame movies are screening in our minds, we judge ourselves through these stored images. We actually shame ourselves in exactly the same way as others once shamed us.

A parent's look of disapproval leaps across space and time with enough force to alter the child's brain chemistry; it causes cortisol levels to spike and inhibits the flow of wellbeing hormones such as endorphins, oxytocin and dopamine. If we suspect that our children feel ashamed, it is important to soothe and reassure them. It is through the way we soothe and repair the effects of shame that children learn to do this for themselves later in life. It is the emotional memory of a soothing adult that provides the template by which children learn to soothe themselves later. Psychologists call this "shame-repair." Accumulated memories of shame-repair give our children the resilience and strength to deal with experiences of shame later in life.

How shaming is used

The child's vulnerability to shame is what makes her so open to being controlled. Shaming is probably the most commonly used discipline method.

Shaming involves a comment or a look that says there is something wrong with the child. Rather than a complaint about the child's behavior or its effect on others, shaming is a comment about the child as a person. By describing the child in negative terms, shaming strikes at the heart of how she views and feels about herself. Shaming has hit its mark when the child shrinks, hangs her head and retreats quietly with eyes downcast. The unwanted behavior has stopped—at least while the shamer is watching.

Incredibly, even babies are shamed for their behavior. They are told they are naughty or difficult for crying or for not falling sleep. While they do not understand the caustic words, they certainly pick up on the tone.

How shame affects children's behavior

Children view themselves according to what we feel about them and what we say to them. As parents we have the greatest power to shape their self-image.

What they are told about themselves is taken deeply to heart, and it becomes the script for their unfolding personality.

That's how shaming becomes a self-fulfilling prophecy. The more you tell a child (through your words or through the way you look at him) that he is bad or naughty, the more that's what he'll become.

Shame is a powerful emotion

Shaming hurts worse than physical punishment. While physical pain passes, it is the shame that sticks, and once it is recorded in the mind, it is not easy to erase. Children are enormously vulnerable to shame. It is shattering for a child to be ignored or told they are bad. Children take shame far deeper into their hearts than many parents realize—and in doing so, their confidence and trust are eroded.

Why we shame our kids

For moments after it is meted out, shaming produces "good" behavior. This small reward reinforces the shamer's enthusiasm for shaming. As we will see later, rebellion, the child's retribution for having been humiliated, tends to come later—long after the shamer's temporary victory. Few people recognize that the child's subsequent acting out is a direct response to the violation felt at hands of the shamer. Mistakenly, shaming is often spared any responsibility for the behavioral chaos it creates.

And so, the role of shame as the prime inducement for good behavior goes unchallenged. Many people have asked me, "If it wasn't for shame, why would anyone behave well?" The belief that without shame we would not be considerate to each other is pervasive, but if we are considerate toward each other only because we'd be ashamed to do otherwise, what does that say about humanity? Doesn't that sound a bit grim to you? Could respectful and caring behavior ever be the offspring of empathy, rather than shame? Is it possible for our children to develop empathy-based, rather than shame-based considerateness? You bet it is (see Chapter 13).

If so many of us are convinced that shame must be at the epicenter of socialization, it's because most of us were shamed into good behavior, frequently if not daily, by our parents and our teachers. Our reluctance to believe in empathy as a motive instead of shame, says a lot about how we were related to as children and how our parents and our forebears were raised. Shaming is the familiar method we cling to, like an old and trusty pair of shoes.

What does shaming look and sound like?

Shaming of children comes in many guises. On the following page is a list of some of the most widely used forms of shaming; you will probably find most of these quite familiar. You probably have had some of these things said to you or done to you as a child, and perhaps you have even shamed your own child in some of these ways. It is not an exhaustive list. You might be able to think of more examples.

The cost of shaming

Imagine your child as a large tree covered in myriad, glittering fairy lights. Each time you shame your child, one of these little lights is switched off and your child's radiance is reduced. Your child might do as she is told, she might say please and thank you at all the right times, but she is no longer fully there with you. Without necessarily being conscious of this choice, the child says: You can have my good behavior, but you will not have the real *me*. Children instinctively resist feeling controlled, and when they must give in, a part of them retreats inside. The full spectrum of their emotionality fades from view, while only the apparently pleasing colors remain on display. Something of great value is lost from the parenting relationship, and the parent-child connection is weakened.

Shame makes us feel diminished, inhibited and helpless. It speaks to us through the inner voices that tell us "Don't be silly," or "You're just being ridiculous," a replay of whatever shaming messages we received as children. Sometimes we even repeat those shaming messages to ourselves right out loud.

Many of the wonderful things we would love to do are nipped in the bud by shame. There is the guy who would like to ask a girl out but freezes in shame, afraid he'll appear too needy. Or the child who, having been chided by his father for crying, learns to cover up by acting cool and aloof. A woman longs to be gregarious, to go dancing with friends and have fun, but she holds back: as an adolescent she had been shamed for being flirtatious, and any attempts at independence were castigated. A man secretly longs to express some creative or artistic impulse but keeps cutting himself off from it because his father had shamed him for any displays of his more sensitive nature. Another man finds it excruciatingly difficult to complain if he ever receives inadequate service, such as in a restaurant, hotel, bank or government office. As a result, his inability to protest leaves him wide open to being taken advantage of. As a child he had been continually shamed for complaining, while often being patted on the back for taking adversity on the chin.

SHAMING TYPE	EXAMPLES
Direct shaming	Shame on you! You ought to be ashamed of yourself!
The put-down	You naughty boy! You're acting like a spoilt child! You selfish brat! You crybaby!
Moralizing	Good little boys don't act that way. You've been a bad little girl.
Age-based expectation	Grow up! Stop acting like a baby! Big boys don't cry.
Gender-based expectation	Toughen up! Don't be a sissy! That's not very lady-like! Girls don't do that sort of thing.
Competency-based expectation	You're hopeless! Loser! You're not even trying!
Comparison	Why can't you be more like your brother? None of the other kids are acting like you. What are people going to think of you?
Ignoring	Turning away in exasperation. Acting like the child is not there. Walking away from the child as if to leave them behind.
The shaming look	Rolling one's eyes. Shaking one's head and muttering to oneself. Glaring at the child, looking at the child with disgust.

These are just a few common and painful examples of how shame cripples our ability to be ourselves and to freely and openly relate to others. Can you think of some of the positive things you would love to do but hesitate to do because of shame? Perhaps there is a job or a promotion you want to shoot for, a change in career, a person you are attracted to and long to connect with, a part of yourself that wants to be expressed and shared with others? But you keep holding back, hamstrung by a suspicion that maybe you are not good enough, that you should not aim too high. You did not invent your shame on your own; it was given to you by others, probably a long time ago. Shame is the greatest impediment to joy, love and personal fulfillment. A shame epidemic, generated through cultural attitudes toward child discipline, robs so many communities of some of the greatest potential talents and contributions of its members.

Many people who have sat with me in counseling sessions have said, if tears come to their eyes, "Oh, I am just being silly"; sometimes they even apologize for crying. This painfully self-censoring voice is a reproduction of others' voices—the voices of whoever shamed them for crying as children. Most of us were so often shamed for showing our feelings as babies and children that we become profoundly embarrassed if our feelings come to the surface in front of others.

Shame makes us inwardly preoccupied: we get consumed with secret, inner dialogue: What's wrong with me? How can I get them to like me? How can I stop them from seeing my awful faults? Shaming has this in common with corporal punishment: by making us so busy with self-doubt and self-reproach, it gets in the way of empathy. The more we shame our children, the more ashamed they become—and the more their capacity for empathy suffers.

The road from shame to fury is often straight and short. Psychologists have uncovered a strong link between shame and outrage; they call it "shame rage" or "humiliated fury." No child—or adult, for that matter—takes suppression or humiliation kindly. The angry retort too often comes later, and is inappropriately aimed at innocent and unrelated victims. The more a child is shamed, at home or at school, the more raw and open is the shame wound, which leads to more hypersensitivity to slights and taunts. Children who suffer heavily from shame can be highly reactive, explosive in their anger and are prone to taking their rage out on others without even realizing why. Scratch the surface a little and you'll find in the most intimidating of school bullies a long and agonizing story of shame and fear. Anyone serious about combating the incidence of bullying at school or in the workplace must put the shaming of children at the top of their list. Along with corporal punishment, shame is a major culprit in the creation of bullying behavior.

EXERCISE

Pay close attention to your self-talk. Notice whenever you say something to yourself that begins with "Don't be a...," or "You are being too..." Listen inwardly to the way you might criticize yourself for having an emotion or a desire. Perhaps you are critical of your sense of humor, your temper, your anxieties, your grief, something or someone you long for, a desire to ask others for help, or about some aspect of your sexuality.

Take careful note of any shaming things you say to yourself inside and write some of these statements down. Then, for each one of these shaming statements, ask yourself these questions.

- How did I first learn to say those things to myself?
- Where did I first hear that said to me?
- Did anyone ever look at me in a way that made me feel those things?
- Who were the people who most often shamed me? A parent? A schoolteacher? A brother or sister? Other kids at school?
- What kinds of things was I shamed for, and what, exactly, was said to me?
- How do I feel these shaming statements have affected my moods, my relationships and the way I feel about myself today?
- Have I ever shamed my own child in ways similar to those in which I was shamed?

Talk with your partner about the things you discover by doing this exercise. If your partner is willing, do the exercise together. This will help you to understand each other better, and by listening to each other with compassion you might be able to help each other heal old shame wounds. Support and encourage each other to give more freedom to those parts of yourselves that may have been suppressed through shame. This mutual support and healing will help you to avoid passing your own shame onto your child.

But not all the shamed join the ranks of bullies. Those who inherit a softer or more introverted nature wear the yoke of shame in other ways. Easily intimidated and victimized, they fall prey to their more aggressive peers. They sabotage themselves, cause harm to themselves or become prone to illness. Some others adapt by adopting a compulsively good boy or good girl personality, they are obligingly servile, unassuming, self-effacing, stretching to the sycophantic.

Still others turn to obsessive perfectionism and can be self-deprecating to the point of paralysis. Playfulness and productivity suffer; joy remains out of reach. Different kinds of shaming interact with our genetics to produce a rainbow of reactions to the wound—but no matter which way you look at it, shaming is destructive, it brings great suffering to our lives and is responsible for much needless conflict and social isolation.

THE PSYCHOLOGY OF SHAME

Children who have experienced more verbal aggression at home, are more at risk of aggressive, antisocial and even delinquent behavior. In his book *The Psychology of Shame*, a review of clinical and research findings, clinical psychologist Gershen Kaufman, PhD, identifies shame as a major cause of anxiety, personality disorders, compulsive disorders, phobias—especially social phobias—and sexual dysfunction. Shame is also strongly associated with addictive disorders and eating disorders. The strongest link established by researchers is between shame and depression.

The cost of shame to relationships

Shaming alienates your child from you—its sting adds distance and damages trust. Each incident of shaming puts a tear in your connection, and if shame accumulates in your child's mind, it ruptures the bond between you.

It is shame that prevents us from opening up emotionally to our partners and our friends, since there are so many feelings that shame tells us we are not supposed to feel. Our connection to the people who matter most suffers as a result of our emotional anonymity. Shame alienates us from each other and leaves us walled in and isolated.

Shame is one of the weedy vines whose tentacles choke out empathy, obstructing its growth toward the sun. Shortness of empathy robs relationships of their vitality.

Pride is not always a healthy alternative

Having intuited the corrosive impact of shame and wishing to steer clear of it, it might be tempting to overcorrect by leaning toward the opposite pole, instead showering our children in praise: "How wonderful you are, you are such a star!" and, in the words of that stirring old song by Tina Turner and Jimmy Barnes, "You're simply the best."

But as we'll see in later pages, praise, which sometimes can appear more like massaging the child's ego, can bring problems of its own. Pride in ourselves is a delicious enough feeling, but is not quite like self-love. Self-love and self-acceptance reach deeper into the soul than pride about this or that positive attribute because self-love enables us to accept and, indeed, have a sense of humor about, even those aspects of ourselves that aren't so great. Conditional pride, on the other hand, requires achievement, or positive attributes, and at times it can be unforgiving of failure.

And yet, have you noticed that pride—in ourselves, in each other, in our children—can at times be a beautiful, shared and heart-opening emotion when freely expressed without expectations? How do we tell the difference between generous pride in our children, versus manipulative, ego-stroking pride—the kind that is calculated to sweet-talk the child to please us again?

If you are confused, I don't blame you! I confess I don't always know, when I show my daughter how proud of her I feel, if my underlying motivation is to get her to produce more goodies. I like to ask myself: can I also be proud of my daughter when she is not, for instance, getting good grades or being "well behaved"? Since the way we affect each other springs from our *intent*, then there is no substitute for ongoing and honest self-inquiry. I would like to differentiate between *appreciation* (healthy pride) and *conditional pride*. Healthy pride or appreciation is not competitive; it does not grade, keep score or compare one child to another. True joy is free from "better than." In Chapter 14 we will look at ways to express healthy pride in—or appreciation of—our children, non-manipulatively. But in the meantime, let's see how we can encourage our children to consider the impact of their behavior, without resorting to shaming them.

What, then, is the healthy alternative to shame?

Humility is entirely different to shame. It flows from emotional security and enables us to be realistic and honest about our limitations. Humility is what allows us to acknowledge when we have things to learn, when we could do better—without feeling deflated or less worthy of love. In shame we feel diminished and we hang our heads, whereas in humility we remain upright and interested in others.

Shame makes us avoid relationships, makes us want to hide. Humility connects us with others. In fact, it attracts love to us. Haven't you noticed that when someone is open and humble, you want to be with them?

Humility reflects an unconscious recognition that love shines too strongly to be swayed by our "good" or "bad" qualities, and this is what helps us to recognize our limitations with grace.

Many times over we will want to show our children when their behavior impinges on others and when we need them to be more aware and considerate. Shaming is a blunt instrument for this task, and stands in contrast with engendering in our children a healthy humility. We will take a closer look, in Chapter 14, at how to foster considerate behavior from our children by inspiring their humility, rather than by imposing shame.

The guilt trip

What is guilt?

Guilt and shame come from the same family of self-conscious emotions, that is, emotions that cause us to shrink, turn inward and become preoccupied with ourselves. However, there are key differences between guilt and shame. Whereas shame is a loss of self-respect, guilt is a morbid anticipation of punishment.

Guilt is the gnawing sensation that, having done something to offend, you are awaiting sentencing. Whereas shame makes us slink away into the shadows, guilt makes us reach out, quite frantically at times, to repair damage we have caused, not out of concern for the injured parties, but so we can be pardoned and avoid any penalty. Guilt is the altogether selfish desire to be forgiven, to be let off the hook, to be relieved of obligation. Guilt is probably the most self-centered of all emotions, as it is not driven by a real concern for the wellbeing of others.

The emotion of guilt and the behavior it inspires do not deserve the merit they are often given. Guilt gains credibility by masquerading as its opposite: remorse. Although guilt and remorse are often felt alongside one another, they should not be confused with each other; they are quite separate and different. When we feel genuine remorse, we are deeply sorrowful for any pain we may have caused another person. Remorse is empathetic, we feel hurt for the other person and we reach out caringly to repair any damage we may have caused. Guilt reaches out for acquittal, it begs for leniency. Remorse asks for neither: it seeks to heal, to mend what has been broken.

What is guilt tripping?
When we lay a guilt trip on a child, we are trying to make the child beholden to us, as if she owes us something. The guilt trip is an investment that causes the child to feel indebted to us—and we aim to collect our dues, the child's good deeds or his non-demanding behavior—at a future date. The guilt tripper holds the keys to the child's release from anxiety, so he can count on the child feeling duty-bound. Weighed down by guilt, the child will promise to be good until we elect to forgive her or otherwise release her from her liability. Guilt is a very powerful method of control.

The guilt-ridden child will work very, very hard to please, but this is not an expression of their care for you. They do so because they are desperately trying to be released from their sentence of guilt, the ever-present threat of punishment.

Guilt tripping requires a martyr
In order to lay a guilt trip on a child, you need to play the "woe is me" card with finesse. The guilt trip involves some measure of wallowing, until you have seduced your child into assuming responsibility for your pain. If you are to master the guilt trip there is a certain degree of artistry involved, and some of us have developed it into a fine art form.

Some examples of guilt tripping:

- ✞ "After all the things I do for you…"
- ✞ "How could you do this to me?"
- ✞ "You children make me so-o-o-o-o tired."
- ✞ "Just wait until you grow up and have your own children; then you'll know what I go through."
- ✞ "If you really cared about me, you would do this and not that…."
- ✞ "Do you know there are people starving and you won't eat my cooking?"
- ✞ "If you knew the pain I had to go through to give birth to you."
- ✞ "When I was your age, I had to walk two miles to school every day, and I had only one toy."
- ✞ "Do you think money grows on trees?"

In some of these examples, the message is: "I am hurt, and it is all up to you to make me feel better." The parent's pain is on display and the child is expected to be the healer. In other instances, the message is: "You are asking me for more than I had when I was your age, and more than I want to give to you. How dare you."

Guilt trips are powerful

When the arrow of guilt finds its target, it gives parents great power over the child, but it is an indirect and manipulative power. Guilt operates covertly, but its toxic effects are soon evident. Guilt does not help us to connect to each other, it sours relationships. The child who has been saddled with guilt will want to break free of the guilt-tripping parent; guilt tripping is a recipe for the parents' eventual loneliness.

The effect of guilt on your child

The guilt trip is a role reversal. The parent becomes the child, the one who is helpless and emotionally overwhelmed. The child is expected to grow up and become the adult in the relationship, taking care of the wounded parent's feelings by trying to be less demanding, more grateful, or whatever the parent seems to be fishing for.

There are few things more disempowering than guilt, and many children collapse under its weight. Their shoulders sag with obligation and they lose their ability to assert themselves. When children are made to feel as if they are a burden or a pain to their parents, they walk through life as if treading on eggshells while carrying the weight of the world. The light of childhood is extinguished—as they grow up prematurely, stifled by an exaggerated responsibility for how others feel.

It is not unusual for the martyr parent to lose the child's respect; the child senses the parent's weakness and insecurity. Guilt tripping arouses a powerful resentment in children, who detest the manipulation and the expectation placed on them to wear the parent's pain. They hate their parents depending on them emotionally, when it should be the other way around.

One thing is for sure: guilt tripping does not produce more love in the world. It has no more power to elicit real empathy than corporal punishment or shaming. It does not lead to a more empathetic connection, but produces quite the opposite.

Why we use guilt

In a nutshell, when any of us have learned backhanded ways to express our needs, it's because we were not allowed to be assertive as children. We were not allowed to strongly express our wishes, feelings and opinions, to ask for attention openly and directly, to say what we wanted. It was not enough for our parents or caregivers to set boundaries with us—we were actually admonished for daring to have wants and needs. When assertion is squashed, it merely goes underground and finds devious ways to emerge.

Self-assertion is the antidote to guilt tripping. When you notice an urge to guilt trip your child, that's a sign that you have a need or a boundary that you are having difficulty expressing. It may even be a need that should be met in an adult relationship—attention, understanding and support—not through your child.

EXERCISE

Next time you hear yourself guilt tripping someone, stop. See if you can identify your need and express it directly. Ask yourself: What is it I actually need right now? Is it care? Is it attention? Is it for someone to respect my boundaries? Then, turn this around. Instead of using guilt, see if you can express your wishes in a more direct and assertive manner. It is OK to need what you need, but using guilt actually prevents you from being heard and understood, and thus from receiving what it is you need. In Chapter 14 we will look at strategies that will help you to do this.

12

Rewards, Praise and Appreciation

The problem with positive discipline

Slowly but surely, most parents around the world are walking away from child punishment—at least the harsher varieties of it. When, in May 2007, the New Zealand government prohibited its citizens from hitting their children, it was a decision that received near-unanimous support in parliament: in a 121-seat parliament, 113 voted in favor of the ban. In fact, social surveys in many countries are revealing a decline of old punishing ways. An evolution in parenting is unfolding before our eyes, but as punishment, shaming and guilt tripping become more and more distasteful to our collectively opening hearts, a vacuum is being created. If not through fear and shame, how will we guide our children's behavior?

A new means of controlling children's behavior has emerged from the rubble. Researchers and academics like it, and it is spreading like wildfire. The era of punishment and shaming is over. Today we praise our children and reward them for their good behavior. We give our children ice cream if they are good, gold stars if they eat all their greens, little smiley stickers if they do their homework, money if they get good grades at school, extra time watching television if they clean up their rooms and pats on the head if they say please and thank you at the right intervals. The home is a busy marketplace where we barter with our kids, wheeling and dealing prizes and privileges for their good conduct.

The sting of shame has been supplanted by a new tactic—honey to the bee. Praise, approval and an appeal to the child's pride are our new bargaining chips. "Good boy!" and "Atta girl!" is what our children now hear when they comport themselves to our liking. Psychologists and educators have elevated the strategy into complex star charts, and the growing constellation on the corkboard shows the child what great progress he is making. A child's stellar performance is within reach of any parent well versed in this modern psychological device. At school, the weights and measures of a child's worth come in a steady stream of As, Bs and pluses, with the aim of teasing them to greater heights. These days we don't goad, we coax. We don't coerce, we seduce.

Praising and rewarding envelop us and, like the fish who can't see water, we don't notice them, we take these methods for granted. Praise and rewards flow from us like second nature. The more high-tech reward systems (such as school grades and star charts) are celebrated, are sworn by, are omnipresent, but they are seldom held up to scrutiny.

Why rewarding and praising are so popular

Since rewarding and praising good performance became the default mode of behavioral correction, it has brought great relief to parents and teachers who'd rather not punish, blame and/or threaten. This seems like a more enlightened and kind-hearted approach. The praising parent hopes to steer the child's behavior without worrying about wounding or alienating him. Praising and rewarding are often done carefully and thoughtfully by parents with the best of intentions.

A large throng of researchers has given rewards and praise an official green light. There is today a ton of evidence demonstrating that you can modify a child's behavior with far greater efficacy by rewarding them than you could have ever hoped by punishing. It is a very promising system, and to behavioral psychologists it is the goose that laid the golden egg. Sound rosy?

So, what's wrong with praise and rewards? On the surface, nothing at all. But as with any instrument, we should understand its limits and know what it can and can't do for us; the pitfalls of praise and rewards are what its advocates seldom tell us about.

Praise is conditional

When we praise our children for meeting our wishes and deny them praise at other times, they experience love as conditional. If you are going to use rewards and praise to shape your child's behavior, the power of this method rests on your withholding the goodies until your child delivers. The highs that come from receiving positive strokes are sweet enough, but the cost is that children feel defeated when the strokes dry up.

Praise and rewards are addictive

When praise and rewards are tied to our child's compliant behavior or good performance, they are the kinder face of authoritarian parenting. When kids learn to depend on praise and rewards they crumble when these don't come, and then go fishing for your compliments. Kids who learn to expect praise end up doing things to impress, to gain recognition and flattery, rather than doing things for themselves, guided by the joy of doing what they love. In order to gain your approval, they lose their connection with themselves. There is a trade-off between the child being a pleasing person and being a person who is authentic or real. As with any addiction, the child's enthusiasm and motivation collapse when the rewards aren't there—these are the withdrawal symptoms. And that is precisely what gives the praiser and rewarder his power: "You want my approval? Earn it."

What happens to children who feel a deficit of true connection with their parents but who are plied with praise for dazzling performance and for pleasing the adults? The craving for approval that results can bear all the hallmarks of addiction. Everywhere there are adults who are heavily dependent on appearing radiant in their successes, on outshining others and claiming rewards. Though they can be highly motivated and accomplished individuals, failure to impress can stir these individuals to rage, self-loathing and depression. Think of the retired executive who feels meaningless out of the boardroom, the celebrity who becomes miserable when the show is over, or any child who becomes crestfallen when he is not ahead of the pack.

We should never underestimate the despair and the anguish that strike those who are addicted to flattery when their limelight fades away. Nothing is more important to our wellbeing than a fulfilling connection to ourselves and to others—based on honesty rather than on positive strokes. Praise and prizes are a poor substitute for more sustaining kinds of human connection.

Praise pumps up conditional pride
Well-praised children feel good about themselves, so long as they are performing well, that is. But feeling good *about* yourself is not the same as feeling good *in* yourself. Praised children's good feelings come from being pleasing to others and getting the recognition they have come to expect. The good feelings are based on whatever attribute earned them some approval. That can be a nice experience, no doubt about it. But should our children become dependent on positive strokes in order to feel happy? Isn't it more important for children to derive their good feelings from doing the things they are passionate about, from playing and creating, from sharing intimate moments with family and friends, from being in nature, and from caring for others? These are just a few of the most healthy and fulfilling sources of inner pleasure and wellbeing, and they have nothing to do with flattery and positive strokes.

The good behavior doesn't last
Once we embark on an external reward system to manage our child's behavior, we risk becoming imprisoned by our own reward scheme. It is a principle of psychology that once the rewards stop flowing, the rewarded behavior will become extinguished. This is called "behavioral extinction," and researchers have found that the good behavior does not endure if it is driven by goodies and prizes. If you think about it, this makes sense. Why would you keep doing something that doesn't come from your heart if the enticements—the pay that

motivated you—are cut off? If you want to rely on the external rewards method, you'd better be prepared to keep those gold stars coming.

When praise is slimy

Praise is seductive. It can feel really, really good, good enough to make us work hard to get some. Who doesn't like praise from time to time? But praise can also feel cloying and condescending. So often, praise contains a hook, and is laden with the expectation that the recipient will be nice. The good boy with impeccable table manners draws a chorus of accolades and "Oh, how sweet" from his adult fans, a star power he will rapidly lose if he strays from his self-control. The girl who obeys her parents, doesn't complain or make demands, is acclaimed by family and neighbors. Flattery gets us far with children, but the flatterer skates on thin ice. As children wise up to the manipulation, they increasingly resent what they need to do for us in order to score points. Some begin to show their disgust for this as toddlers, some start feeling repulsed when they reach teenage years.

I think you'd understand if I said to you, "What a good reader you are," and patted you on the back each time you read another chapter in my book. I might even give you a "Smart Reader" pin if you finish the whole book by the end of this month. How would this make you feel? Would you feel patronized? A tad angry?

When rewards are a shortcut

With external rewards as your behavior modification arsenal, you don't have to take the trouble to find out why your child is not behaving the way you'd like. You just offer her a reward for changing her behavior, and presto.

Take a toddler who refuses to go to sleep at her bedtime. Perhaps you could persuade her to curl up quietly and resign herself to the darkness by trading her favorite treat, a hot chocolate drink, say, promised to her for the morning. Who knows? It might work. But what if it means overlooking your child's need for connection? Have you asked why your child can't ease into sleep? Is she afraid? Is she stressed from something that happened at preschool today? Might she be feeling cut off, anxious or insecure? What if all she needs is to have those feelings recognized and to be held close until she settles into slumber? If this is true, then your child might feel even more cut off and alone as she bravely strives to put herself to sleep for that early-morning hot chocolate. The promised reward glosses over the very thing that would have helped her to fall asleep happily: feeling heard, and connected to you.

Think of a young violin student who has a slump in his progress and loses interest in his violin practice. You could get him to willingly draw out his agony and stick to it a while longer by giving him a dollar each time he dutifully drones up and down the scales. Sure, this might work for a while, but that dollar will never get him to love the violin, in fact, it may further sour his experience of it as he lines his pockets. The dollar is a shortcut. Why not ask him why he doesn't like playing the violin any more? What if he has discovered he'd much rather be playing the saxophone? What if he gets no pleasure from the style of music he is made to practice? Is he languishing in classical when he would rather be learning jazz or bluegrass? What if his music teacher is mean and he doesn't like going to her any more? What if he is being teased by other kids for playing what they judge to be an uncool instrument? What if he feels lonely when he sits and practices by himself but would regain his enthusiasm if someone played duets with him? What if he feels frustrated about the lull in his progress, and if he could just let it all out and be heard, plus take a break for a few days, it might rekindle his will to go on?

Think of all the possible things that your child might need to share with you, or might need your support with. All these possible scenarios and more are overlooked when you reach too soon for that dollar in your purse, and the opportunity to connect with your child in the most helpful way is lost.

Rewards and praise kill authenticity

The more children are seduced by rewards and praise, the more they learn to act according to what is scripted for them so they can win our applause, like the child who sweetly spouts please and thank you but comes across as rehearsed, contrived, not genuine. The child's natural self is obscured by a made-to-order, phony self. Praising adults risk training an approval seeker.

What makes us feel truly connected with each other is emotional authenticity. This realness is sacrificed in our striving to create a well-trained and pleasing child. When their good behavior is contrived to win our approval, it can cause us and our children to feel estranged from each other. To put it bluntly: Do we want an act, or the real thing?

Can we get by without rewards and praise?

Probably not. Most people, myself included, gladly get paid for our work. Most of us probably wish the pay were bigger and better. Can any of us seriously claim we wouldn't love to be told from time to time what a wonderful job we are doing? If it weren't for the moolah and the recognition, would we even get out of bed in the morning?

Your answer to that question depends on your view of what makes us, as human beings, tick. How self-serving are we at our core? Is self-interest the only thing—even the main thing—that drives us?

What about the millions of hours freely given by volunteers for causes they care about? What about the growing number of people who would rather do a line of work that they love, who would rather be their own boss, or only do work that is rich in personal meaning and purpose, even if this means earning less? Musicians, artists, small-business people, doctors and nurses who work in disadvantaged parts of the world, lawyers in public service—the list is endless. A rapidly growing social trend toward deliberate downshifting reflects the dawning realization that relationships—and the time to have them—are far more rewarding than the shiniest material goods and the most glowing praise. The happiest, most fulfilled people are those whose work brings them spiritual meaning in line with their hearts. Status, fame or handsome pay packets are powerfully magnetic, but never fulfilling. There is no prize in this world that rewards us like connection does: connection to our own hearts, following our own bliss, and connecting deeply and honestly with one another. There are some types of reward that foul up our interpersonal connections, others that enhance them. We will look at the difference between these two distinct types of reward a little further on, but first let's look more closely at why rewards and praise appear to work so well.

DID YOU KNOW?

That in the world of business, better pay does not necessarily produce better work, and in fact, it can often *reduce* the quality of work? Almost everybody has believed the idea that increased salary packages, monetary bonuses and similar enticements lead to greater performance in the workplace, but while this might be true up to a point, it is largely a myth. It might surprise you to discover that the "more pay = better work" fallacy has been debunked by 50 years of scientific analysis. The best quality work and productivity are not motivated by money or material rewards. Hard to believe? Watch this short talk by lawyer, business analyst, former White House staffer and author Daniel Pink: ted.com/talks/dan_pink_on_motivation.html.

When praise and rewards succeed

Have you ever watched children swinging frantically at a birthday piñata, and when at last it has been burst open, they hurl themselves at the scattered sweets as if it was their last meal? Kids strive. They compete against each other—if we set them up to. They go all-out for prizes, gold stars, the tick of approval from the teacher's pen.

Children try especially hard to please if they don't feel emotionally secure. For children who feel alone, neglected or afraid, rewards and praise are a matter of emotional survival. If love fails them, pride will do. Children can be quite vulnerable to the shaping forces of praise and reward; they behave themselves in exchange for some approval. If we agree to measure no more than temporary behavior change prompted by external rewards (or enduring changes maintained by *endless* external rewards), then this method passes muster—and it has been given shining report cards by an impressive pedigree of behaviorist researchers.

Where rewards and praise fail

The main problem with this method rests with the superficiality of the objectives, and of the results. We can tinker with children's behavior by regulating their diet of rewards and praise, but this will not reach their hearts. Praise and external rewards are not all that meaningful; they do not bring about a fundamental, personal shift in what children care about. Let's have a look at what that means.

In his book *Punished by Rewards: The Trouble with Gold Stars, Incentive Plans, A's, Praise, and Other Bribes*, psychologist Alfie Kohn talks about the less acknowledged studies that expose the fragile underbelly of manipulative tactics. In one study for instance, an American fast-food chain wishing to make a name for itself by sponsoring a literacy drive, offered school kids food vouchers for reading books. At first this program appeared to be a runaway success, and children's appetite for reading soared. But as it turned out, although they were reading more books, they were picking smaller and less-challenging books, their comprehension levels were falling, and they were reading fewer books in the unrewarded situation (at home). The junk-food rewards program earned some impressive points, but as far as helping children to love reading, this method was entirely impotent. The children weren't reading for reading's sake—they were reading for greasy treats. It would be worth remembering that rewards used in this way create no love.

Again and again Kohn shows us studies on the impact of external rewards in the classroom, finding that children tend to avoid challenges, they play it safe, and they tend to do the minimum required in order to claim the coveted reward. Children's creativity suffers under these conditions, and the *quality* of their work is impoverished. Education based on rewards and coercion loses much of its depth. Nothing produces a passion for study and a consistency of good learning outcomes like the power of love, that is, when children are allowed to learn the things they find *intrinsically* rewarding.

Two kinds of reward

Earlier on I mentioned that there are two very different types of reward. One is intrinsic, the other external. External rewards are used to encourage a person to do what he doesn't want to do. Examples include giving a child money for doing his homework, ice cream for being well-behaved or extra time in front of the television for sharing his toys nicely with friends. All these goodies and privileges, external to the task itself, would not have been thought necessary if the task had been attractive or meaningful to the child.

Examples of external rewards

Here are just a few examples. You may be able to think of more.

- ✞   Saying to the child, "Good boy," "Good girl."
- ✞   Giving the child food treats, money or extra privileges, such as more time in front of the television.
- ✞   Giving the child our conditional approval or affection.

External rewards and praise work—well, sort of

The first thing to say about these external rewards is that they work, like clockwork in fact. You can train or seduce a child into behaving the way you want by supplying them with a pat on the back, a "good boy," a piece of candy. In other words, you can certainly change a child's behavior with the promise of external rewards. But external rewards do not have the power to change a child's heart. As with the violin-playing child mentioned earlier, a dollar per practice might encourage perseverance and his technique will probably improve, but we mustn't fool ourselves that this external reward can help the child to love the violin, or to play it with genuine feeling.

External rewards can sway your child to do good things, but they don't help your child to mean them. In other words, external rewards cannot improve your child's emotional intelligence. Bribes do not create genuine, heartfelt connections between people, they don't create love or genuine care. And in the classroom, as Alfie Kohn explains, external rewards can temporarily reinforce some behaviors, but they can never ever reinforce *understanding*.

External rewards are used because they persuade children to do something they don't want to do or something they don't like. But if they love what they are doing, if it has meaning for the child, you don't need to make deals and offer prizes in order to encourage them. Similarly, when your child is feeling most secure in his connection to you, he is far more likely to listen to you and to be considerate and helpful because of his love for you rather than for rewards. Love and caring for those we feel close to is *intrinsically* rewarding.

What external rewards can't give you

Can external rewards teach your child lessons in morality? Jellybeans awarded for "please" and "thank you" can certainly teach your child manners, but they cannot possibly teach your child why we have good manners. I don't mean the ideology behind manners—any one can learn that—I mean external rewards cannot hope to give your child a genuine, heartfelt feeling of care and respect for others. A chart full of gold stars teaches your child none of the important things about relationships.

While your child is busy maneuvering for the gold star or the ice cream, he is not connecting to a feeling of care for you and he is certainly not connecting to you—he is just after what he can get from you.

Stop to think about this. Are you prepared to settle for this? Wouldn't you prefer that your child be considerate and helpful toward you because she loves you, because it is intrinsically rewarding to act respectfully toward you?

Wait a minute... is that even possible?

Do you believe that it's possible?

What is truly rewarding?

My father would often tell me how his high school history teacher would keep all his students, even the most unacademic ones, on the edge of their seats by weaving ancient stories so compellingly that you could hear a pin drop in his class. My father still remembers much of his high school history lessons in great detail. No one, not even the rowdiest kids, had to be cajoled to pay attention in this class, or praised for being attentive. This was the only teacher in whose class the children would behave so attentively, and he offered no gold stars for good behavior. No magic was involved here; the teacher was simply committed to making the kids' lessons fascinating.

Many times I have observed little children sharing food with each other, or comforting friends who get hurt, without receiving any praise or immediate compensation. So, what it is that makes children apply themselves in the classroom or offer spontaneous acts of kindness without any recompense whatsoever?

Human connection is the greatest reward, and, ultimately, the only truly fulfilling reward. It is a reward that does not diminish us when we seek it, but makes us stronger and more loving. In contrast, material rewards and praise are bleached-out versions of love at best, at worst, merely symbols of love. They are the junk food of human relations: marginally nutritious but ultimately not sustaining. You can collect trophies, such as gold stars and high grades, but these are not what will bring the biggest smile to your face when, in old age, you look back over your life.

Intrinsic reward also comes from doing the things we most love to do because this connects us to the joy we have inside us and because when we do our heart's bidding, our contribution to society is at its best. The human brain has an internal biochemical reward mechanism, designed to make you want to do things that are good for you, the things that bring meaning to your life, again and again. Accordingly, if we want our children to work solidly at school, then right from the start we should make sure we connect their curricula to their personal interests and passions. As much as possible children's activities in school and elsewhere should be chosen to match their personal loves, so what they spend their days doing is what is intrinsically rewarding to them.

Toddlers and children love to join in and help us with many of our daily activities. Remembering the principle of intrinsic reward, you can invite your child's joyful participation by giving her things to do that she finds pleasurable. Shopping in a supermarket is one example of a weekly activity that for many parents of toddlers is an ordeal. Bored toddlers and busy parents are an incendiary mix. So why not make shopping fun, even exciting, for your toddler? Maybe you can sing a song together as you push the trolley around the aisles. Why not ask your toddler to help you find some of the items you are looking for? As she gets a little older, you can even send her on missions to find items for you on her own. You can also turn chores such as picking up a roomful of toys, getting dressed or brushing teeth into an intrinsically rewarding game by turning it into a race (see who can pick up the most toys, or see who can finish getting dressed first), or perhaps there is a special tooth brushing song you can sing together (or hum, when your child has a mouthful of foam). There are endless ways to win your child's cheerful cooperation if you commit to making her activities intrinsically rewarding for her. You can invent your own ways to turn everyday jobs into games with your child, turning struggles into fun for both of you.

By far the greatest and most enduring intrinsic reward is felt when we connect with one another in ways that are rich with feeling. A deep and fulfilling connection comes from parents and children listening carefully to each other, and from mutual honesty. If we want our children to behave respectfully, we need to be good listeners to them, to be open with them and to spend time with them in order to nurture and maintain our bond. When the connection is strong between you, considerate behavior will follow. That's because it feels immediately, automatically and intrinsically rewarding to act lovingly toward those we feel close to. The more we nurture our connection with our children, the less need there is to think in terms of behavior control or discipline.

FIRING UP THE MIRROR NEURONS

Is it possible for children to behave lovingly and respectfully simply because it is intrinsically rewarding to do so? Definitely, especially if respectful relating has been consistently role modeled for them and if they feel heard and cared for. There is a biological basis for the pleasure that altruism brings us. Neuropsychologists have discovered mirror neurons in our brains that enable us to empathically tune in to others' feelings. When we cause someone we care about to feel good, we immediately experience some of this good feeling ourselves—our mirror neurons fire in sync with the other person's delight.

Is it ever all right to praise a child?

I certainly wouldn't wish for you as parents to constantly censor yourselves every time your heart is full of praise for your child. Many times over you will feel proud of your child; there is no reason to hold this back and everything to gain from showing it. So stay tuned; later we will look at how we can, wholeheartedly, unreservedly, non-manipulatively, express our appreciation and admiration for our children in a way that directly connects our hearts and theirs (see Chapter 14). You will see there definitely is a way, and that basically it involves what we say about our own feelings, rather than hailing our child's virtues—but more on that later.

Emotionally secure children are less interested in praise

I have noticed that children who feel secure in themselves only seem to get a mild and passing pleasure from being praised. Praise, to them, is less interesting than the good feelings they already have inside. They don't need you to butter them up. They are already feeling good in themselves, so they are not looking to you to help them feel good about themselves. Like anyone else, they do like praise if it is genuine, but they are not hanging out for it. Children who feel less secure in their emotional connections to their family are more likely to hunger for praise and are more likely to overextend themselves in order to get it.

Intrinsic rewards in education

Most schooling systems today reflect an anxious preoccupation with how to persuade children to work hard at learning. Why is education so unattractive to so many children, to the extent that persuasion is needed in the first place? All manner of points-based and highly competitive testing is imposed on children, involving external rewards for some, shame and humiliation for others. Schools classify children into winners and losers, playing them off against each other in comparative grading, to whip them into studiousness. This coercive approach is entirely unnecessary when curricula are adapted to each child's natural interests and to each child's unique learning profile. When the subjects studied are made relevant, meaningful and enjoyable, children no longer need to be pushed, shamed or seduced into study. An intrinsically rewarding learning path instills a joy of learning that, regrettably, many schools seem to lack.

New strands of education theory are emerging that urge schools to individualize curricula. Modern educators have found that we don't have to force children to learn. When children are allowed to pursue knowledge in the classroom according to their personal interests and their individual learning styles, they tackle learning with incredible gusto. The question then changes from how to persuade children to study to how to stop them when they need a rest! When class work is made intrinsically rewarding, children sometimes even *ask* for homework. We can say this today from a scientifically derived standpoint: love—not fear, shame or pride—is the greatest motivating force in all human endeavors.

DEMOCRATIC SCHOOLING

Progressive models of education give children of all ages considerable influence over what they choose to learn and how they will learn it. Teachers are partners in shaping each child's curriculum; they guide rather than dictate the children's work. This new approach to education, which is growing worldwide, is grounded in research showing that intrinsically rewarding schooling produces excellent academic results, makes school life far more pleasurable and exciting for children, and makes them far more self-motivated.

This new educational approach is yielding impressive results not only in N. America but also in Israel, Japan, the UK, Australia and New Zealand (see References).

Helping children be true to themselves

It would be both dishonest and unfair of me to condemn anyone for manipulatively using external rewards. We all use them from time to time; I catch myself doing it every now and then. Often I am unconsciously manipulative, only to realize it later. It is hard to avoid straying down that path when conditional rewards have been such a regular feature of our lives. The idea of using external rewards to manipulate behavior is so embedded in our minds that we live by and expect them.

I am not insisting that we stop praising and rewarding our children; rather, I am pointing to something else we can do that connects with our children far more meaningfully. Nor am I saying that children should learn to do all that's important without any rewards. Of course they need and deserve rewards—but the rewards that really work are about connection.

So, how can we help our children to be true to themselves, and how can we set appropriate boundaries without punishment, shaming, guilt tripping or manipulating them? The way forward is by connecting rather than controlling, which involves listening to our children's feelings, and it involves our emotional authenticity, as we will see in the next two chapters.

13

Listening

Connection is a two-way street

What are our deepest aspirations for our children? We want them to grow in physical and emotional health, with the capacity to love and be loved, to know themselves and what they want from life, and to have the confidence to go for it. We want to enjoy close and trusting bonds with them, and we want them to have clear personal boundaries and respect for others. All of these goals flow from the quality of connection we establish and maintain with our children, and connection relies on two-way communication. Later, we will look at how our own clear and emotionally authentic communication is the key to a strong, intimate and caring connection with our child, and how this authenticity is what makes interpersonal boundaries very clear (see Chapter 14). In other words, the way we speak—the way we share our thoughts and feelings—is half of what decides the quality of connection with our children. The other half is determined by the way we listen to them.

Listening is the crux of human connection. It mends broken relationships and resolves conflicts. Listening carefully to our children's feelings, from the beginning of their lives, is the best insurance for their considerate and caring behavior. Best of all, when we make the space and time to hear—and be touched by—our children's feelings, we can help them to heal from painful or traumatic experiences. Listening is crucial; it's so important not to begrudge the time, attention and compassion it requires from us. Lending an ear to our child is an investment that cannot possibly be overestimated. In terms of better relations and our children's emotional health, it yields returns tenfold.

But there are more immediate and fundamental rewards than our child's considerate behavior. When we let down our adult guard, and really let ourselves hear our children without judgment, they can touch our hearts so deeply as to transform us forever. The purity of a child's emotions can rock the very core of our being, if we let them, evoking from us more love, loyalty and courage than we thought we had. Although at times this scares us or makes us uncomfortable, our souls crave such depth of emotional connection, and our hearts grow from it. When we open up to hearing our children's voices, they enrich us and provoke us to become better persons.

How do I get my children to listen to me?

This is one of the questions most frequently asked by parents. The answer lies partly with the way we speak to our children, as we will see in the following chapter, but more fundamentally, it depends on how we have listened to them. If we want our children to listen to us, the number one step is for us to become good listeners. Children listen to us in direct proportion to how well they feel heard.

Why does my child so often not listen?

It is true that there are a number of neurological and psychological conditions that make it difficult for a small minority of children to listen to others, to focus their attention, to make eye contact, or to detect and understand others' emotions. These can include Asperger's syndrome, autism, ADHD or even hearing impairment. If it appears chronically difficult to make contact with your child, speak to your child's preschool or schoolteachers, and consider a diagnostic consultation with a child psychologist.

But when otherwise healthy children don't listen, it is often a sign that they don't feel strongly connected to us. When children's feelings are not seen, heard and responded to, they begin to detach from us emotionally. They don't reach out to us as much, and they lose interest in listening to us. Even the earliest life experiences of not feeling heard can have this effect, as we saw in earlier chapters.

So there may be many reasons why your child fails to listen to you sometimes, but the first question should be: How well does my child feel listened to? Perhaps your child has felt that some of his feelings have gone unheard. Fortunately, there is good news: when children have become used to not being heard and they behave accordingly, this can be remedied through patient listening.

More than likely you have listened to and responded warmly to your child most of the time, which has already stimulated your child's natural empathy. When your child shows a genuine interest in you, it is because you have shown an interest in him.

A child's right to receive attention

One of the most commonly heard parental laments is about how children try to get attention. So many behaviors that adults don't like are brushed off as "merely" attention-seeking devices. "Don't worry about him," we say, "he is just doing it to get attention."

When children use oblique ways to get attention, such as causing a ruckus, exaggerating or feigning their hurts, picking on other children, showing off, being coquettish—they risk being ignored or put down, as nearby adults roll their eyes in exasperation. Sometimes, this also happens to children even when they directly and openly call for the attention they crave. Instead of scorning the child, why don't we ask these questions: When a child is being manipulative, instead of direct, how did he learn to do this? How did he come to feel that he shouldn't openly ask for a hug, an answer to his question, sympathy or just to be noticed or played with?

All children begin their lives with complete frankness about their needs. Babies and toddlers reveal their longings with no compunction: what you see is what you get. If a child reaches out for attention and for warmth and she gets it, her ability to be open and directly assertive is reinforced. By begrudging our children's healthy attention-seeking behaviors, we unwittingly train them to be indirect. We leave them little room for much else, so they go for the attention they need and deserve through the back door.

Our society tends to consider children's needs for attention as a bother. No wonder children become indirect attention seekers, some even going to great lengths to fall ill or get injured in order to be noticed. Children who have too often been denied attention can become insatiable, as if no amount of limelight ever fills their cup.

Attention is life giving—a basic need and a human right. Children deserve all the attention they want.

When you wholeheartedly give a child the attention she asks for from the beginning, she soon has her fill. This is precisely what helps her to become more autonomous. As she grows, she asks for less of your attention (research shows that well-attached babies grow into children who are more independent), and when she does want attention, she asks directly, boldly and clearly.

Punished for feeling

Time and time again children are heavily reprimanded for committing the offence of crying or being angry. Let's get this straight: emotions are not bad behavior. Emotions don't hurt anyone. Suppressing children's emotions does, on the other hand, cause them harm; over time, if done repeatedly, it unbalances their brain chemistry, it stresses their immune and digestive systems, and it undermines their ability to relate to others.

Emotional censorship starts early. One of the most common things we say to a crying baby is "Shhh!" We say it soothingly, but why exactly do we shush them? Think of all the lullabies that start by telling our little babies to "hush," and "don't you cry." Have you ever paused to wonder why, in trying to comfort our babies, we ask them to be quiet? It seems as if the first thing we want is for the crying to stop—instead of connecting with our baby until the reason for crying has gone.

Instead of berating your child for feeling her feelings, give her the space to feel, and comfort and support her if she needs it. Sometimes when our children cry, sob or yell in anger we feel overwhelmed, irritated or burdened. Our children don't deserve the blame for this. When our child's emotions press our buttons, we need to own the problem. We need to somehow honor our own need for support or rest without making our children responsible.

What does listening mean?

The listening I am talking about here is not just about receiving and storing information, not just about remembering what your child said. I am talking about listening with your heart, not just with your ears. Real listening is all about feelings. All you need to be a good listener is a genuine interest in your child's emotional world. When you truly want to hear, no special skill is needed. Your child senses your interest in the tone of your voice, in your body language and the look in your eyes. You know you have listened when you feel moved. You might feel compassion, protectiveness; you might feel some pain about your child's hurts, pride or excitement about his achievements, or joy to meet his joy. Listening means letting yourself feel touched somehow, and being aware of the feelings that move through you.

What listening is not

Sometimes listening comes easy. You find yourself intently listening in stillness, without even having decided to, and there is a wonderful and natural flow between you and your child. But sometimes listening can be hard. Our children's emotions spark off our own, and in discomfort we turn away, or we try to talk them out of their feelings. Whether it's because we cannot bear to see our children in pain or because they are freely feeling something that we were never allowed to express—anger, joy, sadness, fear, passion—we block them out, we nip the connection in the bud.

I remember the embarrassment many of us felt as students of counseling psychology as we awkwardly practiced our listening skills together in the classroom, how often we appeared to be listening, while inside we were miles away, disengaged from the person speaking to us. It was often funny, and always quite confronting, to ask ourselves and each other: Are you listening right now, or just nodding your head a lot while you wait for your turn to speak? Are you actually listening, or sitting in judgment? Are you really listening, or just taking mental notes and storing facts? Are you listening, or just thinking about how you can change me?

How often we tell ourselves we are listening intently when in fact our minds are wandering elsewhere. It is unlikely that consistently good listeners exist. For most of us, good listening is a skill that comes and goes with our fluctuating moods. All counselors, psychologists and anyone in the helping professions are imperfect (and sometimes lousy) listeners, and we should be honing our listening capacity for the rest of our lives. It is humbling to note that anyone can be a profoundly good listener without any training whatsoever, since all it takes is an open heart and an interest in the other person.

Blocking empathy

It's a fact of human relationships that our capacity for listening is elusive; we lose it; we regain it; we lose it again. Sometimes it is hard to see whether we are listening so that our children really feel heard. We kid ourselves. We think we are listening when really we are avoiding contact—and then we are bewildered by and surprised at our child's frustration. It can be very useful to get a clear picture of what is listening and what is not. When our own fears, our shame, our jealousies or our emotional exhaustion get in the way, we tend to play some pretty clever games to deflect our children's communications so that their feelings won't touch us. One of the biggest reasons we avoid listening is because our children's disappointments make us feel guilty. Our evasive tactics are called "empathy blockers." Empathy blockers save us the trouble of listening, but they cost us our connection with each other.

Sometimes we use empathy blockers inadvertently because we are anxiously trying to save our children from emotional pain. Ironically, the greatest salve for our children comes from being heard, not from us trying to change how they feel. For all of these reasons, we all use empathy blockers from time to time, quite automatically and unconsciously. You could say we are all quite skilled at blocking. Here are some of the most common examples used when children become emotional.

EMPATHY BLOCKER	EXAMPLES
Downplaying	Oh, don't cry. I'm sure it's not that bad! It's not the end of the world.
Denial	There is nothing wrong; nothing for you to be upset about. Everything is OK.
Reasoning	Don't cry. Can't you see that the other child didn't mean to hurt you?
The positive spin	Look on the bright side. Can't you see, this probably happened for a good reason?
Cheering up	Don't worry. Here, let me tell you something funny I heard the other day. Here have an ice cream. That'll cheer you up.
Advising/giving options	Why don't you try doing this, or that? I think you should just ignore that so-and-so.
The expectation	You should have known better. Get over it. Don't let it get to you.
Put down	Don't be silly. Don't be ridiculous.
Diagnosing/labeling	You are being over-sensitive.
Distracting/diverting	Hey, have a look at the pretty puppet.
Stealing the thunder	Now you know how I felt when the same thing happened to me.

As you can see, on the surface most empathy blockers are not malicious, they are not ostensibly attempts to shame the child, and sometimes they can even be well intentioned, but they do not help the child to feel heard and connected to you. It might seem surprising, even bewildering, to hear that when you try to cheer up a child who is upset, this can often backfire—she might even feel more distressed, even angry. This is because she feels that her feelings are not accepted when what she actually needs is support for feeling the way she does. If this is hard to understand, then think of the last time you felt deeply upset, offended or anxious and someone told you to lighten up. How did that make you feel? Empathy blockers leave anyone on the receiving end feeling shut out and frustrated, and as if there must be something wrong with them for feeling the way they do.

Take a few moments to check this out for yourself.

Have you ever heard yourself use one, a few or perhaps even all of the above empathy blockers with your child? How did your child respond? Can you imagine what you could have done instead? Now, in case you're tempted to become self-critical, remember—we all put up barriers to listening from time to time. Those of us who teach others about empathy blockers know them too well because we've used them so much ourselves.

By the way, not all of the responses in the table above are always inappropriate. There sometimes is a place for advice or a helpful opinion, but unless we take the time to hear our children's feelings first, advice comes too soon and it alienates our child from us. Before jumping in with advice, we need to ask our children if they want it. The most important thing for us to get is that primarily, our children just want to be heard. First and foremost they want evidence that they are not alone, that someone sees how they feel and cares about them. This makes more of a difference than all the advice in the world.

Empathy blockers really muddy the connection between parents and children; they create detachment and distance, and they frustrate children's attempts to reach out. The more we use empathy blockers, the less our children are inclined to come to us with their feelings, the less they want to tell us about their lives and the less they want to listen to us. When we are concerned that our children don't listen to us, perhaps we need to take an honest look at how well we have listened to them.

It is sad when blocked empathy diminishes our sense of closeness with each other, and particularly worrisome when our children feel lost or in some kind of trouble but don't turn to us for help. Our children's trust in us is a function of how safe they feel to open up to us without feeling manipulated, expected of, judged, put down or criticized. Listening is at the heart of connection, and if we can't listen well, we cease to be an influence in our children's lives.

How do we listen?

Listening requires you to do nothing. There is no complex skill or special talent needed. Listening is about allowing and about feeling, not about doing. It's more than likely that you have already been a superb listener to your child umpteen times, and that has helped you to feel connected to each other.

Let's look at how simple listening can be. To listen, simply make a space and set aside the time. Invite or just allow your child to speak, to let his emotion flow. Let your child decide if he needs you to hold him while he talks.

Notice your own reactions, the feelings that are triggered in you by your child's emotions. Accept these feelings, but delay your own responses for a little while—give your child his space first, watch and listen openly. Resist the temptation to interpret your child's feelings, to cheer him up or to resolve his problem; just be with him and let him pour it all out.

When your child has expressed all he needs to, you might like to reflect back to him a very simple summary of what you heard to check with him that you heard him accurately. This can help him to feel that you were with him all the way. Only after your child feels fully heard, ask him if there is anything he would like you to do for him. Would he like a hug? Would he like some help with his problem? If he is very young or can't think of what kind of help he'd like from you, you might like to suggest the kinds of help you could offer.

Love is a space in which all other emotions can be expressed. When your child knows he can count on you to hear his feelings through, you become a sanctuary for him. The way you listen to him gives him the template by which he will take care of his own emotions as he grows up. Children who are listened to without interruption learn to process and move through even their most difficult emotions more swiftly, emerging refreshed and renewed. Our listening and acceptance becomes the model for their self-acceptance, the basis for their resilience and a cornerstone of their emotional intelligence.

Listening involves trusting your child

Listening may involve going against your impulses to quickly make your child feel better, because if you are trying to change how your child feels, she is likely to feel frustrated, ashamed of her own emotions. Listening involves doing nothing to change how your child feels, because it flows from an acknowledgement that no child ever becomes emotional for trivial reasons. There are only two reasons why any child becomes upset: either something upsetting has really happened, or something has triggered an emotional memory of something painful that occurred a long time ago. Either way, your child's feelings are always real, they always have valid reasons, and she always deserves to be heard.

This is quite a big leap of faith that we all fail to take from time to time. It takes courage to trust your child, to trust that if you just connect with her and listen to her feelings, that is precisely what helps her to find the inner resources to get through her distress. Feelings change soon when we feel that someone has made a connection to us. Simply put—connection heals.

The moment we try to change how our children feel, they resist our intervention and they are more likely to remain emotionally stuck. Our children don't like our expectation that they should feel differently—it makes them feel disconnected from us. Have you ever noticed that children recoil from our efforts to cheer them up? They might feel even more upset when someone tries to lift them out of their grief, they might even get angry with the well-intentioned helper. Other children turn away from us; they withdraw and become defeated when we try to cheer them. The fact is, this holds true for adults also: none of us like to be told how we should feel ("OK, you've cried long enough now, time to get over it')—it makes us feel invalidated and inadequate.

Painful emotions behave paradoxically: when we give painful emotions our full acceptance, they begin to dissolve or to transform. When we try to change or eliminate them—they stay put, or they merely get buried only to resurface later. The opposite is true for love and joy: if we fully embrace those feelings, they grow, and they spread to others.

Listening is an art, not a science

Science can demonstrate why listening is so important and so healing, but the act of listening itself is an art. Like dance or any other creative skill, it is a faculty that we can—and should—keep honing throughout our lives, as it keeps bringing more love into our relationships. Psychologists and counselors are professional listeners, yet none of them can say that they have no need to keep improving their listening ability in order to be more effective in their work.

What do our children want us to listen to?

If we remember how we felt as children, it's easy to relate to our children's longing to be heard. They want us to hear about their fears, their pain, their hurts, their anger, their joy and their delight. They want us to know about their loves, their hates, their hopes and fantasies. They want to share with us their triumphs and their failures, their stories and their dreams, their discoveries and inventions, their confusion and uncertainties.

At times, they need us to hear of their disappointments, and although this may be most confronting for us, this will include their disappointment in us. If we allow our children their voice without interference, if we respect their right to their feelings, it will do a lot to heal any rift in our connection. When our children feel understood, love flows more easily. When we speak our truth to each other, even the uncomfortable truths, this brings us back to love.

Why attention can be hard to give

The main reason we sometimes struggle to give our children the attention they ask for is that we didn't get enough of it ourselves. Each new generation of parents does its best to give their children more than they received, but this is not always easy. Many of us were shamed or punished for having emotions, we were told things such as "Stop crying or I'll give you something to cry about!" Many of our role models for listening were not that great.

> ### EXERCISE
> Do you remember having strong emotions as a child? Think about these questions:
> * When you cried, were afraid, were angry, or when you were overcome with joy, how did your parents, your caregivers or teachers listen to you?
> * What kinds of things were said to you, or done for you, when you showed each of those emotions?
> * How did this make you feel at the time?
> Now think about how you feel when your child becomes emotional.
>   How might the way your childhood emotionality was treated affect the way you listen to your child today?

Share your discoveries from the exercise above with your partner or with your most trusted friends. In order to be nurturing, we need to be nurtured ourselves. Parents are called upon to be listeners more than anyone else, and this means we need to honor our own need to be heard, to share our deepest feelings with others. There is something about simply being heard that is immediately healing and restorative. The deepest need in each one of us is to see evidence that we are not alone, and each time we connect deeply with others, it replenishes our hearts and charges us with aliveness. The more we establish meaningful and nourishing connections with others, the easier and more pleasurable we find it to listen carefully to our children.

Inner barriers to listening
There are all kinds of personal aversions to hearing our children's feelings, and they vary from parent to parent. Below are some of the most common triggers that typically make us want to pull out our best empathy blockers, and use them. See if you can relate to any of the following:

☥ **The issue.** You are worried that your child is going to stay upset for ages. You feel that, unless you cheer her up, she will stay stuck in negative emotions and you will be overwhelmed and exhausted.
What to do. Trust your child. When you simply seek to connect with her, this is what gets her through, what awakens her own resources and what gives her emotional resilience.

☥ **The issue.** You feel that unless you teach your child how to climb out of any painful emotions, she will have no resilience in future and will be helpless in the face of grief or anxiety.
What to do. Realize that it is your unencumbered listening, with genuine interest and without expectation, that gives your child her resilience. Your expectation to feel better can be intrusive and can make her feel invalidated. Over time, the way you listen intently becomes the

way she listens to herself—your patience and your trust in her will be replicated in the way she trusts her own feelings. A person who can recover from adversity by natural self-soothing, is usually a person who was well soothed as a child. We all tend to treat ourselves the way we were treated as children.

ϯ ***The issue.*** Your child's emotions bring up memories of your own childhood pain. You can't bear to think that she might be feeling what you once felt—it is as if you are reliving a painful part of your childhood.

What to do. Here, you would benefit from having some healing yourself. Talk about these feelings with your partner, a trusted friend or a counselor. When you find relief for your own emotional hurts, you will feel less troubled by your child's.

ϯ ***The issue.*** You feel terribly helpless and inadequate in the face of your child's distress, you can't think how to fix it and you're convinced it is up to you to find a way.

What to do. You need to trust that by simply listening and holding your child you give her more than you know. Your connection will help her to feel that even when things are at their worst, she is not alone, that someone loves her and cares about her. This will give her the strength to cope with life's irresolvable problems.

ϯ ***The issue.*** You feel resentful of the attention your child receives because you didn't get this kind of attention as a child, and perhaps as an adult you still feel a lack of emotional support in your life. Understandably, it is hard to keep giving what you have missed out on.

What to do. This signals a time for your own needs for attention to be acknowledged and taken care of. You need to reach out to someone you trust and be listened to yourself. Talk to someone who cares about you, about how you have been feeling, and let yourself be supported. To bring water to your child, your own well must be replenished.

ϯ ***The issue.*** Your child has a bone to pick with you. He feels let down and is angry with you. Perhaps this is the greatest challenge, and the deepest fear for each parent: to hear firsthand from our children when we have let them down. Our child's appraisal of us as parents presses our most painful buttons. When parents feel sorrowful, guilty, unappreciated or inadequate, the empathy blockers come tumbling out.

What to do. Even the best parents in the world let down or disappoint their children from time to time. So consider this: if your child can come to you with his grievances and you hear him out, it will go a long way to deepening the trust between you and bring more love to your relationship. It is so empowering for your child to be allowed to speak up for himself because if he can do so with you, he can do so with anybody. Imagine how you would have felt if you were allowed to stand up to your parents and your teachers. All children have a right to express their disappointments, even if it makes us uncomfortable. We are far more likely to earn our children's respect when we are not defensive, when we give them a fair hearing and acknowledge their right to feel the way they do. It requires a lot of self-assurance for us to do this for our children, and it is something children look up to.

When you discover that you have failed to listen to your child, don't beat yourself up. Just have an honest but compassionate look at the personal issues that got in the way.

The feelings that parents most often have difficulty with are the ones we call "negative"—fear, anger or envy. We fight these feelings, we work hard to stop them, we deploy tremendous resources to make them go away. Let your child feel his feelings. It is by giving these feelings space that they begin to resolve—as long as we listen with acceptance. The moment we try to change these feelings, we have stopped listening, which breaks the very thing that makes healing possible: connection. Almost all of us have some difficulty trusting this process, so we can all stand to learn how to allow our children to feel and express their negative feelings. It is not our efforts to induce positive thinking, but our undivided empathy and acceptance that enable our children to move through their most difficult emotional terrain.

It's worth repeating this: the feelings we call negative tend to pass when we listen without expectation and with an open heart. When we listen to—and join in with—our children's joy, their joy does not pass—it increases. With listening, you and your child win, no matter what.

When does hurt become damage?

All children are hurt from time to time, and as parents we all do things that are hurtful to our children from time to time, often without realizing it. It is important to acknowledge this fact of human relationships, but we don't necessarily need to be consumed with worry that every hurt causes damage. Our children have natural healing mechanisms that help them to regulate their emotions and move through their hurts until they can feel love and joy again. In fact, that's one of the main purposes of emotion. When children are hurt, frightened, disappointed or shocked, they cry, they scream, they emote. Children protest their pain and reach out to be heard, validated, held and comforted. When we acknowledge their feelings they feel connected to us once again and can move on.

It is when we deny children the right to feel as they do, when we try to convince them that there is no good reason for them to feel as they feel, that their pain sets in and risks becoming damage. Children whose feelings are repeatedly denied tend to internalize their pain, become ashamed for how they feel, doubt themselves and blame themselves. Everywhere there are wounded, depressed and angry adults who once tried to talk to their parents about their hurts, only to be faced with a parent who felt threatened and guilty, became defensive, hushed them, told them their treatment was normal, and berated them for complaining or for not being grateful. The message that there is nothing to complain about can do more to wound children than the mishap that first aroused their complaint. Even abused children can begin to recover once a caring and empathetic individual listens to their story and honors their right to feel angry and hurt. But often, children are plunged into a deeper gloom or driven to outrage when they are told there is no good reason to feel as they do.

That's why listening with empathy is immeasurably important, it prevents emotional wounds, heals the wounds that have already occurred, and renews a loving connection.

But whining *really* drives me mad

Like anyone, your tolerance and patience have limits. Almost everyone finds it hard to listen to their children when they drone on, complaining in a whiny voice. If you want to get your child past the whining, it certainly doesn't help to judge him or to shut him up. Instead, help your child to be assertive by encouraging him to express his needs and feelings in a strong voice—and reinforce his self-assertion by listening with unmitigated empathy. If you want your child to be assertive (rather than whiny), then be sure that you are letting him be that. Hear him out and let his emotions be powerful.

Whining is anger leaking out through a small opening. —Anonymous

When your child's problems seem unfixable

From time to time, it will seem impossible to fathom our child's feelings and to understand the source of his pain. Read the following anecdote and you will see what I mean. Who knows why Roger was crying so hard? Perhaps he was tired, perhaps he hated the fact that he couldn't fix the train all by himself, perhaps moment his train stopped moving, it triggered an emotional memory of when his puppy dog was hit by a car and couldn't be fixed. Understanding can make a big difference, but it is not always essential—and it is certainly not always possible. We give so much by simply acknowledging the strength of our children's feelings and staying with them as a comforting presence. Connection is what counts.

ROGER—AN ANECDOTE

Roger is a seven-year-old boy who became hysterical one day when his favorite toy, a battery-operated train, ceased to work. Roger seemed inconsolable, no matter what his dad did to comfort him. With some effort Roger's dad fixed his train and got it running again, but to his surprise and frustration, this did little to settle Roger down. None of his efforts to calm Roger made a difference. Tired and cranky, Roger's dad was ready to walk out in a huff, but he sensed that there was something deeper than a broken train bothering Roger. Had the father tried to convince Roger that there was nothing to cry about any more, it would have made matters worse.

Roger's dad decided to let go of trying to stop the crying.

He sat with his son, held him and said, "I'm not sure why you're so upset right now, but I'll just sit with you and hold you if you want. Is that OK?"

At first Roger cried even harder, but he was now crying for relief.

Finally, someone had seen into his private emotional world. Even if he didn't feel understood, Roger felt validated. When he began to feel emotionally supported, Roger began to sniff and calm down.

Within moments he was playing again as if nothing had happened.

Listening is healing

It is possible for you to help your child to heal quite considerably from emotional wounds and traumas by listening with empathy. We live in a society in which parents have only a fraction of the support they need, and where many parents are isolated from the communal and extended family safety nets that make childrearing far less stressful. Sadly, parenting can be compromised by the stressful conditions in which we do it, a lack of up-to-date and reliable information, or a lack of good role modeling—and none of these impediments are the parents' fault. Your child may have endured emotional stress *in utero*, trauma at birth or in a battle with early weaning, conflict in the family, hurts from other children, siblings or teachers. Whatever circumstances have caused your child to feel wounded, healing is possible, and listening to her feelings is the key to healing.

Our children have a powerful healing mechanism inside them—their emotions. When they cry, scream, shake or sob their hearts out, this is Nature's way of restoring their nervous systems to a healthy balance. If they are listened to and allowed to feel, if they are held, comforted and helped to feel secure, this goes a long way toward restoring their emotional wellbeing.

Even children who have survived severe traumas can recover significantly and learn to trust and love again if they are in an environment in which their feelings are consistently validated and compassionately heard. Loving and empathetic human connection has the power to literally rebuild damaged areas of the brain's emotional centers. An empathetic connection causes new and healthier neural pathways to grow, and can restore brain chemistry to a healthier balance. Since a child's brain becomes progressively less amenable to change as she grows, then the older the child is, the more sustained attention emotional healing requires.

And this is the most important thing to understand: in order to heal, children need to feel welcome to express their feelings—their grief, their sorrow, their outrage—without anyone pressuring them to get over it or to feel better.

EMPATHY MAKES MIRACLES

In 2005, a team of Sydney psychologists delivered a paper regarding a grant they were given to test preschool children who had emotional and behavioral problems with the healing power of empathy. By instructing their teachers on how to be a steady and consistent presence for the children, always available to listen to their joys and grievances, they were able to dramatically reduce the levels of emotional and behavioral problems. The children felt emotionally secure and far more settled within the preschool environment, and the staff enjoyed the children a lot more. The success of this experiment exceeded the participants' expectations.

In the Blue Mountains west of Sydney, Youth Insearch operates healing workshops for some of Sydney's most troubled teenagers. Over 27,000 teenagers have had their lives transformed by attending these remarkable programs. The stunning achievements of this organization moved Australia's prime minister to speak at their twenty-first birthday celebrations in 2006. I urge readers to visit the Youth Insearch website (see References), download and view the audiovisual clips; they show profoundly moving evidence of how empathetic connections can heal some of the deepest wounds. Even some of the most hardened, mistrustful and abused adolescents are able to melt their armor, rediscover their innocence and learn to love again, if they are immersed in an empathetic community.

The Heal for Life Foundation (see References), another success story, has for years demonstrated how survivors of childhood abuse can rebuild their lives and learn to love again by being surrounded by an empathetic community where they have the freedom to express their feelings.

Researchers from the Australian Catholic University in Melbourne recently set out to test a new approach to healing some of the most severe childhood psychological disorders. Instead of treating the child, they instructed parents on ways to increase their empathy and improve the emotional care of the child. This strategy was highly successful—the researchers proved that empathy can greatly alleviate childhood depression and anxiety, even when symptoms are severe.

Nobody knows how far psychological healing can go, and we don't know if *complete* healing of emotional trauma is even possible. What we do know is that we can't afford to be blasé about the things that emotionally wound children and assume that children simply bounce back. Children can heal only when there is a patient listener who validates their feelings just as they are, without pushing for change. For healing to be possible, connecting emotionally with the child is the key and listening is the conduit.

There is a central ingredient that each of these projects has in common, an ingredient that has underwritten their outstanding successes as healing ventures. In each example, it is necessary for the participants—preschool children, adolescents and adults alike—to be allowed their feelings, no matter how uncomfortable, including their hatred, outrage, terror, despair, grief and confusion. The healing journey begins with letting them have their truth and listening to them without judgment. Empathy can work miracles and, as parents, it is the most important relationship skill for us to cultivate.

The emotional wounds of childhood last until old age; they shape personalities because they change the brain, redirecting neural pathways and altering brain chemistry. Healing is only possible if it does the same thing in reverse. That's why healing takes time. Healing does not come from one single experience. Children need to be regularly immersed in a more nurturing environment for emotional healing to take place. It takes time for new neural pathways to develop until the child begins to see himself and others differently and to relate to others in new ways. The older the child, the longer the healing process, because the brain becomes less amenable to change after early childhood. Empathy is not a one-stop shop: it is an ongoing commitment.

Helping your child express joy

Empathy is not only about listening to children's emotional pain, but is also about meeting their joy and celebrating it with them. Kids need to see that their joy is mirrored; if this seldom happens, they risk losing touch with it. When a child jumps for joy and sees her joy reflected in her parents' eyes, her joy is multiplied. Give in to your child's joy and you will be infected with it—it is contagious.

The more we listen to our children, the more they listen to us and the more considerate and cooperative they are likely to become.

A child who feels heard will be in tune with her own feelings, needs and wants, and her sense of self-worth will be strong. Her connection with her parents will be rich and close, and she is more likely to confide in them when she needs their help and support.

14

Talking

Connection, as I said earlier, is a two-way street. One direction, the one we looked at in the previous chapter, is all about listening with empathy. The other direction involves an open communication of our needs and feelings. Together, these two streams of expression forge a fulfilling connection, which is what creates trust and closeness in relationships.

Communicating to really connect

When our children take our words to heart, this has a lot to do with the quality of emotional connection between us. We would like our children to hear us not only with their ears, but also with their hearts. What this requires from us is our emotional transparency. If we want our children to care about how we feel, then they need to see how we feel.

When we are emotionally open with our children and when our words are congruent with our feelings, we earn their trust. This approach involves a shift of our focus from "How do I change my child's behavior?" to "How do I role-model the respect that I want my child to learn?"

What is emotional authenticity?

Being authentic doesn't mean gushing your feelings everywhere, being theatrical, wallowing or being emotionally explosive—it is not about the size or the volume of your emotionality—it means congruence and transparency. Sometimes just a flash of feeling showing in your eyes is enough to connect meaningfully with others. If you feel annoyed, then frown a little, let your voice sound annoyed. If you are sad, let your eyes look sad. If you are feeling happy or excited, let that come through in your smile, and the timbre of your voice. That's how simple it is.

What does inauthenticity look like?

Another way to understand emotional authenticity is by looking at what it is not. When someone is saying one thing to us but we sense they mean another, or when someone seems dispassionate and emotionless, they seem to have an unreal quality to them and we find it difficult to get to know them.

None of us express ourselves authentically all the time. We hide, we pretend, we conceal our feelings from each other—even from ourselves—quite frequently. Often we are unaware that we are doing so. Here are some of the ways in which many of us typically cover up so our children won't see our true emotions:

- Trying to sound sweet and gentle with them when we actually feel annoyed.
- Setting boundaries in a syrupy, singsong voice while feeling angry. Sounding reasonable and rational when we feel fervently about the boundary we are trying to set.
- Trying to sound annoyed or strict when inside we really feel hurt by something our child said to us.
- Trying to sound cheerful when we are feeling sad.
- Trying to sound rational and calm when we feel alarmed.
- Hitting a child, and insisting that we are doing this with love.
- Holding back excitement when we are feeling proud of our children (for fear it would go to the child's head).
- Acting serious and composed, pretending we are not having just as much of a great time as our child, when we are sharing an amusement park ride or playing a game together.
- Acting reserved when inside we want to shower our child with love.

What's wrong with inauthenticity?

It is quintessentially human to conceal our emotions, to keep our feelings private. But when we are communicating with our children, when we are setting boundaries with them, we are most effective when we are real, so it is worth taking the risk of letting our feelings show. Many of us have become so good at ignoring our emotions, that it sometimes takes a deliberate effort to tap into our feelings and a further act of courage to reveal them.

Most of us learned in childhood that for one reason or another we should mistrust our emotions and not let them show. We have learned to fear what others might do if we seem vulnerable, and so we guard our hearts warily. But for our children's sake, we need to unbuckle our armor. Our kids can sense what we are really feeling from a mile away. When we are acting in a way that belies our feelings, they are onto us and we don't connect with them. They feel confused, even suspicious. Should they respond to what we feel or to what we are showing on the surface? Our children don't like feeling that perhaps we don't really mean things as we say them. When we seem inauthentic, we lose our ability to influence them.

Your children want to know your spirit

When you are authentic, your emotional presence carries a substance, an essence that touches and nourishes your child. Your child thrives from being in contact with you when you are real. He will often be looking for your presence, which he picks up through your emotions. When this occurs, your realness moves your child and reaches his heart, he will feel closer to you and will want to respond to you.

Test this for yourself. Do people who seem more emotionally real have more of an impact on you? I don't mean people who get hysterical or people who wallow interminably. I mean people who are clear about their feelings. Compare how you feel when you are with them to the way you feel when you are with individuals who are detached, remote or insincere.

We all look for connections that feel real

Although emotions sometimes frighten us and make us squirm, the fact is that we all look for emotional aliveness in others and somehow intuitively know that feelings are what connect us to each other.

We flock to the movies and read novels seeking to connect to the characters through what they feel, and we don't just want to know their pretty feelings; we want to see characters feeling anger, grief and fear, and we want to feel moved by them. When characters in a story show no emotion, we don't feel close to them, we don't care about them as much, we don't miss them much when the story is done.

Have you ever noticed your attention drawn to people whose feelings are easy to read? Or to people who, without making a big deal out of it, make their feelings known? Have you noticed yourself feeling a little guarded around people who appear aloof, detached or emotionally dry? We look for some emotional transparency in others, but dare we cultivate it in ourselves? When we are emotionally remote, others, including our children, find us hard to get to know. We are known through the way we make our feelings discernible to others. That is the essence of connection. And without being consciously aware of it, that's what our children look for in us.

How do we communicate with emotional authenticity?

You probably already do so without trying, more often than you realize. Your emotional transparency has already meant a lot to your child, brought you closer together and won her trust many times over. There are myriad ways, unique to each individual, to be real. Authenticity is basically about not getting in the way of our spontaneous body language.

Speaking with authenticity involves speaking about ourselves, about how we feel, without blaming or shaming another person. This is important, because when we blame or shame another person we trigger their defensiveness and, as a result, our own feelings and needs will not be recognized. Blaming and shaming are the fastest ways to ensure that we will not be seen, heard or cared about.

You speak most authentically when you use your own words as they come to you. That said, I would like to offer a starter kit, a simple formula that helps to bring your feelings into the foreground while keeping blame and shame at bay.

The "I statement"

Setting boundaries with our children respectfully involves making a clear statement about you, about how you feel and about what you want, in other words, making an "I statement." It does not involve making a negative statement about your child—you could call this a "you statement." You statements undermine your influence because they invariably cause your child to feel ashamed and she is likely to react defensively. The advantage of an I statement is that it powerfully engages your child's attention to your feelings and needs while freeing her of guilt or shame.

We saw in an earlier chapter how, starting at the toddler stage, our children need to learn from us how to express anger responsibly and safely, how to embrace it as part of a loving relationship. An I statement is the key to expressing your anger responsibly and non-threateningly, and in making them your child is far less likely to feel threatened or crushed. Anger is destructive, frightening and alienating when the focus is on putting down, guilt tripping or shocking your child. The goal of an I statement is to command your child's attention, to show yourself in a way that compels her to see you as an Other, with needs and feelings that she can relate to. That's what draws the line between your being assertive and your being aggressive. The more you assert yourself with your child, the less you will feel angry.

I statements can be used to communicate your whole rainbow of feelings in a way that deeply connects with her. Here is one easy version of the formula:

HOW TO MAKE AN "I STATEMENT"

Start by saying, "When you..." (here you describe your child's behavior, the one you want to refer to).

Continue with, "I feel..." (say how you feel about your child's behavior; you may need to explain why you feel this way).

Finish with, "And what I'd like is..." (specify the behavior change that you are asking for).

Let's see how this might work with a live example. Say, for instance, your son keeps banging on a glass tabletop with his spoon while you are trying to talk to someone on the phone. You could say to your son, "Hey! When you bang so loud with your spoon, I feel frustrated. It's too hard to hear on this phone and I'm scared you're going to break the glass. So I'd like you to stop banging the glass now."

Get the drift so far? But did that sound a bit too wordy, a bit too formal or unnatural? If you are thinking that such a lengthy and involved sentence might work better with older children and adults, you are probably right. With toddlers and younger children, the language does need to be simplified. So for the sake of practicing, you could start with the formula below, even though at first it might sound a little contrived. Over time, let your I statements become more spontaneous, more natural to the way you speak. What is important is that you stick to the main elements, which are:

ቶ   talk about how you feel
ቶ   don't make comments about your child, only comment on his behavior
ቶ   ask for what you want
ቶ   don't blame, shame or threaten your child.

Aside from these basic guidelines, give yourself the freedom to make assertive I statements in your own style. Below are some examples of I statements that you might use when setting boundaries. You will see that I stray from using the original formula so you can be free to use your own language in a way that feels natural for you.

YOUR CHILD'S VEXING BEHAVIOR	YOUR BOUNDARY
Your toddler runs away from you in a crowded supermarket, though you have told him to stay close.	I'm very upset with you. When I ask you not to run away, I need you to listen to me. I thought I'd lost you and I was really worried.
For the umpteenth time, your teenage daughter leaves her belongings strewn all over the living room.	I'm really angry about the state of the living room. I can barely use it as it is. I want it cleaned up.
At the beach your toddler keeps carelessly kicking sand on you as he runs back and forth.	Hey! You keep kicking sand on me—I don't like it.
Your toddler insists on playing piano on your computer keyboard.	This is my toy and it's really special to me. I'm afraid it might break, and that would make me sad. I don't want to share it.
Your 7-year-old son starts shooting you with a water pistol just as you settle down to read a newspaper in the backyard.	Hey! I'm not enjoying this game. Cut that out.
Your little boy wiggles around so much it is almost impossible to dress him to go out. You have already asked many times for his cooperation, to no avail.	I feel really frustrated. It's too hard to dress you when you jump around like that. Please be still.

Expressing healthy (non-manipulative) pride and appreciation

As we saw in Chapter 12, praising our children and giving them accolades such as "Good boy" or "Atta girl" might make them feel approved of, but it can also make them feel manipulated or patronized. So, what do we do when we are bursting with pride for our children? What about when we feel grateful or appreciative for something they have done for us?

There is every reason to freely express such wonderful feelings as your pride in your children, your admiration of them, your enjoyment of who they are and your appreciation of what they do. Telling your child "I'm so proud of you" is a sunburst for your relationship; pride only burdens your child if it is used to manipulate. Here is a way to show your pride and admiration that shares your heart more fully than praise would. It works the same way as with the feelings you express when setting a boundary. It involves showing your child how you

WHEN YOU RUN OUT OF ENERGY	YOUR BOUNDARY
You have been playing an intense game of hide-and- seek with your 5-year-old daughter at the end of the day, and you feel worn out.	(Gently): OK. I think I'm getting tired of playing now. I'm going to need some space and some time to myself.
Your 7-year-old son insists that you read him one more bedtime story, though it's getting late and you're tired.	I know you'd love another story, but I need to say no. I'm really tired now, and I need some time to myself so I can rest.
SITUATIONS THAT MAKE YOU SAD	**YOUR BOUNDARY**
At a party your daughter keeps ignoring one of her girlfriends, who keeps making overtures to play with her.	I didn't like the way you ignored your friend, I felt really sad for her.
A DANGEROUS BEHAVIOR THAT SCARES YOU	**YOUR BOUNDARY**
You see your child crossing the street without properly looking in both directions.	I was so scared when you crossed that street. You didn't look both ways. You could get really hurt. Please don't ever do that again.

feel about him, instead of just complimenting or flattering him. If you connect with your child by sharing yourself, your child's heart will be touched far more deeply than if you merely tell him how wonderful he is.

Here are some examples of what I mean. I have included an I statement and a you statement so that you can compare the different flavor and emphasis of each.

Imagine yourself as a child, hearing each of these statements spoken to you. How do each of these comments make you feel? Can you sense a difference?

One of the hardest things to do is to define the borderline between buttering up a child's ego and using flattery to manipulate, versus showing your child your admiration and appreciation. The difference is determined by your intent, not merely by the words you choose. Manipulative praise is a carrot we dangle in front of children in the hope that they will keep doing what we like them to do. There are many children who resist manipulation, who find it a turn-off. But when we simply express our admiration or appreciation, the motivation is the pleasure of connecting.

YOUR CHILD'S BEHAVIOR	YOUR I STATEMENT	A PRAISING YOU STATEMENT
Your child plays a piece of music on the piano that he has been practicing for weeks and you love it.	I loved how you played that piece. You sure put a lot of passion into it. It made me want to sing. And I'm so proud of how you persevered with it.	Well done. You are such a talented pianist.
Your daughter runs a great race in a school athletics carnival.	I loved watching you run. I was so excited.	Good girl. You're a top athlete.
Your toddler helps you to pick up toys and tidy up the lounge room.	Thanks for your help; I really appreciate it. I like how neat the room looks now.	Good boy. Aren't you such a tidy boy?

Because an appreciative I statement shows your feelings for your child, it touches him far more deeply than approval or praise—and it won't get him addicted to seeking approval.

Helping your child connect with her own good feelings

When your child has done something well, something caring or mastered a new skill, she is probably already feeling wonderful as a result. When she does something successfully, she may already be enjoying her accomplishment and that intrinsic reward is the most powerful, more powerful than anyone's praise. You could help her to revel in those good feelings and to be empowered by them by asking her to tell you how she feels. It is wonderful to celebrate the triumphs and the rewards of success together.

Imagine, for instance, that your daughter has just stood before her entire class and made a speech for the first time—a magnificent achievement for anyone her age. You could tell her how fantastic you think she is, but that might make her feel uncomfortable, under the spotlight. Instead, why not ask her about her own experience? How did she feel as she approached the stage? Was she nervous? What was it like for her to see the audience in front of her? Did she enjoy the experience? How did she feel at the end? Your interest in her emotional world can be so nourishing, far better than receiving your praise. Your attention feels loving and appreciative, and it allows her to relive the excitement of her success as she shares it with you.

It's far more empowering for your child to know how to draw from the good feelings inside instead of getting hooked on positive strokes from others. This can mean the difference between her growing up to be self-motivated or approval seeking.

Setting age-appropriate and reasonable boundaries

When we set boundaries that guide our children's behavior, how do any of us know for sure if our expectations are fair or realistic, and if the boundary is really necessary in the first place? How do we decide whether saying "don't," "no" and "stop" is burdening our children and crushing their aliveness, or whether it is bringing more security, love and respect into their lives?

These are ongoing questions for all parents, to which there are no definitive or universal answers. Advice from child development experts, parenting books and courses can be very helpful, and the more we learn about what can be reasonably expected from children at each developmental stage the better. But many of our common-sense expectations turn out to be culturally based, and a product of the times. Cultural norms are like shifting sands and often have little to do with what is good for children's development, which leaves it up to us to strike a balance between relying on outside sources and listening to our own hearts, honing our instincts and watching how our children respond. So rather than encumber you with a bunch of rights and wrongs, here are some suggested questions. You can ask them of yourself, and, hopefully, you will keep on asking them. When deciding whether to set a boundary on something your child is doing, ask yourself:

☩ Is your child's behavior actually harming or invading someone, or clearly risking harm to himself or others? If, for example, your child is jumping around, being noisy and exuberant, why not ask others if she is disturbing them before you restrain her natural joy?

☩ Is this boundary actually relevant to my child or am I just repeating history? We sometimes tend to automatically say "no" to something our child does in a way that mimics how we were treated as children, even though what our child is doing couldn't possibly hurt anyone. Just because, say, our parents scolded us for climbing on the furniture, does that mean we have to do the same thing with our own child?

☩ Is the behavior you are asking your child to change normal and healthy for her age? Is it realistic for her to learn what you expect her to at her current age?

You wouldn't expect your three-year-old to be, for instance, the best at sharing her toys with other kids. You'd be unrealistic to expect a four-year-old boy to never show any aggression toward others, or to think of saying "please" every time he wants something. It's one thing to begin teaching children to be aware of others' feelings, but we save ourselves and our children a lot of pain when we accept that this will take quite a long time.

When we think about the kinds of boundaries we will set with our children, we have four main sources of wisdom to combine and weigh up.

- ♱ Listen to what your heart is telling you; it knows far more than you realize.
- ♱ Remember how you felt as a child, what worked for you and what didn't.
- ♱ Watch your child, pay attention to how she feels and responds.
- ♱ Inform yourself about developmental norms.

If you are willing to keep learning from all these sources and to adjust your approaches as you do, you are the best person to make the decisions about how and when to set boundaries.

Don't use your anger to shock or terrify

Your child might feel unafraid of your anger if you express it moderately; without blaming, shaming or exploding into a rage. But it is hard to predict how he will experience your anger from the viewpoint of a small and vulnerable child. Showing your child that you are angry goes too far if you intimidate him. If your child is afraid of you, this tells you that you have been too overpowering and that next time you need to moderate the intensity of your feelings to a level your child feels safe with. The goal of showing your feelings is to make contact, to capture his attention, to let him know how important something is to you. The goal must never be to frighten or dominate your child.

We should remember that we are several times larger than our children and that they depend on us for love and survival. This makes them especially vulnerable to us. Because sometimes you will unintentionally startle or scare your child, it is important to check in with him after any conflict to see how he dealt with your emotions. Ask your child, "Were you scared when I raised my voice earlier?" or, "How did you feel when I was cranky with you?" If you find that your child became frightened of you, let him tell you about that. Consider saying "I'm sorry" if you were too overwhelming, and comfort him if he needs it. Your willingness to care gives him back his sense of personal power and he will be less intimidated by you in future. Your child's feedback is essential so you can adjust your emotional levels within limits that feel safe for him.

If you also respect your child's right to be angry with you and to show you his anger, he will be far less frightened of your anger and the anger of others.

A caution: showing anger or other difficult emotions to babies is inappropriate and too overwhelming for them. We can begin showing our feelings gradually, starting carefully with small doses, when our child enters the toddler years. Let your child be the guide for how much of your emotionality he can take, and thrive from, and be watchful of his reactions.

More power, less anger

Anger can be, as has been mentioned, a force for making contact, but you will notice that the more you foster communication between you and your child, the less you will find yourself rising to anger. Often, all you'll need to get your child's attention is to be clear and direct, strong and calm about your needs. If you are comfortable with your sense of personal power, you are more likely to be heard than if you become angry.

The difference between emotional authenticity and guilt tripping

As our children enter their toddler years, we want them to learn, one little bit at a time, a sense of responsibility for their actions. We want them to begin to see that their actions have an impact on others, that the caring things they do feel good to others and the hurtful things they do can hurt others. So how do we teach them responsibility without saddling our children with a burden of guilt? How do we show them our feelings without guilt tripping them? What is the difference between guilt and responsibility?

Authentic contact with your children means owning your feelings, which means an honest expression of feelings without blaming. Guilt is the fear of punishment; if you don't use punishment at home, your child won't be tormented by guilt, so let her know your feelings but show her that you are big enough to take care of your own feelings. If you are asking your child to stop doing something that bothers you, that doesn't mean asking your child to come and make you feel better. "Hey! Can you please stop that noise? We can't hear each other talking here" doesn't need to be followed up with "Look what you've done; now you've ruined our conversation." She needs to see that her actions have an effect on you; she does not need to become your counselor or your nurse.

Self-awareness fails us sometimes. We may not know whether we are trying to make our child feel guilty or trying to introduce to them a healthy sense of responsibility, but our children do know; they sense our intentions and the difference shows up in their behavior. A guilty child can become submissive and sycophantic, whereas a child who feels some age-appropriate responsibility for her actions can remain assertive.

The child as counselor and confidant

Being emotionally real does not mean leaning on your child for emotional support and telling him your personal problems. This issue merits special attention because it is a problem that happens in many families. Sometimes parents confide in their children and lean on them for emotional support when they should really be turning to another adult. Sometimes parents are not aware that their children don't have the maturity to be emotionally supportive of them. This is often a parent who was once emotionally exploited as a child, or one who is suffering through a crisis and is deprived of supportive adult company. Some parents who are separated or divorced enlist their children's loyalty while estranging them from the other parent. There are few things more damaging of children than using them in these ways.

MARCO—AN ANECDOTE

At the age of 7, Marco lost his father in a tragic accident. His uncle took him aside soon afterward and said to him, "You are now the man of the house, so you must look after your mother." Sure enough, over the years, Marco's mother would confide in him, telling him about her hardship and her loneliness. He felt her pain overwhelmingly and resolved to do nothing to upset her. He helped out around the house well beyond what any other children might do. He gave up much of his child-like playfulness and adopted a rather serious demeanor.

Marco remained this way until adulthood. He had an overdeveloped sense of responsibility to his wife. He was subservient and submissive, and could not stand to ever see her upset. Although he was incredibly sensitive and considerate, she found him to be frustratingly passive and, at times, a pushover.

Selflessly, Marco plodded on but inside he was very angry. Occasionally, his anger would boil over, but then he would be tortured by guilt, so he would squash himself down again.

Being his mother's little man and adopting the role of caretaker and rescuer (as he was appointed to be) had led Marco to lose his ability to speak up for his own needs.

Children are exquisitely sensitive to our needs and feelings, and if we turn to them with our problems, they grow themselves up prematurely—they readily become our comforters. This tends to happen in homes where one of the parents is distant, unreliable or absent and the remaining parent is lonely and unsupported. This latter parent turns to the child for solace. Usually, such solace is sought from an older child, but can at times happen with toddlers. Children learn to play the role of rescuer very quickly at the expense of enjoying their childhood. They assume the role of parent to the parent, and a needy or lonely parent can too easily take advantage of this. The precocious child appears wise and serious beyond his years, surprising adults around him with his advanced capacity for sympathy and understanding. The right to be a child is traded for the admiration of adults who remark how grown up and caring he is for his age. This dynamic condemns the child to being self-negating and self-sacrificial, which leaves a legacy of problems with relationships. It is enormously important that all parents receive the love and support they need, but from other adults, not from their children.

The authoritarian voice

What is an authoritarian statement? Making an authoritarian statement is when we set a boundary by invoking a standard or code with no mention of why we are insisting on our child's compliance, and without showing our child how his actions affect others or how it would make others feel if they did as we suggest. The authoritarian statement is impersonal—in making it, we assume the role of arbiter of all that is right, and penalties await those who don't comply. These kinds of statements very frequently create resistance, first of all because they don't create connection. Additionally, our authoritarian voice can make children feel ashamed and defensive.

Have you ever noticed that when you sound authoritarian—"Do as you're told, or else"—your child resists you or grumbles as he kowtows to your demands? Well, that's perfectly natural; all people naturally resist being bossed around. We ought to be worried about a child who doesn't. Often, children who become oppositional or defiant or passively resistant are blamed and branded as disobedient. They are labeled as behavioral problem children without anyone considering what this might be a reaction to.

We can be far more effective guides of children's behavior if we keep attending to the quality of connection between us and by being mindful of how easy it is to slip into authoritarianism. Below are some examples of very common boundary-setting statements that use the authoritarian voice.

Say, for example, your child uses a word out loud and in public that could, in certain company be considered a borderline swear word. You respond in the authoritarian voice like this:

ቀ "It's not appropriate to speak like that."
ቀ "It's bad behavior to talk like that."
ቀ "Stop that; it's bad manners."
ቀ "It's wrong to speak like that"

The voice of authority does not talk about you and me—it invokes an unseen code of conduct—the right and wrong of behavior that the child simply has to accept. It does not seem real enough to the child. The parent acts as the censor, the guardian of an abstract book of rules that shows the child nothing about human connection. The rule-bound child might behave better, but without a feeling for why, and he will feel oppressed. Obedience is nothing like genuine caring, even if at times the two produce similar behavior.

We have all heard these seemingly harmless phrases a thousand times when we were children, which is why they so automatically roll off our tongues. It's not that such language is necessarily harmful; it's just that when we talk about appropriateness or correctness, we give nothing of ourselves; we make no personal connection with the child and we do not invite the child's care. When we talk in the abstract instead of the personal, we leave the way wide open to rebellion.

The thing about rules

Every house needs rules, right? Parents need to take charge, to impose rules about children not running away, not crossing a street without looking, not breaking valuables, not hitting each other, not taking things without asking, and so on.

Without rules we have anarchy—but if all we do is make the rules of behavior and expect our kids to follow them, we will be disappointed. Toddlers and children see the rules and they break them. So do we: take a poll among everyone you know and see how many people bend their tax obligations, or knowingly speed while driving. When children don't break the rules, they forget them. Rule books can feel oppressive, and when they do feel that way, children instinctively reject them, although children do at times like to know some rules—because a world that has boundaries helps them to feel secure— their behavior is not reliably or consistently guided by them. And the heavier the book of rules, the more brazen the rebellion.

The reason children love to break rules is that rules are impersonal. Rules tell us what we mustn't do, but they are faceless, they don't show us who gets hurt when they are broken. Like the rest of us, children are most powerfully affected by direct human contact, by seeing how others feel. They respond to people, not clauses. They need to know the why and the who, not just the what. More assertive children will always rebel against rules because rules do not satisfy their need for human connection.

By themselves, codes of behavior are ineffective and a recipe for trouble. We are far more effective with our children when we can strike an emotional connection with them. A million times over we will need to say "no" to our children, to set boundaries, but quoting a rule ("We don't do that kind of thing around here') is far less powerful than explaining the reason for the boundary and showing our children how we feel about it ("when you swing that stick around, I am worried that someone could get really hurt').

Rules need to be explained in terms of the effects brought about by breaking them and the effects of adhering to them. Children live more happily by rules that they have helped to write and that they have agreed to in advance. When we let rules be more important than people, and when we let rules speak for us, then rules become a substitute for true human connection, a blunt and unreliable tool for creating good behavior.

Be consistent? Who's consistent?

So many parenting books and courses implore parents to be consistent with their rule setting; there are few messages more consistently repeated. Keep the rules consistently, penalize consistently, and both parents must be consistent with each other about the rules they ask their children to follow. I can appreciate why we are so concerned with consistency these days—we don't want our children to get confused.

But we should give ourselves a little breathing room. No one feels the same way about the same things every day. No two parents feel the same as each other about all childrearing issues. We all grow and change, and our sense of boundary changes with us. A decision to keep the rules consistent appears to make things easier, in that you never have to think things through or weigh up your feelings any more, just quote the rule book—consistently.

Your children need more than that. Here are some of your children's needs that are not served by your being rigidly consistent:

- ✝ Children need to see your honesty and authenticity—no real relationship is a forever-unchanging monotone. Feelings and needs change over time.
- ✝ Children need to learn how to negotiate, to understand others' needs as they change, to express their own changing needs and to adapt to changing conditions in relationships.
- ✝ Children need to see that their parents are willing to grow, change, recognize their own mistakes and change their expectations accordingly. As parents grow, their views grow, and so will their sense of boundary. Some parents need, for instance, to learn how to have firmer boundaries, whereas others need to learn to let go.

Sure, it confuses our children if we subject them to chaotic and repeated change. But at the same time we should allow for the reality of some graded change. What matters is that we clearly explain to our children why our expectations and boundaries are amended.

Ultimately, it's up to you to decide where the balance is, by weighing up the need to be consistent with the need to be real. Experts can tell you far less about how to find this balance than you can discover for yourself by listening daily to what your heart—and your child—tell you.

Here is another to way to think about it: is it more important to be consistently real than to have consistently static rules?

Should there be consequences for vexing behavior?

Even when our children are feeling most lovingly connected to us, they can still do things that offend or disappoint someone. This is also true among the kindest and wisest adults. Remember that children take many years to learn to be aware of other people's feelings and needs, and even then, it is natural for this awareness to come and go. You can fully expect any child to behave insensitively from time to time. While playing rough-and-tumble, they get carried away and someone gets bruised, or they lose or destroy valuable possessions. Sometimes, children get distracted and cause you to run late. Sometimes when school buddies get frustrated or hurt, they ignore each other, or they say mean things to each other. The list of misdemeanors is endless. Often our children do something that lets us down even though we had already made our needs very, very clear. So, when children breach our most carefully expressed boundaries, should there be consequences for their behavior?

If you think about it, there probably *are* consequences, whether you intend them or not. You don't have to make them up. Your child's behavior triggers some consequences, because you feel things in response. Even if what you feel is compassion toward your child because you see that her vexing behavior is motivated by something that hurt her, your compassion is a consequence that springs from a combination of her behavior and your relating style. Since it springs naturally from your heart, this is a consequence that will make a difference.

Your children learn about boundaries through the way you role-model them, so there *do* need to be consequences to follow from inconsiderate or vexing behavior, when saying how you feel does not seem to be enough. The problem arises when consequences are arbitrary and not related to what the child has done. Unrelated consequences feel like punishment—they might shame your child, but do not help her to become more considerate. Here are some examples to help illustrate what I mean:

Unrelated consequences

Let's say that your child, ignoring your clear instructions, has played with your camera and broken it beyond repair; in fact, he has dropped it into the toilet. You're fuming, so you resolve to impose some consequences:

Time out

This is a very popular consequence. Parents send children to their room and order them to stay in there for a period. Enforced isolation can be devastating, so unless your child needs to be physically separated from a sibling or friend he is fighting with, or unless he wants to be left alone for a while, think twice before sending him into solitary. If you are thinking of imposing a time out, of sending your child into isolation, ask yourself if being separated has anything to do with the thing your child did to upset you.

No dessert tonight
This is another consequence that most people are familiar with; even our grandparents used it. If you are actually concerned with your child's dietary excesses, this might make sense. Otherwise, what does withholding dessert have to do with what he has done to upset you, and what is it teaching him other than punishment?

Sit on the naughty stool
This consequence—actually a fancy form of punishment—gained in popularity as a result of a popular reality-TV parenting show. Your child will certainly be upset and reluctant to trouble you again too soon if she does time on the stool, but she will probably wonder for the rest of her life what sitting on a stool had to do with what she did to offend you.

All of the above are arbitrary punishments that tell your child he is at fault while teaching him nothing about responsibility. If your child is to learn about responsibility, consequences need to bear some kind of relevance to his actions.

Examples of related consequences
When I turned 17 and earned my driver's license, I loved to borrow my father's car to take my mates out on weekends. Some of us smoked cigarettes in those days, and against my father's conditions, I let my friends ride in the back with their cigarettes lit. I thought that if we drove with the windows wide open there would be no smell of tobacco in the morning and my father would never know the difference—which, of course, was a total disregard of my father's wishes.

One morning, my father found a cigarette burn on the back seat. There was little fanfare, my father didn't get into blame or shame, but he did not hold back how angry and disappointed he was. Thinking back, if that had been my car, I would have felt exactly the same way. I was not punished, but there were clear, natural and sensible consequences. It was up to me and my friends to take responsibility for the damage. We had to organize quotes from car upholsterers and pay for, and oversee, the repairs to completion. My father made his feelings clear and there was no conflict between us. My bank account took a thumping, as I had only managed to save a small amount of money at that time.

But I actually felt empowered by the consequences my father imposed, and I still feel strongly about the need for all of us to clean up our own messes. This taught me something of value—it helped me become more respectful of others and their property, whereas punishment may have given me nothing but shame and resentment. To this day, this remains for me a good example of consequences that are natural and directly related to the offending behavior.

It is worthwhile thinking carefully about how to respond to children of all ages with consequences that are relevant, and consequences that teach an age-appropriate level of responsibility (don't worry, I wouldn't ask a toddler to pay for property damage).

Connection happens when the consequences have something directly to do with the behavior. This is what enables children to learn to feel an appropriate sense of responsibility.

Here are some examples of related consequences:

ℙ You have asked your son clearly not to play roughly with a toy that is a special family heirloom, yet he continues to throw it around. You begin to feel annoyed and disrespected. You let him know that if he does it one more time, you will take it away from him. When he does, you follow through with your warning.

ℙ While playing in a park with some friends one day, your son keeps pushing his friends down. You hate to see his friends mistreated and worry that this could cost your son their goodwill. Though you show him how upset you are about this and you have done all you can to understand what has aggravated him, he soon returns to his abusive behavior. You warn him in no uncertain terms that if he pushes his friends one more time, you will take him home. He learns that you mean this, because when he pushes someone again, you follow through.

ℙ You are helping your daughter with some difficult homework, but she is grumpy and dismissive of your attempts to offer suggestions. You soon realize that you are feeling irritated and offended. You tell her you don't like the way she is speaking to you and that you feel unappreciated for the help you are offering. You let her know your enthusiasm for helping is waning, and tell her that if she does not desist, you will withdraw your help. In spite of this she continues to bicker with you, so you do as you warned and stop.

ℙ Your daughter bends the rules to gain advantage in a game of cards, and you feel annoyed and cheated. This spoils the fun of the game for you and sours your experience of togetherness. You notice you are no longer enjoying playing with her, so you say, "When you cheat, I don't feel like playing with you any more." If she continues, you stop the game.

How do you find appropriate and natural consequences? Did you notice that each of the above examples involved first checking in with how you feel? The aim is to make the consequence come from how you feel about what your child is doing that bothers you. It works best when you are honest and when the consequence is geared to shield you or someone else from the effects of your child's behavior.

By the way, natural consequences can also include acts of compassion. Usually, underneath a child's aggression or rudeness, there is a genuine hurt. You might see that your child's behavior is driven by something painful that happened earlier. Perhaps one of your children is acting out because she felt bullied by her older sibling earlier. If what you feel is compassion, trust your feeling and show it, give her a hug, sit quietly with her and ask her to tell you what is going on for her.

Taking care with consequences

It's valuable to always be mindful of our own motivations when issuing consequences for our children's transgressions because if our intention is to punish, this will be reflected in the tone of our interactions and our children will feel punished rather than educated. If we impose consequences too quickly, without first taking the time to connect with our child, the relationship will suffer.

So, the following three points summarize the steps of effective and connective boundary setting.

1. *Begin by listening.* Ask your child if she knows why she is behaving the way she is. There may be something very important for you to understand about what is troubling her and why she is acting out in a bothersome way. When children misbehave, it is always, without exception, for a reason. Inconsiderate behavior happens because children's sense of connection to family or friends has somehow been disrupted or has not been nurtured enough.

2. *Always make sure you express your feelings and needs first* with an I statement that makes your boundaries clear to your child. Give your child a chance to hear you and to respond.

3. *Introduce natural consequences if steps 1 and 2 don't resolve the problem.* Give your child some advance warning. When there are rules of behavior that you have all agreed to in your home, give your child a clear notice that you will be implementing these rules if your stated boundaries are not respected. Consequences are not meant to replace communication— they are meant for when your best attempts to listen and communicate go unheard.

What about consequences for good behavior?

We all like to see evidence that our care has made a difference to someone. None of us would keep doing nice things for others if we felt our behavior had no impact. So, why not show your child how her considerate behavior has affected you?

When you think about it, there are plenty of ordinary, everyday consequences for caring behavior. When we help a neighbor carry their shopping up a steep driveway, they smile and say thank you. There are always natural consequences inside you in response to the loving things that others do for you—*if you take the time to notice how you feel*. What a shame it is to hide these feelings from each other.

When your child does something that touches you, helps you, gladdens your heart, take a moment to stop, look inward and notice how you feel. Then let this feeling guide you. Let your child know how she has affected you. You could simply thank her, smile warmly, let her know how much you appreciate what she has done (for helpful examples, see section above about "Expressing healthy (non-manipulative) pride and appreciation" page 252), or give her a hug.

When you show your child appreciation, you are role-modeling appreciation. Your child understands the real meaning of "thank you" by feeling what it is like to be thanked.

The way of connection

The best discipline measure by far is the care and maintenance of a strong emotional connection with your child. If from the beginning we listen to our babies' feelings, and as they enter toddlerhood we share our own hearts with them, close relationships and caring behavior will naturally follow. Ongoing attention to the quality of our connection will save us, and our children, many conflicts and heartaches as they mature into school age and adolescence. When you and your child know each other's feelings, when you both can have limits and respect them, you forge a partnership that can carry you through any conflict.

At first this might not seem like the easiest way to go. The way to foster connection is not always clear—it requires your unshakeable (but entirely justified) faith in your child, getting to know and trust your child intimately so you can see the hurt, the loneliness, the shame or the fear that drive his difficult behaviors. It requires your recognition that connection heals, and that disconnection is at the root of every conflict. The way of connection asks you to search earnestly for how you feel inside, for what your needs and your limits are, and to create your own way of setting boundaries accordingly. Since disciplining your child can seem so much simpler (at first), and since it requires little thinking and feeling, it might be tempting to revert to old ways. But the damage wrought by authoritarian approaches is much too great a price to pay for such expediency.

Connection is not just about effort, and it is not just a matter of setting behavioral standards. It is what affords us the deepest pleasure in our relationships, with our children and with each other. It is what makes our relationships fulfilling, and it paves the way to a most rewarding and joyous parenting journey. Although in our efforts to connect we make many mistakes, each one is an opportunity for learning. The way of connection yields a pay-off that is immense and irreplaceable—you and your child will feel much closer and more trusting of each other.

When you listen, and communicate with authenticity, you role model for your child how to attend to his own feelings, how to be clear about his needs and boundaries, and how to respect the feelings of others. This is morality in action, written into his neural pathways, embedded as instinct. Connection is the fertile ground on which emotional intelligence grows; it is the foundation of trusting relationships.

There are times when tending to our connection with our children asks us for patience—a precious commodity. A great many of the problems we stumble on as parents arise because we are unsupported. When we are alone, or without community, we are less likely to find the space inside ourselves to really listen to our children and to express our feelings and needs appropriately. We become emotionally overwhelmed. We fly off the handle and are more likely to become punitive or shaming. Support from others lifts our mood and energizes us, and helps us to view our child differently. The more help and support we have as parents, the more parenting becomes an enjoyable and fulfilling adventure.

Part 6

Parents Need Nurturing Too

15

The Well-supported Parent

We were never meant to do it alone

Thinking about all the parenting literature that abounds these days, I was recently struck by this question: In most instances, why are only two people mentioned—you and your child? As I read, I feel like saying, "Hey, where is everyone else? Where is all the help and support? Where are the grandparents? Where are the uncles and aunts? Where are the friends, neighbors, and community? Is it all up to Mom and Dad?"

Most of what we read about parenting has been produced in the past 20 years in industrialized and affluent societies, so it reflects cultural biases—no surprises there. Extended family and community have become so fragmented, family life so private, that it doesn't even occur to us any more to turn around and ask where everyone went. When we get tired, confused or grouchy, we think the problem lies with us as parents, or with the child ("He needs to learn to behave"). Is this normal?

When it comes to our perceptions of what parenting is all about, we need to virtually start from scratch because of this remarkable phenomenon—the way we perceive our children changes altogether when we feel emotionally supported. Did you realize that? Check it out for yourself. When you feel at peace, when you are feeling loved, supported and fulfilled, your vision of your child is transformed; the child you see is very different. When we are stressed, the child seems irritating and over the top, and the baby seems difficult and strident. When we feel connected, supported and have time on our hands, the very same child seems playful and exuberant, the same baby seems healthy, deserving, and in need of holding. Our choices and responses are entirely different according to how well supported we are and how fulfilled we are in ourselves. Parenting is a pleasure and our children are more settled and happy when we parents have enough support.

When you get tired, frustrated, exhausted, there should be someone with you who can take over, someone else to play with your child, someone else to hold your baby while you catch forty winks. If you renew and replenish yourself, your heart opens again. Cooperative parenting is actually Nature's design for humans; most problems with our children arise when we stray from this design. Cooperative parenting is the natural inoculation against depression, postnatal depression, anxiety, attentional and behavioral disorders, and a broad range of social ills.

WHAT ANTHROPOLOGISTS KNOW

Anthropologists have known for a long time that grandparents and alloparents (see Chapter 7, "Group cooperative parenting") are essential for family wellbeing and children's health.

In some mammal species, the female, through menopause, becomes infertile while still young and strong- this includes some whale species, elephants, and several primates (including us). There is a good evolutionary reason for this. In primates, survival rates are much better among groups in which the grandmothers are free to join in the care of the young.

Children always seem to do better in societies that surround parents with supportive elders. Isolated nuclear family parenting is inherently problematic; we are not designed to cope well with it. We have taken a wrong turn and need to re-establish cooperative parenting.

Your baby or toddler probably prefers you to anyone else, and if you're his mother or father, that's normal and natural. But when you get tired and irritable, and the pleasure goes out of parenting, your baby will be better off spending some time with his third or fourth favorite person for a while until you can refresh yourself. We need to weigh up two needs: your baby's need to be with you and your baby's need to be with someone who is energized, emotionally available and ready to connect with him. That's why I emphasized that your child, as soon as he is able to, should be given the opportunity to bond with more than one or two special people who can be responsive and loving (see Chapter 7). I am also thinking of you here—you deserve your parenting journey to be as enjoyable and pleasurable as it can be.

You might scoff and say this is unrealistic. We all lead lives that are too busy, everyone has their own problems, our own parents live many miles away. Besides, who can afford the extra pair of helping hands? Well, I think it is unrealistic to do it alone, and in our society, most of us have been doing it unrealistically for quite some time. As parents, we have become cut off and deprived of the sustenance that we are meant to receive, so we get exhausted, angry and depressed.

For hours each day we hand our babies and toddlers to professional strangers who have little personal investment in our child, with whom our child will never properly bond. At home, we let a video screen do the job, perhaps for several hours each day, so we can scratch out some time to get things done.

Communities are disintegrating. The need to spend time with people is being rapidly replaced by spending money on things. Depression rates are spiraling out of control, a recognized result of the deprioritizing of human relationships. This trend is unsustainable—alarming—but it is a trend that you can personally help to put the brakes on, and even put into reverse.

The cost of parenting in the fast lane

The more you learn to listen to your heart and your parenting intuition, the more you come to realize how many of today's parenting strategies are shortcuts that you can no longer accept, and this can be quite confronting. These shortcuts can hurt you and your child, undermine your relationship and lead to behavior problems. Shortcuts, like early weaning, sleep training, electronic babysitting (videos) and early daycare seem to give you, the parent, freedom and support in the short term, but they can borrow heavily against your child's long-term emotional health and the quality of your family's relationships. All of us collectively inherit the social problems generated by the fast food, fast living and fast parenting trends. Humans, and especially children, simply cannot do without regular doses of sustained, loving connection—without it we soon break apart. The classroom, the street and the marketplace become the stage on which the emotional wounds of broken attachment and social disconnection are destructively acted out.

So, what do we do to resist the pressures, financial and cultural, that force us away from our children? It's made more difficult for us in some countries, such as the US and Australia, where parents receive far less financial and social support than in other democracies. Even less developed and less privileged democracies, such as Bulgaria, give a great deal more support to parents than we do. Europeans have come to understand and prioritize something that we have yet to recognize.

Meanwhile, if we want support, we have to create it.

It's time to take our children back

Children and parents are spending less and less time together. As we saw earlier, the average child spends more time bonding with a TV screen than with her own parents. Increasingly, babies only a few weeks old spend many more hours in daycare centers with well-meaning strangers than they do receiving the vital bonding they need with their parents. Everywhere I hear parents shocked by the massive amounts of homework given to their children today, and their children are often at near breaking point under the weight. Are we saying goodbye to childhood?

Parents are working longer hours than ever, we are more affluent than ever and we are more depressed. Governments and industries cry "Socialist!" when anyone calls for more time for parents with their children. How many families enjoy nightly dinners with everyone present, sharing conversation, laughter and stories—around a table and not in front of television? If it weren't for the fact that many parents take children to sports events on weekends, and to tennis, ballet or piano lessons, etc., after school, I would say we are hardly watching our children grow up anymore. How much time do any of us spend with our children each day, just talking with them and listening to them?

If the pressures of our productivity-mad culture are driving a wedge between family members, this is not through necessity, it is by choice. If you ignore for a moment our astronomical levels of debt, we seem very well off financially, but when it comes to relationship, community and time, we are indigent.

It's time to fight for the staples of daily family life (in all the diverse family styles that exist)—the dinner and conversation, the parents rocking the baby, the noise of children playing in the street—it is time to take our children back. It's time to review our shallow sense of economics and bring relationships into the equation. Our assets and techno-goods are wonderful, but they are not more important than our children, not more important than time to ourselves, not more important than our need for loving relationships and time to just hang out together.

Institutions that care for babies will never replace Mom and Dad; they can't come close to a parent's love, no matter how high quality they are. As far as your child is concerned, no one can do it like you can. You are your child's hero. And all heroes need a team.

Creating the support we need

It makes a world of difference to not be alone, to have a group of familiar people around us. Those of us lucky enough to have an extended and supportive family nearby who we get along with, are indeed blessed. But there are many of us who need to think of joining a parent support group or creating a parent support group ourselves in our locality.

Starting your own group

If you don't find a parent support group that you feel comfortable with, why not start your own? Call it whatever you like—"parenting support group" would do fine. Alternatively, you could come up with a name that represents your values as a parent.

Mothers' and fathers' groups that meet regularly are a wonderful new feature of our times, but many people end up joining parenting groups by default, based on who happens to be available in the neighborhood center, the birthing classes or at the hospital. They don't get an opportunity to screen the other members for compatibility. Consequently, some of these groups work well, others don't. When participants have fundamental differences of attitudes and approaches, clashes can occur and people move away from the group. We are in the middle of a societal shift in childrearing attitudes in our times, so it is not unusual to encounter a clash of values. Your parent support group, if it is created around shared core values, is more likely to be one you look forward to seeing, that nourishes you and that you have fun with.

How to create a parent support group that works

To help your group get off the ground successfully, try the following steps.

1. Gather like-minded people. It won't work if there is an essential clash of parenting orientations. This doesn't mean you need to stick to people that do everything exactly the same as you, but you will need some common ground on core principles. When a few core principles are shared, everything seems to flow well. Here is a simple list of core values that are endorsed by leading-edge child development research, values that are at the heart of this book and are reflected in a large number of current parenting books:

    ♱ We should do our best to respond to babies' needs, as consistently as possible; their emotional security depends on it.

    ♱ Toddlers and children need freedom to express themselves and to play.

    ♱ Toddlers and children need clear boundaries, assertively set and without punishment or shaming.

    ♱ There are no bad or naughty children; all misbehavior reflects some way in which the child feels disconnected from others. We can help children by listening empathetically and repairing the disconnection.

    ♱ Children are not our adversaries, to be controlled; they are to be cherished, and they need to feel connected to us.

    ♱ Children deserve as much respect as we do.

    ♱ Parenting is an ongoing journey that requires us to keep learning and growing.

    ♱ There are no bad parents, only wounded parents or parents who need a lot more support.

        You might like to add some more core values of your own. Not enough stated values and group cohesion will be loose and vague, with an elevated potential for mismatch and discord. Too many values and the group risks becoming legalistic, rule-bound, exclusive and alienating. Try to strike a balance that feels most supportive and remember that you are supposed to have fun together.

2. Share parenting resources with each other, discuss together the books, DVDs, websites and parenting courses that support your approach. You'll need to be discerning in making sure that your resources reflect up-to-date research. Child health practitioners increasingly understand the implications of the new attachment science, and new developments in brain science, but although this knowledge is now mainstream, it is yet to be adopted by all practitioners.

3. Avoid fundamentalism. Remember that most parents do their best to give more than they received as children. Don't ostracize or judge a group member who struggles to meet your group's parenting criteria, and give them all your support to be as nurturing and emotionally available as they can be. The fact is that, at times, every parent falls short of their own aspirations and we don't help by shunning someone for breastfeeding less than two years, for occasionally being too lax or too oppressive with boundaries, for not managing to co-sleep with their toddler, or whatever. We are all limited beings. The main thing is that we agree with the objectives we are all trying to grow toward, while respecting our own limits.

4. Acknowledge that each of you has parenting difficulties, even if you follow the best guidelines. All parents are learners. Be open with each other about your personal difficulties and ask for support.

Some things you could do together:

 ♱ Give each other practical help—cook and clean together, do shopping for each other. Hold each other's babies and help each other to catch up on sleep.

 ♱ Get to know each other and allow your babies and toddlers to develop attachments to others.

 ♱ Share baby massage sessions on the floor. Massage each other, too.

 ♱ Swap children's clothes, toys and books.

 ♱ Be sensitive to each other when making parenting suggestions. Remember, many parents are very delicate about receiving advice. Do it in the form of I statements, and own your *own* needs.

 ♱ Share your own childhood memories with each other. You might like to do some of the exercises in this book together, or simply discuss with each other some of what you discover when you do the exercises at home. Share your feelings with each other: your joys, your sorrows and your frustrations. Listen to each other, offer empathy and emotional support.

 ♱ Indulge yourselves in stimulating adult conversation, while your children play around you or near you. Have fun together, laugh, and don't make it all about your children—remember you are there for yourselves too. Sing songs together, dance, play music, do art or craft, go on picnics—make it up as you go along!

✝ When there are people around whom you can trust to connect with your baby and child, this can give you and your partner more opportunities to be alone together, to enjoy each other and fulfill your need for intimacy. When your own relationship needs are met, you have more energy and warmth to offer your children.

The people with whom you share a commitment to creating a child-friendly world will form a deep bond of friendship with you. Don't be surprised if you make some of your life's warmest and most enduring friendships through your parenting community.

How often should your parenting group meet? As often as you'd like. How about meeting with at least one other parent (if not the whole group) every day? For a short while at least? Or almost every day? Can you allow yourself to envision never having to be alone? Can you imagine only being alone, or alone with your child, when you actually want to be? What if your time of early childhood parenting can be the best time you have had in your life?

A starter kit for gathering like-minded parents

The first thing to do is to see if you have existing friends or relatives who share your core values about how to raise children and just talk to them about how you might be able to help each other and spend time together in cooperative parenting every so often. It could be that the best people for you are right in your neighborhood and you might even know them already. Think about your existing circle of friends and acquaintances, your sporting club, church group, yoga class or book club—are there any other parents in those circles whose style might be compatible with yours?

If you don't have people in your life who share your values, then you may need to reach out and find some. You could post notices in local online parenting forums, in your local newspaper, on notice boards in your area, at the community center, the shopping mall or the family health clinic.

People don't always take the time to read posters, so the more eye-catching and easy to read you make your notice, the more likely it will be read. Make it friendly, inviting, warm and personal. You might even consider including a photo of yourself.

Here is a basic template for your ad, which you can vary as you see fit:

NATURAL PARENTING SUPPORT GROUP

Do you have a baby, and/or small children?

If you believe that:

- babies' needs for secure attachment are paramount,
- clear boundaries are needed with our toddlers and children, without shaming or punishing them,
- children deserve as much respect as their parents,
- mothers and fathers need support to listen to their hearts and follow their natural instincts,
- meeting children's natural needs, such as breastfeeding, co-sleeping, carrying in-arms, is best,
- parenting can be less stressful and more enjoyable within a cooperative support group,

then, would you like to help me form a cooperative parent support group in our area?

Please contact: (name)

Telephone:

Email:

Some of you may feel turned off by the prospect of fielding calls. What if, for instance, you occasionally have to turn someone away if you feel that you won't get along with them? If so, you might prefer to team up with at least one other parent you know to begin with and share the work of growing a group. Alternatively, you could keep looking around for an established group that shares your values.

Established groups

Starting a parenting group can be very daunting for many of us who have grown accustomed to living privately. It can, therefore, be helpful to find an already established parenting group. Local community centers and maternity facilities are increasingly acting as hubs for forming parenting groups. This is a truly positive trend, although groups formed around a locality don't guarantee a commonality of attitudes.

Tens of thousands of parents around the world have joined support groups that help them to embrace the newer and more natural parenting styles. These groups have adopted a range of names such as, attachment parenting groups, natural parenting groups and continuum parenting groups. The label matters little—what counts is making supportive connections with others who basically share similar views. There are many ways you can tap into a wider community of parents who share your values (see References).

From control to connection—a paradigm shift

It saddens me to see how many children are treated as objects to be controlled rather than as people to be connected to, appreciated and learned from. The moment a child behaves in a way that scares us, frustrates us, embarrasses us, hurts us, makes us feel inadequate or helpless, we grab in our toolkit for a technique to correct the child's behavior, to make the child good. This is the managerial model of parenting, a child husbandry of sorts. Being close with our children means so much more than this.

All misbehavior starts with fear or hurt. Difficult behavior is usually a sign of emotional disconnection—from the child's own sense of self, from you or from the peer group. This does not mean that we have to excuse disrespectful behavior in our children. Our efforts to connect with our children by listening and being real with them will do more for long-term family harmony than any behavior management strategy.

Since every family member is intricately connected to the whole, if we only consider our child's behavior we are narrowing our view and doing our child a disservice. Children are not the sole creators of their behavior. A child's behavior reflects a context; it is his best effort to respond to how his relationships feel to him. Instead of only asking how to change our children's behavior or attitudes, we should be trying to understand what motivates our child, to see the world through his eyes.

Every difficult moment in parenting is also an opportunity for our healing and growth, and very often when we work on ourselves, our children's behavior changes as we change. Could a recurring behavior problem be showing us that we ought to be learning to be more empathetic? Could it be showing us that we need to learn to be more emotionally authentic? More assertive?

Sometimes, our children's acting out is a response to our stress or our marital conflicts. Sometimes, their behavior is natural for their age but it presses our buttons because it triggers some of our own unresolved childhood issues. The best results happen when we choose to learn and grow along with our child.

There is more to parenting than trying to raise a happy, healthy and successful child. We too can grow as our children grow, and learn to become more loving and more authentic. That's the secret to the most fulfilling, enriching and enjoyable parenting journey.

Parent care—the deadlock-breaking question

Remember Chapter 2's deadlock-breaking question: "What was going on for me at this age?"? Whenever you encounter an impasse in your relationship with your child, ask yourself what was going on at the same age for you. Whenever you find yourself resenting or otherwise not enjoying your child, ask yourself what your world felt like to you at your child's age.

Remember that your child triggers your emotional memory. This can sometimes help and sometimes hinder your relationship. When the emotional memory triggered involves a painful memory that you have not come to terms with, or feelings in yourself that you cannot accept, it can block your empathy toward your child. Until you can connect with your own grief and give it some expression, your own childhood issues can get in the way and make it hard to connect with your child.

There are also times when your emotional memory can help you to empathize and to offer your child meaningful guidance. When you remember how you felt at your child's present age, if you accept your feelings you gain invaluable insight into what your child might feel and need. The emotional memory that lives on inside you is probably your greatest source of expertise and wisdom as a parent, there to tap into whenever you need it. The key that makes all the difference is your compassionate and wholehearted acceptance of all that you felt as a child.

RUTH—AN ANECDOTE

Jessie was a teenager who was often angry with her mother. She believed that her mother, Ruth, was overprotective, overbearing, and too controlling, and that she was stopping her having any fun. Whenever Jessie was angry, Ruth felt rejected and inadequate. As a result she would become defensive, which made Jessie feel invalidated, frustrated and increasingly estranged from her mother.

When Ruth asked herself the deadlock-breaking question, she remembered how her own mother had been so critical of her as a teenager and how ashamed this made her feel. All Ruth had wanted was for her mother to listen to her and to stop judging her and putting her down.

Ruth remained vulnerable to shame well into her adult years. Unused to having good feelings about herself, she longed to be seen as a good mother, to the point that she could not bear to hear Jessie's genuine grievances. When Jessie complained, Ruth felt ashamed all over again and became instantly defensive. She wished she could find a way to teach Jessie to stop complaining and to appreciate her more as a mother.

But as Ruth connected to her own memories of teenage anguish, this helped to deepen her perspective; she resolved to give Jessie the empathy she had wished for herself.

Of course, it was helpful to Ruth to confide in a caring and understanding friend, who helped her to see that just because her daughter was mad at her did not make her a bad mother. When, finally, Ruth allowed Jessie to speak and really heard how she felt, far from hurting their relationship, it brought them closer than they had been in many years. What's more, Ruth found herself trusting Jessie more and was less compelled to be so restrictive of her freedoms. Jessie and Ruth even began to have fun together again.

The solution did not come from trying to change Jessie's behavior—it flowed from Ruth receiving the emotional support she needed so her long-standing shame would no longer get in the way of their relationship.

GARY—AN ANECDOTE

Gary, the father of a six-year-old boy, Max, worked long hours and was often weighed down by problems related to his business. Gary found himself spending less and less time with Max. Meanwhile, Max was acting out a lot and becoming increasingly defiant and provocative. Gary kept looking for new ways to manage Max's behavior: he tried timeouts and removing privileges, but none of these strategies made a lasting difference; Max was becoming more erratic and angry.

Things began to get better only when Gary started to remember how he felt when he was six years old and his own dad seemed remote and unavailable. Gary realized that since his own father had spent so little time with him and played with him so little, he felt awkward around his son, as if he didn't quite know how to be with him. Gary had no role models for how to enjoy hanging out with a little boy.

While speaking to his wife about this one day, Gary began to realize how sad he had always been, how much he had missed his dad as a child. This opened him up to feeling sad about the distance between him and his own son. Instead of continuing to think in terms of managing Max's behavior, he now resolved to learn how to play with him more, how to listen to him more, and how to share himself with his son. Although this did not come easily at first, in a short time Max became more settled and more cooperative.

These anecdotes illustrate how changing a child's behavior is not necessarily about focusing on the child, but about changing the child's environment. Usually, when we fix ourselves instead of trying to fix our children there is an instant flow-on effect—they become happier, calmer and more responsive. What is healing for the parent is immediately healing for the child. The payoff from this holistic approach is that everyone in the family grows together, not just one individual.

Emotional maintenance for parents

Bringing up children can sometimes be maddening. If sleep deprivation doesn't drive you batty, sibling rivalry, a bad week for tantrums, or the daily battle to get to school on time might be what does it. Each one of us has our thermostat set at a different level. While some parents are naturally endowed with a bottomless supply of patience (and the rest of us envy you), others' blood starts to simmer early in the piece. We fear that, in spite of our best efforts to dam up our temper, it will burst its banks and scald our child.

For the sake of our physical health and our emotional balance, we all need to find a safe outlet for our anger. When anger is appropriately expressed it can build connection, but sometimes excess emotional charge needs to be safely released away from our children. We all need to realize that it is OK to be angry—that it is normal. Even passionate anger is nothing to be afraid or ashamed of, as long as it is safely expressed away from your child. What is not OK is to let our frustration turn into hostility toward our child. Most of us tend to be afraid of our anger—we become shocked with ourselves: "What is wrong with me? How could I be so mad at an innocent child? Am I a monster?" Remind yourself that anger is not violence. In fact, venting anger safely is the best measure to prevent violence.

So, parents, care for yourself enough to look after your emotional wellbeing. Whenever you need to, beat on a pillow. Break a plate. Have a game of squash. Hit a punching bag. Kick the garbage can. Write down everything you are angry about. Go for a brisk walk or run. Anger is a powerful physical force and it wants movement.

To each their own. Everyone finds a method that works for them. I know a couple who have a wrestling match on the carpet whenever their willful toddler drives them crazy. They have strict codes of safety so that no one gets hurt. It really works for them. And believe me, the male does not always win.

What an emotional jungle parenting can be sometimes. We become sad for our children when they have a bad day, we feel lost, helpless or inadequate when we cannot console or guide them. We feel abandoned when they trade us in for the company of their peers. I cannot say this often enough—we needn't bear these feelings alone; we should share them with our partners, closest friends, family or someone in our parent support group. That's one of the main advantages of cooperative parenting.

If you are not used to disclosing your emotions, doing so might feel uncomfortable at first, but it is worth taking the risk and extending your comfort zone a little. When you express your feelings and receive emotional support, you will notice how much more space you have for your child afterward, and how much more loving you feel. Emotional maintenance is essential for parents if we want to keep renewing the joy of being a parent.

Our culture tends to be shy about all kinds of feelings; we don't seem to value our emotions. Even joy is understated; we seem to hold it back as much as the other emotions. Often, life's pleasures pass us by simply because we don't take a moment to focus on them, much like walking past a beautiful view without turning our heads to see—without saying "Wow!" So why not make a point of noticing something about your child every day that gives you pleasure, that uplifts your spirit or tickles your heart. It could be something new your child learns to do, one of her smiles, something funny he says, or a small act of kindness. Stop to breathe in the joy of this moment, and then tell someone about it. Share your joy and revel in it.

When your joy is savored, and then shared, it is magnified—it is as if your body becomes better at producing it. You deserve parenting to be more than a job—it could be your most exciting adventure.

The guru in the house

Children challenge us in every area of our selves that needs healing. They frustrate us, irritate us, alarm us, wound us and sometimes disappoint us—and often these feelings show us where we need to heal and grow. Every day our children also remind us of the lightness of being and how to have a playful attitude to life. They love us more loyally than anyone else in this world. They forgive our mistakes and our lack of patience every day. For all of these things, our children deserve our deepest gratitude.

To become a parent is to enroll in a school of love, and our children bring us the lessons. In this school, it is not appropriate to grade ourselves as good parents or bad parents; here, we just need to accept that all of us are learning and growing. Each one of us is a contributor to the ongoing evolution of parenting—we learn from each other and we teach each other, as we share our stumbles and our triumphs.

We say that we are bringing up our children—but this is only half the truth. Growth is mutual, and in so many ways our children bring us up.

So, here is our challenge as parents: can we embrace parenting as life's most transformative personal growth course? If we do, the most profound fulfillment is guaranteed.

EPILOGUE

A letter to US parents, grandparents and teachers

In today's world, it is increasingly true that no one can thrive unless all are thriving together. Our communities are becoming more and more interconnected and interdependent. Malaise in one corner will inevitably, sooner or later, affect the whole. On the other hand, a burst of happiness anywhere in the world sends ripples that touch all of humanity eventually, if only subtly. As we strive to create a loving environment for our own children, we should pause to think how the children around us are faring. The babies and children of other families will one day be the leaders of our children's world. They will be our children's doctors, lawyers, senators, and community leaders. Every one of us has a stake in the wellbeing of *all* children; and so it is well worth "taking the temperature" of childhood in our nations and around the world.

American children are not doing well in comparison to the children in the rest of the developed world. You may be shocked by what you are about to read. Across a number of key indicators, the care of children in the United States lags behind that of nearly every other industrialized democracy.

In 2007, the United States earned second to last place in a ranking of children's wellbeing among the world's affluent and developed nations.[1] Why is that the case? What else is going on for American children today? Let's take a closer look:

- ✝ The US has the highest child abuse death rate in the developed world. In the last 10 years, over 20,000 children died at home at the hand of family members – that is nearly four times the number of US soldiers killed in Afghanistan and Iraq.[2]
- ✝ Corporal punishment in schools is still legal in nineteen states, where teachers strike children on the buttocks with a wooden paddle.[3] Only two developed nations, the US and Australia, have failed to enact a nationwide ban in schools. This practice is now illegal in the education systems of well over 100 nations.
- ✝ Troubled American teenagers are sent to unregulated, privately owned juvenile boot camps in various locations throughout the nation. At

---

2. Innocenti Report Card 7: An Overview of Child Wellbeing in Rich Countries: unicef-irc.org/publications/pdf/rc7_eng.pdf
2. everychildmatters.org
3. nospank.net/classrm.htm & stophitting.com

many of these boot camps, discipline includes physical beatings and solitary confinement. A number of unintended deaths have occurred.[1] Outraged citizen groups have been formed to expose and combat this widespread institutionalized mistreatment of children.[2]

ቀ The United States is the only Western nation that imposes life sentences without the possibility of parole for juvenile offenders. Children as young as 13 are imprisoned for life. This violates several international human rights treaties.[3]

ቀ The United States has the highest rates in the industrialized world of the following indicators: teenage pregnancy, teen birth rate, sexually-transmitted diseases, illicit drug use, childhood obesity, diabetes, and use of antidepressants.[4] Around 95% of the world's Ritalin is prescribed within the US and Canada.

ቀ The average American child, age three to four, watches around 4 hours of television per day. It is estimated that 25% of children under two; 65% of six-year-olds; and 90% of ten- to eighteen-year-olds, have a TV in their own room.[5] There are many reasons these statistics should be viewed as extremely alarming; we discussed the disastrous effects this can have on children's psychological health in Chapter 9 (see subheading: Television—the play killer). But the devastating effects of television on children's emotional intelligence do not stop there. According to the American Academy of Pediatrics, by age eighteen, the average young American will have seen two hundred thousand acts of onscreen violence.

Is this something we should be worried about? Can viewing onscreen violence actually make viewers more violent? There are now more than a thousand studies that have determined that it can.

ቀ Despite being the world's wealthiest nation, the United States has one of the least generous parental leave provisions in the world; an average of twelve weeks with no pay. This is considerably less than every

1. nospank.net/boot.htm
2. cafety.org
3. amnestyusa.org & aclu.org
4. • nationmaster.com, select "health"
   • Paul Hawken 2007, *Blessed Unrest: How the Largest Movement in the World Came into Being and Why No One Saw It Coming*, Viking: New York, p. 118.
   • Gregory S. Paul 2005, "Cross-National Correlations of Quantifiable Societal Health with Popular Religiosity and Secularism in the Prosperous Democracies," *Journal of Religion and Society* 7:18.
5. Aric Sigman 2005, *Remotely Controlled—How Television Is Damaging Our Lives* Vermillion, London, p 50.

European country, less than all countries in the Americas (North and South), and even less than many African and Asian countries. Compare this to Denmark: 18 months at 100% of pre-birth pay, Argentina: 3 months at full pay and Kenya: 2 months at full pay.[1]

✝ The United States is the only country—besides Iraq—where metal detectors are used in schools.[2]

✝ The United States is the only country in the world in which infant boys are routinely circumcised for non-religious reasons—at a little over 50 percent—despite the fact that no medical association in the world recommends this practice, and despite the fact that it is now recognized as an unnecessary, traumatic, and damaging procedure (see Chapter 5: "To Circumcise or not?" and circumcision.org/position.htm)

✝ The Baby-Friendly Initiative (BFI), spearheaded by WHO and UNICEF, has proven to be crucial in elevating rates of breastfeeding around the world—a key public health issue. But at the time of this writing, merely 5% of American babies are born in BFI-accredited facilities, since there are just 121 Baby-Friendly hospitals and birth centers in the US. In Sweden, 100% of births take place in BFI-accredited facilities, and in Australia, the rate is 1 in 3.

✝ The United States remains one of only two nations, along with Somalia, not to have ratified the UN Convention on the Rights of the Child.[3]

The United States is the most powerful economy in the world. It is the nation that can most afford the best provisions for families and children, and so it is surprising that so many American children have been receiving less than they deserve.

Without a doubt, from coast-to-coast, the US can boast innumerable communities that are prosperous, peaceable and stable—in which the children thrive and are nurtured. But childhood is formative, and when the wellbeing of a critical mass of children is compromised, this can be very costly for any nation. How might the state of affairs for America's less fortunate children be reflected in the general functioning of society?

The US suffers a much higher homicide rate than other Western nations and has the highest incarceration rate in the world.[4] The US also has one of the most dramatic rates of inequality. While 15% of Americans—46 million people—live

1. en.wikipedia.org/wiki/Parental_leave
2. Paul Hawken 2007, *Blessed Unrest: How the Largest Movement in the World Came into Being and Why No One Saw It Coming,* Viking: New York, p. 118.
3. childrightscampaign.org
4. Steven Pinker 2011, *The Better Angels of our Nature —the Decline of Violence in History and its Causes,* Allen Lane, New York, pp. 91-106.

in poverty, an average CEO remuneration tops 500 times the *average* wage, and 800 times the *minimum* wage. Compare this to the British CEO-to-average-wage ratio of 25:1, Australia's ratio of 22:1, France's 16:1 and Japan's 11:1.

Modern advances in child developmental sciences make it quite clear that the above social ills, and many more, would be greatly alleviated in the wake of strong policy shifts towards more support for parents, and the securing of a non-violent upbringing for children.

There is a bright side

On the other hand, the United States has produced some of the world's most innovative movements and organizations for childrearing reform.

- ♱ The United States is a powerful center for promoting natural childbirth, led by organizations such as:
    - bradlybirth.com
    - cappa.net
    - lamaze.org
    - motherfriendly.org
    - birthpsychology.com
- ♱ The La Leche League was formed in the late 1950s in the United States to combat the displacement of breastfeeding by big business (manufacturers of artificial baby formula). The organization helped bring breastfeeding back from the brink of extinction, and today it has branches in more than sixty nations.[1]
- ♱ The Alliance for Transforming the Lives of Children[2] created the Proclamation and Blueprint for Transforming the Lives of Children— what some have called the "missing instruction manual"—outlining infants' and babies' needs for optimal development.
- ♱ The most groundbreaking discoveries in brain development research and emotional intelligence have occurred at American universities. This exciting new body of knowledge is revolutionizing approaches to parenting, education and child health around the world.[3]
- ♱ The "attachment parenting" movement is the brainchild (or should I say "heartchild"?) of American pediatrician, William Sears, MD, and his wife Martha, who interpreted for parents the results of attachment research. A vibrant and fast-growing international movement has emerged to provide supportive communities for parents and to inform

---

1. llli.org
2. aTLC.org
3. mindgains.org

them about leading-edge child development science. Attachment Parenting International has support groups in most states.[1]

A number of remarkable, social-evolutionary movements for child-rearing reform thrive on American soil and from here have radiated outward to strengthen similar movements abroad. For instance, many nations' governments are starting to fund early intervention and home visitation programs to support new parents, and the outcomes so far are very promising. The bulk of the research and development of such early intervention strategies emerged in the United States. As well, the most unequivocal research damning the use of corporal punishment was produced by American researchers. The openness of American society has permitted a broad proliferation of the "democratic education" movement; a modern educational approach that produces the highest academic standards while reducing school violence and enhancing children's emotional and social intelligence.[2] The United States has the resources—in terms of its scientists, its culture of openness, and its wealth—to become a world leader in enacting child-rearing reforms instead of trailing the world's industrialized democracies.

America can become the most peaceful, sustainable, and equitable society on earth, if policy makers simply catch up with what American child development scientists—and a growing number of parents—are so clearly saying.

What can be done?

When confronted with the realities of a social dilemma of great magnitude, it is not unusual to feel a sense of helplessness at first. The problems I have listed here may strike you as overwhelming, and you might be asking yourself, "What can I possibly do about all this?" Good news: there is in fact a number of ways in which you can lend as little or as much support as you would like to the many childrearing reform efforts. Many of the websites I refer to herein are entry points to organizations that you can join or give your support to if you feel strongly about the wellbeing of children.

No society can legislate for good parenting. But there are many policies that can be put in place to provide the kinds of social conditions that enable parents to give their best. Many of these policies have already been tried and tested in many nations, including in the United States. They are proven to be cost effective, and they have resulted in profound increases in childhood wellbeing. Government initiatives that support families have a proven track record for

---

1.   attachmentparenting.org
2.   educationrevolution.org

increasing school attendance and reducing youth violence, substance abuse, crime rates, and rates of depression.[1]

The following are a few examples of effective parent-supportive policies:

- ✝ Government-funded early intervention (home visits) programs that support healthy parent-baby attachment.
- ✝ Legislation that bans all corporal punishment of children at school and at home.
- ✝ Generous parental leave provisions.
- ✝ More support for democratic and progressive styles of education.

To this end, Kelly (aka, Kali) Wendorf,[2] Anne Manne,[3] and I have compiled a Children's Wellbeing Manifesto.

Our Manifesto is a proposal for fifteen family-supportive policies, most of which have already proved highly successful in numerous countries. You can read the full text of the Manifesto at our-emotional-health.com/manifesto.html.

There are so many child-rearing reform movements you can tap into if you wish—we live in an exciting era of change. If you feel moved by the idea of participating directly in some aspect of the child-rearing reform movement, there are many established organizations that can be effective vehicles for your contribution. The organizations I have mentioned here are but a small fraction of a growing international movement devoted to children's emotional health and wellbeing. If you are not drawn to joining or supporting groups that work for change, that's fine. Do not underestimate the gift you bring to the whole world each time you simply offer a child your most heartfelt empathy.

World peace begins at home and at school

Childrearing reform is one of the most powerful forms of social change activism. It is entirely nonviolent; in fact, it is loving and politically neutral.

America finds itself restlessly striving for fundamental change. But unless there are enduring changes to childhood, changes in the politics of a nation may come and go without leaving a lasting legacy—the most exciting new initiatives can easily be overturned by the next administration. As my friend and colleague Kelly Wendorf once said, "We can save a forest today, but if children are not brought up feeling love, connection, and empathy, then that same forest will be cut down tomorrow."

---

1. Robin Grille 2005, *Parenting for a Peaceful World*, Longueville Media, Sydney, Chapter 31.
2. Kali Wendorf 2009, *Stories of Belonging: Finding Where Your True Self Lives*, Finch, Melbourne.
3. Anne Manne 2005, *Motherhood: How Should We Care for Our Children?* Allen & Unwin, Sydney.

As adults, we tend to behave toward others as we have been treated. It follows that the way a nation treats its children is a blueprint for the future health of its society and the driving force of its prosperity. The future of any nation is determined by the happiness of its children more than by any other single variable. Even the foreign policy of a nation is, to a considerable degree, a reflection of its prevailing child-rearing customs.

International studies have repeatedly found that when any nation invests in its parents, so that they have enough *time* with their children, and in its children's emotional health and education; the social dividends will by far exceed the investment.[1]

Conversely, the research shows that sparing investment in childhood is false economy; it creates a costly spread of social dysfunction that bleeds the economy and generates waves of unhappiness through populations. In other words, an economic recession is *not* an excuse to delay investment in families; it is in fact an argument for the opposite. The greatest relief to the national budget, in areas of health, crime, and social dysfunction, will come from diverting more funds toward parents and children.

The world is fraught with violence—in the streets, in schools, across national borders—and our violence toward nature is jeopardizing the viability of this planet. An urgent imperative confronts us all—we must come to grips with the new realizations made abundantly clear by modern neuroscience and child-development experts—*no person anywhere was born to be violent. No gene exists that makes a person unloving.* Think about what this means for a moment; think about the implications! A great leap forward from our collective history of violence is entirely possible and well within our grasp. The way forward at this critical moment in history involves worldwide child-rearing reforms. Driven by a new scientific orthodoxy that has aligned itself with the human heart, this reform movement has already begun, and it is gathering speed.

A new society is eminently possible—one that is driven by love rather than greed, fear, or suspicion. All that is needed is a collective commitment to giving more children an emotionally healthy environment in which to grow, play, love, learn, and feel secure. This requires giving all parents a chance, support and enough time—that increasingly rare commodity—to enjoy their children.

The great family of humanity strives to create a more joyous childhood for all. I dream that this book may inspire you to add your gifts to this universal striving as well as empower you to know the strength of your heart and the role you can play in our collective evolution.

It is my fervent hope that the pleasure of parenting can be multiplied for all parents, and that children everywhere can thrive in a loving world, with the

---

1.   Robin Grille 2005, *Parenting for a Peaceful World*, Longueville Media, Sydney.

promise of a healthy and peaceful planet. Whether you know it or not, you are an integral part of this awakening. From my heart to yours, I thank you for having undertaken your journey through these pages.

Bibliography

Suzanne Arms 1994, *Immaculate Deception II: Myth, Magic and Birth*, Celestial Arts, Berkeley.

Marcy Axness 2012, *Parenting for Peace: Raising the Next Generation of Peacemakers*, Sentient Publications, Boulder, Colorado.

Janice Berger 2000, *Emotional Fitness: Discovering Our Natural Healing Power*, Penguin Books, Toronto.

Steve Biddulph 2005, *Raising Babies: Should Under 3s Go to Nursery?* Harper Thorsons, London.

T. Berry Brazelton and Stanley I. Greenspan 2001, *The Irreducible Needs Of Children: What Every Child Must Have to Grow, Learn, and Flourish*, De Capo, Boston.

Sarah Buckley 2009, *Gentle Birth, Gentle Mothering: A Doctor's Guide to Natural Childbirth and Gentle Early Parenting Choices* Celestial Arts, Berkeley.

Meryn Callander 2012, *Why Dads Leave: Insights and Resources for When Partners Become Parents*, Akasha Publications, Asheville, North Carolina.

David Chamberlain 1998, *The Mind of Your Newborn Baby*, North Atlantic Books, Berkeley.

Helena Cornelius and Shoshana Faire 2007, *Everyone Can Win: Responding to Conflict Constructively*, Simon & Schuster, Sydney.

Sue Cox 2006, *Breastfeeding with Confidence: A Practical Guide*, Meadowbrook Press, Minnetonka, Minnesota.

Louis Cozolino 2006, *The Neuroscience of Human Relationships: Attachment and the Developing Social Brain*, W.W. Norton, New York.

Helen and Clive Dorman 2002, *The Social Toddler*, (also available as a DVD) CP Publishing, Richmond, UK.

Sue Gerhardt 2004, *Why Love Matters: How Affection Shapes a Baby's Brain*, Brunner-Rutledge, East Sussex, UK

Anni Gethin and Beth Macgregor 2007, *Helping Your Baby to Sleep: Why Gentle Techniques Work Best*, Rex Finch Publishing, Sydney.

Ronald Goldman 1997, *Circumcision, The Hidden Trauma: How an American Cultural Practice Affects Infants and Ultimately Us All*, Vanguard Publications, Chapel Hill, North Carolina.

Thomas Gordon 2000, *Parent Effectiveness Training*, Three Rivers Press, New York.

Robin Grille 2005, *Parenting for a Peaceful World*, Longueville Media, Sydney.

Paul Hawken 2007, *Blessed Unrest: How the Largest Movement in the World Came into Being and Why No One Saw It Coming*, Viking, New York.

Sarah Blaffer Hrdy 2000, *Mother Nature*, Vintage, London.

Sally Inch 1984, *Birthrights: What Every Parent Should Know about Childbirth in Hospitals*, Pantheon Books, New York.

Deborah Jackson 1999, *Three in a Bed: The Benefits of Sharing Your Bed with Your Baby*, Bloomsbury, New York.

Sheila Kitzinger 2001, *Rediscovering Birth*, Atria Books, New York.

—— 2003, *The Complete Book of Pregnancy and Childbirth*, Knopf, New York.

Alfie Kohn 1999, *Punished by Rewards: The Trouble with Gold Stars, Incentive Plans, A's, Praise, and Other Bribes*, Houghton Mifflin, Boston.

Frederick Leboyer 2002, *Birth Without Violence: Revised Edition of the Classic*, Healing Arts Press, Rochester, Vermont.

Thomas Lewis, Fari Amini, and Richard Lannon 1999, *A General Theory of Love*, Vintage Books, New York.

Lloyd de Mause (ed.) 1982, *The History of Childhood: The Untold Story of Child Abuse*, Peter Bedrick Books, New York.

Pinky McKay 2006, *Sleeping Like a Baby*, Penguin Books, Melbourne.

Nancy Mohrbacher 2005, *Breastfeeding Made Simple: Seven Natural Laws for Nursing Mothers*, New Harbinger, Oakland, California.

Lynne Murray and Liz Andrews 2005, *The Social Baby: Understanding Babies' Communication from Birth* (also available on DVD), The Children's Project, London.

William Sears 1999, *Nighttime Parenting: How to Get Your Baby and Child to Sleep*, Plume, New York.

Daniel Siegel 1999, *The Developing Mind: How Relationships and the Brain Interact to Shape Who We Are*, Guilford Press, New York.

Aric Sigman 2005, *Remotely Controlled: How Television Is Damaging Our Lives*, Vermilion, London.

Margot Sunderland 2007, *The Science of Parenting*, DK Publishing, London.

Michel Odent 2005, *Childbirth without Fear: The Principles and Practice of Natural Childbirth*, Pinter & Martin Publishing, London.

Joseph Chilton Pearce, *Magical Child*, Plume, New York

Daniel H. Pink 2011, *Drive: The Surprising Truth About What Motivates Us*, Riverhead Books, New York.

Steven Pinker 2011, *The Better Angels of our Nature: The Decline of Violence in History and its Causes*, Viking, New York.

Marshall Rosenberg 2004, *Raising Children Compassionately: Parenting the Nonviolent Communication Way*, Puddledancer Press, Encinitas, California.

Thomas Verny 1982, *The Secret Life of the Unborn Child*. Dell, New York.

Marsden Wagner 1994, *Pursuing the Birth Machine*, James Bennett Publishing, Sydney.

—— 2006, *Creating Your Birth Plan: The Definitive Guide to a Safe and Empowering Birth*, Perigee Trade, New York.

Laurel Wilson and Tracy Wilson Peters 2012, *The Greatest Pregnancy Ever: Keys to the MotherBaby Bond*, Lotus Life Press, Centennial, Colorado.

References

The list of references that follows is a non-exhaustive guide to further reading as well as internet access to useful resources and organizations.

Chapter 1—Preparing to Be a Parent

Lloyd de Mause (ed.) 1982, *The History of Childhood: The Untold Story of Child Abuse*, Peter Bedrick Books, New York.

Sue Gerhardt 2004, *Why Love Matters: How Affection Shapes a Baby's Brain*. Brunner-Rutledge, East Sussex, UK

Sarah Blaffer Hardy 2000, *Mother Nature*, Vintage, London.

Robin Grille 2005, *Parenting for a Peaceful World*, Longueville Media, Sydney (see parts II and III).

Thomas Lewis, Fari Amini, & Richard Lannon 1999, *A General Theory of Love*, Vintage Books, New York.

Margot Sunderland 2007, *The Science of Parenting*, DK Publishing, London.

Chapter 2—Your Memory is Your Teacher

David Chamberlain 1998, *The Mind of Your Newborn Baby*, North Atlantic Books, Berkeley. The many fascinating anecdotes in Dr Chamberlain's book show how healing it can be to touch upon memories of infancy.

Louis Cozolino 2006, *The Neuroscience of Human Relationships: Attachment and the Developing Social Brain*, W.W. Norton, New York.

Daniel Siegel 1999, *The Developing Mind: How relationships and the Brain Interact to Shape Who We Are*, Guilford Press, New York.

Verny, Thomas 1982, *The Secret Life of the Unborn Child*. Dell, New York.

Chapter 3—Connecting Begins Long Before Baby's Birth

Books

Marcy Axness 2012, *Parenting for Peace: Raising the Next Generation of Peacemakers*, Sentient Publications, Boulder, Colorado.

Sarah Buckley 2009, *Gentle Birth, Gentle Mothering: A Doctor's Guide to Natural Childbirth and Gentle Early Parenting Choices* Celestial Arts, Berkeley, California.

David Chamberlain 1998, *The Mind of Your Newborn Baby*, North Atlantic Books, Berkeley.

Norman Gardner 2005, *The Forbidden Art of Pregnancy*, Aaberation Press, Boca Raton, Florida.

Robin Grille 2005, *Parenting for a Peaceful World*, Longueville Media, Sydney, see Chapter 25.

Tracy Wilson Peters and Laurel Wilson 2012, *The Greatest Pregnancy Ever: Keys to the MotherBaby Bond*, Lotus Life Press, Centennial, Colorado.

Websites

General

Sarah Buckley, "Ecstatic Birth: Nature's hormonal blueprint for labor" at:
sarahjbuckley.com/articles/ecstatic-birth.htm.
Primal Health Databank at birthworks.org/site/primal-health-research/databank-keywords.html.

Massage and chiropractic

icpa4kids.com
iaim.ws/home.html
infantmassageusa.org

Chapter 4—Bringing Joy to the Dawn of Life

Books and a magazine

Suzanne Arms 1994, *Immaculate Deception II: Myth, Magic and Birth*, Celestial Arts Publishing, Berkeley, California.
Sarah Buckley 2009, *Gentle Birth, Gentle Mothering: A Doctor's Guide to Natural Childbirth and Gentle Early Parenting Choices Celestial Arts,* Berkeley, California.
Patrick Houser 2007, *Fathers-to Be Handbook*, Creative Life Systems, Kent, UK.
Sally Inch 1984, *Birthrights: What Every Parent Should Know about Childbirth in Hospitals*, Pantheon Books, New York (see Chapter 5, "The First Stage: pain in labor').
Sheila Kitzinger 2001, *Rediscovering Birth*, Atria Books, New York.
— 2003, *The Complete Book of Pregnancy and Childbirth,* Knopf, New York.
Frederick Leboyer 2002, *Birth Without Violence: Revised Edition of the Classic*, Healing Arts Press, Rochester, Vermont.
Michel Odent 2005, *Childbirth without Fear: The Principles and Practice of Natural Childbirth*, Pinter and Martin Publishing, London.
Smith, Collins, Cyna & Crowther 2006, "Complementary and alternative therapies for pain management in labor," *Cochrane Database of Systematic Reviews*, 4.
David Vernon 2006, *Men at Birth*, Australian College of Midwives, Canberra.
Marsden Wagner 1994, *Pursuing the Birth Machine*, James Bennett Publishing, Sydney.
— 2006, *Creating Your Birth Plan: The Definitive Guide to a Safe and Empowering Birth,* Perigee Trade, New York.

Websites

motherfriendly.org
health.groups.yahoo.com/group/homebirth-usa
midwiferytoday.com
Natural hormone flows that relieve pain: sarahbuckley.com/articles
womens-health.co.uk/alt_pain.html
Numerous accounts of orgasmic birth and how it happens:
unassistedchildbirth.com/sensual/orgasmic.html
orgasmicbirth.com/whatis

Chapter 5—The First Hello

Books

Sarah Buckley 2009, *Gentle Birth, Gentle Mothering: A Doctor's Guide to Natural Childbirth and Gentle Early Parenting Choices*, Celestial Arts, Berkeley California.

David Chamberlain 1998, *The Mind of your Newborn*, North Atlantic Books, Berkeley, California.

Ronald Goldman 1997, *Circumcision: The Hidden Trauma: How an American Cultural Practice Affects Infants and Ultimately Us All*, Vanguard Publications, Chapel Hill, North Carolina.

Lynne Murray and Liz Andrews 2005, *The Social Baby: Understanding Babies' Communication from Birth*, (also available on DVD) The Children's Project, London.

Websites

Excerpts from position statements on circumcision written by Western medical practitioners: circumcision.org/position.htm

jewishcircumcision.org

Chapter 6—Creating a Joyous Connection with Your Baby

Book

Lynne Murray and Liz Andrews 2005, *The Social Baby: Understanding Babies' Communication from Birth* (also available on DVD), The Children's Project, London.

Video

Bijou Blick and Beulah Warren, *Getting To Know You: Recognising Infant Communication and Social Interaction*, Northern Beaches Child and Family Health Services and the New South Wales Institute of Psychiatry, Hilton Cordell Productions, Sydney.

Websites

The full text of the Australian Association of Infant Mental Health Inc. (AAIMHI) Position Statement #2: aaimhi.org/viewStory/Policies+and+Submissions

Baby signing information: signingtime.com

signbabies.com

mybabycantalk.com

Chapter 7—Science and Babies' Emotional Needs

Books

Sleeping

Deborah Jackson 1999, *Three in a Bed: The Benefits of Sharing Your Bed with Your Baby*, Bloomsbury, New York.

Pinky McKay 2006, *Sleeping Like a Baby*, Penguin Books, Melbourne.

Beth McGregor and Anne Gethin 2007, *Helping Your Baby to Sleep: Why Gentle Techniques Work Best*, Rex Finch Publishing, Sydney.

William Sears 1999, Nighttime Parenting: How to Get Your Baby and Child to Sleep, Plume, New York.

Breastfeeding

Sue Cox 2006, *Breastfeeding with Confidence: A Practical Guide*, Meadowbrook Press, Minnetonka, Minnesota.

Nancy Mohrbacher 2005, *Breastfeeding Made Simple: Seven Natural Laws for Nursing Mothers*, New Harbinger Publications, Oakland, California.

Up-to-date books on breastfeeding: breastfeedingstore.llli.org/public

Websites

Babies sleeping separately

A large amount of research has been done to investigate how babies cope with separate sleeping: cosleeping.nd.edu

The UK Foundation for the Study of Infant Deaths launched an awareness campaign called "Sleep safe, sleep sound, share a room with me": fsid.org.uk/page.aspx?pid=420

Co-sleeping: askdrsears.com/topics/parenting/sleep-problems

attachmentparenting.org/parentingtopics/babysleepstrategies.php

Breastfeeding

mothersdirect.com.au/index.htm

International Code of Marketing of Breast-milk Substitutes, World Health Organization and International Baby Food Action Network (IBFAN): ibfan.org/issue-international_code-code.html

Baby massage

infantmassageusa.org

Chapter 8—Helping Parents to Connect

Books

Genes and nurturance

Louis Cozolino 2006, *The Neuroscience of Human Relationships: Attachment and the Developing Brain*, W.W. Norton, New York.

Robin Grille 2005, *Parenting for a Peaceful World*, Longueville Media, Sydney (see, especially, Chapter 21, "The Shaping of Personality and Human Relations").

Daniel Siegel 1999, *The Developing Mind*, The Guilford Press, New York.

Children and daycare

Steve Biddulph 2005, *Raising Babies: Should Under 3s Go to Nursery?* Harper Thorsons, London.

Peter Cook 1997, *Early Childcare: Infants and Nations at Risk*, News Weekly Books, Melbourne.

Robin Grille 2005 *Parenting for a Peaceful World*, Longueville Media, Sydney (see "Childcare," pp. 370–2).

Anne Manne 2005, *Motherhood: How Should We Care for Our Children?* Allen & Unwin, Sydney.

Website

our-emotional-health.com/addendums.pdf; Part VI, Chapter 30, "Who Parents the Parents?" addendum for *Parenting for a Peaceful World*.

Chapter 9—Creating a Joyous Connection With Your Toddler

Books

Helen and Clive Dorman 2002, *The Social Toddler*, (also available as a DVD) CP Publishing, Richmond, UK.

Aric Sigman 2005, *Remotely Controlled: How Television Is Damaging our Lives*, Vermilion, London.

Margot Sunderland 2006, *The Science of Parenting*, DK Publishing, London (see, especially, pp. 96–109).

Chapter 10—The Passionate Toddler

Books

Janice Berger 2000, *Emotional Fitness: Discovering our Natural Healing Power*, Penguin Books, Toronto.

Pinky McKay 2008, *Toddler Tactics*, Penguin Books, Melbourne.

Chapter 11—To Discipline or to Connect?

Websites

stophitting.com

nospank.net

Global initiative to end all corporal punishment of children (including all the countries that have already legislated against it): endcorporalpunishment.org

Chapter 12—Rewards, Praise and Appreciation

Books

Alfie Kohn 1999, *Punished by Rewards: The Trouble with Gold Stars, Incentive Plans, A's, Praise, and Other Bribes*, Houghton Mifflin, Boston.

Daniel H Pink 2011, *Drive: The Surprising Truth About What Motivates Us*, Riverhead Books, New York.

Websites

The democratic education system in Israel: democratic.co.il/en

The Sudbury system in the US and around the world: sudval.org

Examples of democratic education in the US: educationrevolution.org

Chapter 13: Listening

Websites
Center for Nonviolent Communication: www.cnvc.org
Heal for Life Foundation: healforlife.com.au
Youth Insearch (YI) has audiovisual clips that show profoundly moving evidence of how
  empathic connections can heal some of the deepest wounds in severely damaged
  young people: youthinsearch.org

Chapter 14—Talking

Books

Effective communication with children
Thomas Gordon 2000, *Parent Effectiveness Training*, Three Rivers Press, New York.
Marshall Rosenberg 2004, *Raising Children Compassionately: Parenting the Nonviolent
  Communication Way*, Puddledancer Press, Encinitas, California.

Effective communication between adults
Helena Cornelius and Shoshana Faire 2007, *Everyone Can Win: Responding to Conflict
  Constructively*, Simon & Schuster, Sydney.

Website
gordontraining.com/parent-programs

Chapter 15—The Well-supported Parent

Websites
To help you to locate a group near you or to borrow some ideas about how to start your
  own group:
Kindred Community: www.kindredcommunity.com
Attachment Parenting international: attachmentparenting.org
Natural Parenting: naturalchild.org
Continuum Parenting: continuum-concept.org

About the Author

Robin Grille is a father, psychologist in private practice and a parenting educator. His articles on parenting and child development have been published in Australia, the US, Canada, the UK and New Zealand as well as translated into several European languages.

Robin's first book: *Parenting for a Peaceful World* (2005) received international acclaim. Additionally, he is a keynote speaker and workshop leader in the United States, Australia, New Zealand and the UK.

To find out more about his work, books, articles and seminars visit: our-emotional-health.com and HeartToHeartParenting.org.

Photo by Yaramin Grille

Acknowledgments

This book is about family, and in every way it has been a family project. It would have been impossible for me to write it without the mountainous faith and support of my wife, collaborator and first proofreader, Linda, and without the patient and timeless teachings of my daughter, Yaramin. You are the heart of my life.

I believe we live in most exciting times, when more people than ever before are calling in unison for a world more nurturing, more respectful and more honoring of children. I have been blessed with the advice and instruction of some special souls who have devoted their lives to the betterment of children's lives, such as Adam Blakester, Sarah Buckley, Yvonne Devine, Bob Fathman, Mitch Hall, Jan Hunt, Tracy Wilson Peters, Lisa Reagan, Sofi Thompson, and Kelly Wendorf.

Lastly, it is a privilege, a pleasure and a good fortune to have entrusted my Australian manuscript into the capable hands of my American editor, John Travis, MD, who with his infant wellness and neuroscience expertise, has added much value to this book.

I feel deeply honored to count all the above as wonderful friends, colleagues, comrades, and to have received your inspiration and your encouragement.

Index

erases painful events, 28
fetal, 40–42
imaging technology, 10
pleasure centers, 146
seeking system, 162
shame stored in the, 207
breastfeeding
co-sleeping facilitates, 113
daycare and, 151
increasing rates of, 8, 74–75
learning, 9
to full-term, 118–29
breathing patterns, 112
bris shalom, 84
Buckley, Sarah, 46, 47, 64
Bulgaria, maternity leave entitlements, 153
bullying behavior, 162, 211

– C –
Cadogan, William, 119
caesarean births, 50
Calvin, John, 95
Canada
maternity leave entitlements, 153
statement on corporal punishment, 199
Carolyn anecdote, 141
Cassie anecdote, 23
Chamberlain, David, 40
Channing, Walter, 49
child abuse, 7, 199
child as counselor and confidant, 257–58
child labor, 7
childcare. *See* daycare
childhood
cooperative parenting, 59
memories of, 26–29, 38–40, 164–65
throughout the ages, 7, 95
children. *See also* infants; newborns; toddlers
as confidants, 257–58
help you to heal and grow, 26
memories triggered by, 21–24
objectification of, 91–92
chiropractic for infants, 54

cholecystokinin, 123
circumcision, 82–84
codes of behavior, 260
colostrum, 73
communal parenting. *See* cooperative parenting
communication. *See also* listening skills
with infants, 104–6
with newborns, 78–79
community support for parents, 271
compassion, 265
conditional praise, 220
confidants, children as, 257–58
connection
defined, 13–15
from control to, 279
helping parents with, 137–54
prenatal, 37–42
vs. discipline, 195–217
way of, 266–67
with infants, 89–107
with newborns, 43–51
with toddlers, 157–69
conscious parenting, 19
consequences
for good behavior, 265–66
for misbehavior, 262–65
related, 263–65
unrelated, 262–63
consistency, 261
control
over toddlers, 178–80
to connection, 279
cooperative parenting, 59, 130–32, 168–69, 271
corporal punishment, 196–205, 211, 217
cortisol levels
daycare and, 153
from traumatic birth, 51
in toddlers, 168
separation anxiety and, 99, 148–49
co-sleeping with infants, 111–17, 125
crying
advice on, 98–102
communication with, 78–79

CPSIA information can be obtained at www.ICGtesting.com
Printed in the USA
LVOW12s0117030115

421321LV00003B/388/P